ALCOHOLISM, NARCISSISM AND PSYCHOPATHOLOGY

Chapter One

ALCOHOLISM, NARCISSISM AND PSYCHOPATHOLOGY
An Overview

HISTORICAL PERSPECTIVE

THE alcoholic has been a subject of study for hundreds of years (Forrest, 1982a). During biblical and pre-biblical eras, the "drunkard" was viewed from essentially a moral or moralistic perspective. Chronic intoxication and drunkenness were sins according to early church doctrine. This same sentiment continues to permeate modern Western-cultural thought. During the nineteenth century, the drunkard was labeled an "alcoholic" by the emergent professions of psychiatry, clinical psychology, and social work. Alcoholic persons have always comprised a sizable segment of every society. Alcoholics have been perceived as "weak-willed," morally degenerate, and without willpower or self-control

In actuality, the beliefs, superstitions and dogma surrounding the alcoholic have changed very little in the past two thousand years. We continue to speculate about the causes of alcoholism and alcohol abuse. In spite of our many scientific accomplishments, and technological progressions, we continue to understand surprisingly little about the alcoholic. Today, many people believe that the alcoholic is simply in need of more willpower in order to stop drinking. Likewise, the alcoholic continues to be viewed by many people as a "sinner" and a moral degenerate.

With the advent of modern psychiatry and the other behavioral science professions, the drunkard was transformed vis-à-vis the diagnostic process into an alcoholic. The diagnosis of alcoholism can and does lend significant sources of gain to the psychotherapeutic and rehabilitation processes with alcoholics (Knauert, 1980). Nevertheless, diagnostic labels (Szasz, 1961 & 1976) have frequently served purposes antithetical to the mental health and emotional well-being of the patient. The "ic" labels have done much to stigmatize and alienate people with emotional problems.

The problem of diagnosis in the field of alcoholic rehabilitation is paradoxical. The diagnosis of alcoholism needs to be actively shared and discussed with the patient (Forrest, 1978; Knauert, 1980). Utilized properly, this treatment technique results in several sources of therapeutic gain. Yet, some therapists (Burnett, 1976) suggest that rule number one in counseling the alcoholic is that the therapist is never the one to make the diagnosis of "alcoholism." Clearly, diagnosis remains an enigma in the alcoholism and mental health professions.

Various and sundry criticisms have been directed at the newly evolving behavioral-science professions. However, these disciplines have made significant contributions to the treatment of alcoholics and emotionally disturbed people. The behavioral-science professions are both new and not so new. The psychotherapist is akin to the shaman or witch doctor of the past. At the same time, the skills and behaviors of professional counselors and therapists are far removed from these mental practitioners of the not-so-distant past. One common denominator between the modern psychotherapist and the healer of the past is that both have had to rely upon human relationships as a medium of change. Suggestion, persuasion, expectation, and relationships have always remained crucial ingredients in the success or failure of the mental practitioners' work. Variables such as these affect even the surgeon-patient relationship.

Medical research (Wooddell, 1980) has contributed a great deal to our current understanding and treatment of the alcoholic. Medical procedures have been successfully developed in recent years that simply keep the chronic alcoholic alive. Far fewer alcoholics die each year as a result of delirium tremens (D.T.'s). Medical research advances have allowed us to more adequately investigate the etiology of alcoholism. Thus, chronic alcohol addiction has been investigated within the framework of an allergy. Researchers have also studied (Emrick, 1980) the various psychological and psychiatric treatment approaches used to modify drinking behavior. Relatively little basic research has been conducted to validate the "disease" concept of alcoholism. The American Medical Association does define alcoholism as a disease. However, comparatively little clinical research has been directed at confirming or disproving this position. Jellinek (1945) concluded that alcoholism is determined by hereditary influence via constitutional instability to the social risks of inebriation. Efforts to provide evidence of a hereditary or genetic factor in the etiology of alcoholism have been inconclusive. Attempts to prove that alcoholism is caused by a metabolic dysfunction have also proven inconclusive. This list of causative theories of alcohol addiction could be greatly expanded. However, the conclusions germane to each remain the same. Researchers and clinicians do not know what alcoholism is or why select individuals drink alcoholically. As Szasz (1976) so succinctly points out, the medical profession and, more specifically, the psychiatrist have historically responded to these unknowns by defining them as mental diseases. Such a position may or may not be correct. Psychotherapists and counselors need to come to grips with questions such as these.

THE INTERPERSONAL NATURE OF ALCOHOLISM

During my earliest clinical work with alcoholic persons, I was impressed with the interpersonal disturbance so basic to the alcoholic adjustment style. This position has been consistently reinforced vis-à-vis twelve years of clinical experience in the alcoholism field. Indeed, the alcoholic is interpersonally disturbed. Alcoholism is a people problem.

The fundamental psychogenic basis of alcoholism (Forrest, 1978 & 1982a) rests within the interpersonal realm. Obviously, such a position is congruous with the training of a clinical psychologist. At some future time, psychotherapists may know definitively that alcohol addiction is caused by a genetic defect, an endocrine disorder, a nutritional deficit, or that alcoholism is a physical disease process.

Most alcoholic persons do not *appear* to be crazy or mentally diseased. Yet, the alcoholic is always emotionally upset or disturbed. The alcoholic is rarely psychotic with the exception of that interval of time when he or she is experiencing acute alcohol withdrawal. Acute alcohol withdrawal can cause a transient toxic psychosis. Approximately 8 to 12 percent of the alcoholic persons seen in intensive psychotherapy evidence thought disturbance following detoxification and withdrawal (Forrest, 1982b). Therefore, only a small percentage of the alcoholic population manifests severe psychopathology or possible mental disease. With regard to overall symptomatology, ego structure, and adjustment style, the majority of grossly disturbed alcoholics fit within the "borderline" and "narcissistic" diagnostic categories (Kernberg, 1975 & 1980). A small percentage of the chronic alcoholic population manifests gross neurological impairment which results in extreme personality disorganization, fragmentation, and schizophrenic-like behavior.

Chronic alcoholism begins as a result of relatively unique patterns of interpersonal living. A corollary to this supposition is that "people can make people sick." In less-deterministic terms, significant others always play a crucial role in the development of an individual's character structure and symptom choice. In general, people tend to recreate, adopt or somehow manifest the neurotic (as well as adaptive) adjustments and behaviors operational within their primary family constellation. The relatively unique patterns of communication, interaction, emoting, and behaving within any given family system always include a number of maladaptive or neurotic processes. Simply stated, every family system is uniquely adaptive and maladaptive.

Alcoholic persons are the products of family systems (Wegscheider, 1981) which reinforce the predisposition toward the alcoholic symptom choice. A major theme in this text is that alcoholic individuals have experienced profound and chronic narcissistic need and entitlement deprivation within their family systems. The eventual intrapersonal conflicts and behavioral pathology of the alcoholic evolve as a result of these psychonoxious interpersonal experiences. Furthermore, the network of interpersonal relations that the alcoholic develops during the course of his or her addiction career very actively supports, reinforces, and maintains the alcoholic symptom choice. Alcoholics have been involved in various networks of distorted interpersonal relationships that prodromally reinforce the alcoholic symptom choice. Infantile and childhood interpersonal experiences are crucial causative factors in the eventual actualization of the alcoholic symptom choice. Even the adolescent and adult relationships of the alcoholic are conducive to the development of alcoholism.

The alcoholic sustains devastating narcissistic injury within the realm of mother-infant-significant other relationships. Painful interpersonal encounters of this variety continually teach the individual to be anxious in all human relationships and encounters. Feelings of inferiority, inadequacy, worthlessness and a generalized personal sense of non-well-being are associated with prolonged narcissistic injury.

ADOLESCENCE AND THE PRE-ALCOHOLIC

The impact of chronic narcissistic need and entitlement deprivation experiences can be most lucidly viewed via the observation of the adolescent. It is during the adolescent years that the person who eventually develops alcoholism begins to clearly act out the interpersonal effects of chronic narcissistic injury. The adolescent years represent a prodromal stage for the alcoholic. This is true in two basic ways. First of all, the pre-alcoholic adolescent begins to overtly manifest select behavioral symptoms. The pre-alcoholic adolescent often lacks the ability to persevere in any task or activity. Such individuals seem to give up easily. They lack a sense of "stick-to-itiveness." The pre-alcoholic adolescent has a failure identity. This failure identity may persist throughout life. The failure identity of the alcoholic is pervasive and includes academic, athletic and interpersonal matters. Many "tough," seemingly aggressive athletic alcoholics are in reality uncoordinated and generally inept in an athletic sense.

The self-concept of the alcoholic is always steeped in feelings of failure. The pre-alcoholic adolescent behaves in accord with a rather wide range of negative internal affects. During adolescence, the incipient alcoholic begins to recognize and comprehend a number of very unpleasant internal feelings. In part, missing school, quitting school, academic failure, interpersonal conflicts, sexual acting out, family disruption, borderline delinquency, and the various other prodromal behavioral symptoms of alcoholism can be associated with the heightened self-awareness precipitated by adolescence. At this developmental juncture, the evolving alcoholic begins to evidence very obvious intrapersonal and interpersonal psychopathology.

A second, very important process that is actualized by the pre-alcoholic adolescent involves the establishment of a friendship network. The establishment of an adolescent friendship or "chum" network often occurs in combination with the initiation of the drinking career. It is during the adolescent years that most people experiment with alcohol (Forrest, 1983a). At this time, approximately 80 to 85 percent of teenagers drink an alcoholic beverage for the first time. Alcoholics establish a relatively unique interpersonal network with the onset of adolescent drinking. Pre-alcoholic adolescents choose a select peer group with which to drink. Perhaps the "birds of a feather" adage applies to this selective interpersonal process. The pre-alcoholic teenager readily chooses as peers and friends those individuals who also have a significantly greater probability of eventually becoming addicted to alcohol. While it is not atypical for the alcoholic to recall that he or she was the particular adolescent peer group member who consistently drank to the point of intoxication, many alcoholic persons remember in psychotherapy that their interpersonal relationships during late adolescence were constructed around heavy drinking. Cumulative distorted interpersonal experience occurs as a function of the process of selecting neurotic people as friends and peers. The alcoholic recalls in therapy that his or her friends and associates during the adolescent years were quite similar to self. Problems with teachers and school personnel, poor academic performance, encounters with legal authorities, aggressive acting out and family conflicts are central to the recalled characteristics of the friends and peers of the teenage pre-alcoholic. In psychotherapy, the alcoholic eventually evaluates his or her adolescent peer relationships as not being in-depth and meaningful. Many alcoholics report that they had very few, if any, in-depth adolescent interpersonal attachments. Some alcoholic persons can be viewed as essentially chronic loners.

What is so tremendously important about the alcoholic's selection of peers and compatriots during adolescence is the fact that already, as a pre-alcoholic, the addicted individual has established an interpersonal system that supports his or her addiction symptom choice. As long as the alcoholic is actively addicted, he or she must maintain an interpersonal network that will support, maintain, and reinforce the addiction process. By the time of adolescence, the alcoholic has established a pattern of interpersonal relations that in a rudimentary fashion serves the addiction process.

The alcoholic can appropriately be viewed as a "fixated adolescent." Many clinicians and psychopathologists would take exception to this statement, believing the alcoholic-symptom choice to be indicative of personality and characterological fixation specific to earlier developmental epochs. In actuality, both positions are clinically correct. The alcoholic pathologically thinks, behaves, perceives and feels like an adolescent. The character structure of the alcoholic is determined and constructed vis-à-vis the interpersonal experiences of infancy and childhood. However, the interpersonal style of the addicted individual is strongly influenced by the impact of adolescence. As a child and prior to the adolescent years, the alcoholic has effected some degree of personal choice in his or her selection of playmates and peers. However, during elementary school and early junior high, the alcoholic is relatively limited in his or her ability to choose certain peer relationships. The loosening of family ties, loss of familial control, strivings for independence and autonomy, and the various other processes associated with adolescence influence and determine the interpersonal movements and interpersonal choices of the pre-alcoholic adolescent. However, the so-called "normal" dilemmas of adolescence do not explain why the pre-alcoholic adolescent selectively constructs an interpersonal network consisting of heavy drinkers, drug abusers and pre-alcoholics.

Relatively few individuals become addicted to alcohol during adolescence. However, some three million adolescents in the United States are alcoholics or alcohol abusers (Forrest, 1983). This number is small in comparison with the number of identified adult alcoholic persons in this country. Nevertheless, the pathological drinking careers of most alcoholics are initiated during the adolescent years. The interpersonal system that maintains the drinking behavior of the alcoholic is likewise developed during adolescence.

The pattern of initiating heavy drinking and establishing adolescent interpersonal relationships which very actively support the addiction process is more characteristic of the male alcoholic. Recent research indicates (Beckman, 1975; Wilsnack, 1982) that the onset of alcoholic drinking among women alcoholics occurs later in life and can often be associated with specific object loss. Chronic alcoholism (Forrest, 1978) is always a developmental process. Male and female alcoholics of any age simply do not become physiologically and psychologically addicted to alcohol overnight. Characteristically, the alcoholic progresses through a number of developmental drinking stages that end in chronic alcoholism (Forrest, 1978). This process may involve any number of years. Frequently, the individual who does progress to the stage of chronic alcoholism is not identified by society, self, or significant others as an alcoholic prior to the age of thirty-five or forty. This is unfortunate, as the alcoholic rarely receives treatment or rehabilitation prior to being identified or labeled.

The interpersonal nature of alcoholism becomes increasingly obvious as the alcoholic emerges from the adolescent years into early adulthood and adulthood. The alcoholic progressively drinks more and more, and his or her network of interpersonal relationships progressively includes more people who will reinforce and support drinking behavior. Contrary to popular opinion, very few alcoholics drink alone. Frequently, this myth ("alcoholics are people who drink alone") operates to enable the alcoholic to drink for an extended duration of time. Many alcoholics use this myth in the service of their alcoholism. By believing that an alcoholic is a person who drinks alone, the alcoholic can internally and externally reject the reality of his or her addiction.

In reality, the interpersonal world of the alcoholic is one constructed around the addiction process. Close interpersonal scrutiny always validates this point. Even the apparently socially isolated alcoholic retains interpersonal ties that enable him or her to remain intoxicated. In such cases, it is the salesman at the liquor store, the bartender, or even the cab driver who procures the liquor. These people play a crucial role in the interpersonal maintenance of the addiction process. The addicted individual surrounds himself or herself with any number of drinking cohorts who reinforce a rather broad spectrum of addiction-oriented behaviors. The drinking behavior of the alcoholic is reinforced and synergized by drinking with other heavy drinkers and alcoholics.

A plethora of other maladaptive behaviors are actively reinforced vis-à-vis drinking with other alcoholics and problem drinkers. One very important interpersonal ingredient in the process of "drinking with other drunks" is that the individual caught up in such an interpersonal network is continuously reinforced into the role of a deviant. The behavioral parameters associated with the deviant rubric are rather divergent when evaluated from the perspective of the alcoholic interpersonal network. Numerous clinicians and psychotherapists have commented upon the moral deterioration that the chronic alcoholic evidences (Bellwood, 1973; Martin, 1982). Indeed, the acting out pathology of the alcoholic becomes floridly manifest as the addicted person becomes progressively more addicted. Much of the behavioral and transactional craziness of the alcoholic is directly a function of intoxication. The inappropriate, bizarre, socially deviant behaviors of the alcoholic are continuously learned, reinforced and overlearned within the context of the alcoholic's interpersonal network.

A brief clinical case presentation will elucidate the inappropriate pattern of social reinforcement associated with the alcoholic interpersonal network:

> A middle-aged male dentist entered therapy as a result of feelings of intense guilt associated with heavy drinking. Prior to initiating therapy, Doctor B. had fallen into a pattern of stopping at a lounge located near his office on a nightly basis. He

would meet three of his "drinking buddies" at this lounge and consume five or six drinks and then go home. It was significant that two of the patient's friends were divorced and the third, although married, maintained one extramarital affair after another. Soon the patient's drinking acquaintances were able to "fix him up" with a "piece of strange." This pattern eventually entailed staying out all night, involvements with other women, and rather chronic intoxication. Within a matter of months, the patient became entangled in a morass of interpersonal conflicts which were previously foreign to his life-style.

By the time Doctor B. entered treatment, he was struggling with a number of very significant intrapersonal conflicts. In fact, it was rather clear that the patient was not so much guilty about his drinking compulsion as he was about the other behaviors the drinking process precipitated. Within the confines of the therapeutic alliance, the patient revealed that he had grown up in a very religious family and that his life-style and personal value system were at direct loggerheads with his alcoholic lifestyle. One important aspect of our working therapeutic relationship focused upon the impact of Doctor B.'s alcohol-facilitated interpersonal relationships and his subsequent internal and familial conflicts. The patient, within a matter of two months, decided to terminate his drinking behavior and his involvements with his "heavy drinking" friends from the lounge.

Presently, this patient has been sober for over three years, his sexual acting out is terminated, and he is once again productive in his profession, marriage and family life. He no longer suffers with guilt and superego conflicts. The superego lacunae of Doctor B. was such that he could no longer tolerate and live with himself.

This case illustrates a number of the points discussed so far. The alcoholic interpersonal network facilitates drinking and other aberrant behaviors. This case study demonstrates that alcoholic "birds of a feather" stick together. The adolescent dimensions of the alcoholic interpersonal network are also apparent in this case presentation.

THE FAMILY AND THE ALCOHOLIC INTERPERSONAL NETWORK

Chronic alcohol addiction can be viewed as an interpersonal disease. Indeed, the alcoholic suffers from a "cancerous emotional process" (Forrest, 1978). The alcoholic is sick in the realm of personal relationships. The alcoholic interpersonal network covertly supports and maintains the psychopathology of alcoholism.

As discussed in Chapter Thirteen, the spouse of the alcoholic often plays a crucial interpersonal role in the maintenance of the addiction process. It can be difficult to ferret out the exact behaviors and transactions of the non-addicted spouse that, in fact, reinforce the addictive behaviors of the alcoholic. An exception to this situation involves the overt "permitting" or "enabling" behaviors and roles of the spouse. The spouse of the alcoholic is a permitter (Steiner, 1971; Wegscheider, 1981) in the sense that she or he permits and allows the addicted marital partner to drink alcoholically and engage in a multiplicity of other inappropriate behaviors that are basic to the addiction process. Consistently, the spouse of the alcoholic is a permitter as a result of his or her many neurotic insecurities. This issue is also addressed in Chapter Thirteen. As a result of the permitting behaviors and roles of the non-addicted spouse, the alcoholic deteriorates in a rather global sense and the spouse likewise becomes progressively more upset and emotionally disturbed. The alcoholic family system also becomes progressively more pathologic. The interpersonal nature of chronic alcohol addiction means that the spouse and children of the alcoholic become increasingly symptomatic. The interpersonal nature of alcoholism is similar to the Reichian emotional-plague concept (Reich, 1942). As the alcoholic interacts and behaves with significant others, they share in his or her symptoms and, in a resultant fashion, become progressively more disturbed. Frequently, the spouse of the alcoholic is severely depressed, anxious, and emotionally overwhelmed. The children of the alcoholic (Ackerman, 1978) manifest a wide variety of psychological symptoms. Many children of alcoholics develop alcoholism. The modeling provided by an alcoholic parent and the modeling and learning that takes place over a period of many years within an alcoholic family system have profound effects upon the individuals who are exposed to these interpersonal experiences.

The interpersonal impact of alcoholism can be keenly felt by those unfamiliar with alcohol addiction. Certainly, the deaths of some twenty-five to twenty-eight thousand persons each year that occur as a result of the intoxicated driver have a profound interpersonal and intrapersonal impact upon their families and loved ones! This reality can be extended to include assaults, homicides, suicides, rapes, and a variety of other offenses committed by alcoholic and intoxicated persons (Forrest, 1982b).

By the time the alcoholic reaches the stage of chronic alcoholism (Forrest, 1978), he or she is able to maintain very few functional interpersonal relationships. Even family relationships are terminated. The skid-row milieu is a lucid example of interpersonal relations involving primarily drinking and alcoholics. The interpersonal world of the skid-row alcoholic is constructed almost singularly around the process of drinking with other alcoholics. Fortunately, only 4 to 6 percent of the chronic alcoholic population even enter the ranks of the skid-row population (Forrest, 1978). The vast majority of individuals who reach the stage of chronic alcoholism are involved in an interpersonal network which is significantly divorced from that of the skid-row milieu. Yet, the interpersonal relationships of alcohol-addicted persons are constructed around the common denominator of drinking.

Alcoholics in industrial or military work settings are very quick to meet and identify with other alcoholics. Furthermore, the alcoholic "in" group within a work setting is quite adept at hiding and actively supporting the addiction behaviors of its membership. Covering up for each other, purchasing liquor for the alcoholic who is without money, and lying to the spouse of the addicted "in" group member are but a few of the transactional realities that take place within the alcoholic interpersonal network. In the event that an alcoholic begins to experience acute alcohol withdrawal or manifests other extreme medical and psychological symptoms, it is frequently an addicted "friend" who takes such a person to the hospital or physician. This general phenomenon is well known within small communities.

By the same token, it is none other than the members of the alcoholic interpersonal network who facilitate the alcoholic's reengagement in the addiction process following seemingly successful treatment and rehabilitation. Although it is the alcoholic who chooses to drink following treatment, the drinking associates of the rehabilitated alcoholic usually play a crucial role in the patient's decision to initiate drinking again. It is axiomatic that the longer and more pathologically addicted an alcoholic has been, the more interpersonally disturbed and conflicted he or she will be. Chronic alcoholics who are able to establish sobriety are confronted with the task of interacting and behaving in an interpersonal world which demands the utilization of basic social skills that they may not possess.

Alcoholic persons do not know how to behave effectively in interpersonal milieus that are not structured around heavy drinking. The chronic alcoholic spends a great deal of his or her life structuring time vis-à-vis the addiction process. The addiction process is always a unique and prolonged experience in socialization. For the drinking alcoholic, dancing, attending parties, fishing, working, parenting and the global processes of daily living are constructed around the ingestion of alcohol. When the addicted individual quits drinking, he or she must learn or relearn a wide variety of new social skills and interpersonal behaviors. If the alcoholic is unable or fails to learn new and more effective patterns of interpersonal living while sober, he or she will again initiate the addiction process. In short, the chronic alcoholic needs to be resocialized following the establishment of sobriety. Certainly, this is a complex and difficult task for both the patient and therapist.

It is important for the family of the alcoholic to be socialized and resocialized through treatment and rehabilitation. The alcoholic family system (Forrest, 1978 & 1980; Wegscheider, 1981) can and often does play a crucial role in the rehabilitated patient's decision to return to drinking. Alcoholic patients who have been sober for a few weeks or months are typically depressed, extremely anxious and hostile. Living with a newly recovering alcoholic can be difficult and, perhaps in certain respects, even more difficult than living with a drinking alcoholic! As such, the psychotherapist often finds that it is the spouse of the alcoholic who reinforces the alcoholic's return to drinking and continued intoxication. The spouse and children of the alcoholic derive a good deal of secondary gain from the addictive behaviors of the alcoholic. Uncertainty and new anxieties associated with the addicted family member's newly established sobriety covertly reinforce family interactions which can support further drinking. The spouse and family of the alcoholic do not know how to interact, communicate, and behave in the absence of the alcoholic's drinking. Every member in an alcoholic family system (Ackerman, 1979; Wegscheider, 1981) hates and despises the drinking *modus vivendi* of the addicted family member. Nevertheless, the family adjustment and interaction style have been shaped by the addiction process. In the event that the alcoholic marital dyad cannot together modify and change long-standing patterns of interaction, communication, emoting and behavior, divorce may ensue. The alcoholic may discover after sobering up that he or she cannot live with the non-addicted spouse. The non-addicted spouse may similarly be confronted with the fact that he or she cannot live with a sober alcoholic. In some cases, the non-addicted spouse will initiate a divorce after the alcoholic has achieved sobriety and is evidencing significant progress in changing other important areas of daily living.

Alcoholism has been discussed as an interpersonal process. At this point, a schematic model is presented that depicts the interpersonal and intrapersonal psychopathology of alcoholism. This model is presented in Table I. The text will be devoted to a consideration of each of the interpersonal and intrapersonal processes presented in Table I. In essence, the chapter-by-chapter content of this text is a clinical gestalten of the various interpersonal and intrapersonal processes that, in sum, constitute the psychopathology of alcoholism.

THE INTERPERSONAL AND INTRAPERSONAL PSYCHOPATHOLOGY OF ALCOHOLISM

The alcoholic is a product of intense and profound narcissistic need and entitlement deprivation. It is the mother, surrogate

TABLE I.

The Psychopathology of Alcoholism

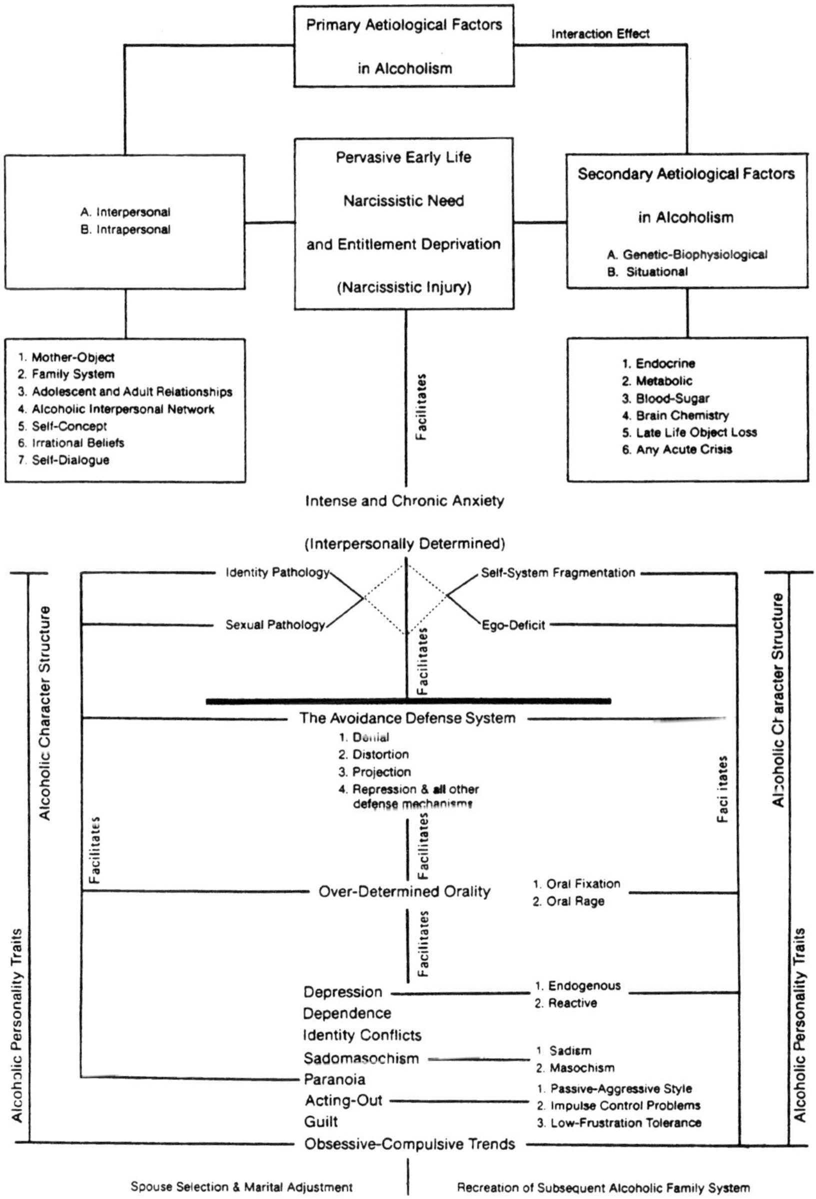

mother and significant others of the infant and young child who most catastrophically inflict narcissistic injury upon the evolving person. The impact of narcissistic injury can result in physical death of the person or, less drastically, chronic schizophrenia. The alcoholic has not sustained narcissistic injury of this magnitude and scope. Physical abuse and neglect are very often important psychogenic factors in the interpersonal history of the alcoholic. Marked narcissistic need and entitlement deprivation experiences affect the later life development of primary character behavior symptomatology. The alcoholic is characterologically and behaviorally similar to the character behavior disorder or sociopath. Neurotic disturbances are very often the result of more inconsistent patterns of narcissistic injury. Hysterical symptoms, phobias, hypochondriasis, anxiety, depression and the other more classical neurotic disturbances can be associated with long-term interpersonal experiences involving vacillating and inconsistent narcissistic injury. The alcoholic does manifest a number of neurotic conflicts. However, the impact of consistent narcissistic need and entitlement deprivation experiences pushes the addicted individual into the alcoholic adjustment style rather than precipitating a more classical neurotic symptom choice. Narcissistic injury has been a *consistent* and *chronic* experiential reality in the case of persons who develop alcoholism.

A second interpersonal factor in the etiology of chronic alcoholism is that of having grown up within a family system including at least one alcoholic parent or parental model. At least 40 percent of individuals who become addicted to alcohol have one alcoholic or chemically dependent parent or surrogate parent (Roe, 1945; Forrest, 1982c). It is reasonable to hypothesize that perhaps 50 to 65 percent of identified alcoholic persons in this country have been parented by an alcoholic. Persons who grow up within the confines of an alcoholic family system continuously emulate and model the behavioral repertoire of the alcoholic family member. Interpersonal learning experiences of this type can be viewed as a form of programming. The individual who (1) sustains chronic and severe narcissistic need and entitlement deprivation during infancy and childhood and (2) has this experience within the context of a family system that includes at least one alcoholic parent or surrogate parent may have experienced the necessary and sufficient interpersonal conditioning prerequisite to developing alcoholism. Many alcoholics are able to identify one or two and perhaps many more alcoholic persons within their extended family system. Some alcoholics report that most of their close relatives and significant others are heavy drinkers or floridly alcoholic. Extended family members can and very often do play an important role in the process of teaching, shaping and modeling alcoholic behaviors.

Intense interpersonal anxiety is the consistent early life result of narcissistic need and entitlement deprivation experiences. Depression of an endogenous nature is also associated with early life narcissistic injury (Della-Giustina and Forrest, 1979). Affective disturbance is associated with narcissistic injury. Interpersonal anxiety is the sine qua non of the alcoholic adjustment mode. Affective disturbance is central to the life-long adjustment of the alcoholic. Father Joseph C. Martin (1974) suggests that the alcoholic is unable to intellectually and rationally control his or her life. In this sense, the alcoholic is emotionally out of control. The internal conflicts and struggles of the addicted person always begin within the interpersonal realm and subsequently become manifest within the intrapersonal realm. The intrapersonal psychopathology of the alcoholic is also maintained by interpersonal relationships.

The early life anxiety experiences of the alcoholic result in severe self-system fragmentation. Psychological identity fundamentally evolves vis-à-vis relationships with significant others. In the event that the individual is unable to assimilate an adequately consolidated nuclear sense of self through relationships with significant others, he or she experiences rather chronic ego pathology and self-system defusion. As a result of intense early life interpersonal anxiety, the alcoholic has been unable to adequately internalize and synthesize ego introjects. The interpersonal and intrapersonal processes of identification, incorporation and emulation are distorted and faulty. Chronic interpersonal anxiety dictates the presence of self-system fragmentation. Thus, the alcoholic always struggles with the issue of "Who am I?" Chronic identity problems most prototaxically stem from self-system fragmentation or ego deficit. In a similar fashion, role and gender confusion are always a function of ego deficit. Every chronic alcoholic manifests identity and role pathology. These matters have never been satisfactorily resolved or worked through by the addicted person within the realm of healthy human relationships. Relationship disturbance is basic to chronic alcohol addiction.

The dependency pathology of the alcoholic can be viewed as a distorted attempt upon the part of the addicted individual to work through relationship conflicts in order to establish an adequately consolidated nuclear sense of self. Parasitically, the alcoholic depends upon and clings to significant others and alcohol in order to establish an identity and feel secure. This solution to identity deficit remains neurotically maladaptive. The overdetermined dependency needs of the alcoholic can only become more pathological as the addiction process evolves. The parasitic interpersonal attachments of the alcoholic are eventually facilitated and maintained through the chronic ingestion of alcohol.

Tension reduction is a major psychological factor that reinforces the addiction process. A plethora of significant stress factors are related to alcoholism (Mines and Yost, 1983). These stress factors are associated with an awareness of such negative interpersonally and intrapersonally determined affects as anxiety, depression, rage and tension. Adult and adolescent alcoholics are consciously aware of these internal affects. By chronically ingesting large amounts of alcohol, the alcoholic is able to significantly reduce and control a rather wide variety of threatening and uncomfortable affective states. This is one aspect of alcohol addiction that continues to be poorly understood by many counselors and clinicians. Most alcoholics control or bind potentially overwhelming anxiety via the addiction process. Many alcoholics are able to manage a diversity of threatening affective states through the medium of intoxication. Identity conflicts, defusion of the self-system, marked anxiety, depression and rage are some of the major interpersonal and intrapersonal stress factors that operate to facilitate the addiction choice. These clinical matters are of great intrapersonal significance to the adjustment style of every alcoholic.

Early in life, the alcoholic learns in an overdetermined fashion a number of particular defensive strategies that make coping relatively easier. The ego defenses of the alcoholic are overdetermined and maladaptive. Paradoxically, these same defensive operations work relatively well for many alcoholic persons for as long as twenty or thirty years. Over reliance upon the oral dynamism constitutes one primitive method for controlling or binding intense anxiety. Alcoholic persons attempt to manage a rather wide variety of threatening affects via their orality. The alcoholic is an overdetermined oral problem solver! The alcoholic neurotically copes with depression, marital conflicts, vocational difficulties, and *life* orally. Ultimately, the pervasive orality of the addicted individual is always destructive. Chronic alcohol addiction is a very destructive oral attack against the self. The alcoholic has primitively overlearned to utilize oral procedures in order to psychologically survive. The alcoholic is prototaxically terrified when the psychotherapist attempts to resolve or take away this defensive style. Clinicians and psychotherapists who do intensive and prolonged therapy with alcoholic patients often find that orality is closely associated with sexual adjustment (Forrest, 1982b). The alcoholic is orally disturbed and conflicted.

Many clinicians believe that the alcoholic is homosexual or latently homosexual (Knauert, 1982). Identity conflicts and ego pathology are basic to the alcoholic adjustment style. However, very few alcoholics manifest primary sexual object deviation. It is germane to the effective treatment process for the therapist to actively explore the sexual adjustment of every addicted patient. Very often, the alcoholic is consciously aware of his or her various sexual difficulties, and the exploration of this area can be an important source of treatment gain. Alcoholic patients who attain sobriety through the medium of a psychotherapy relationship may radically alter their sexual adjustments (Vraa, 1982). In this regard, the compulsive sexual acting out pattern of some alcoholics seen in psychotherapy is frequently modified as a function of the treatment process. The overdetermined pregenital strivings of some chronic alcoholics are likewise amenable to modification within the context of a productive therapeutic alliance.

The pervasive orality of the alcoholic can be viewed as a defense against interpersonal involvement, attachment and intimacy. The alcoholic also neurotically effects attachments and intimacy via his or her pathologic orality. Even the paranoid and sadomasochistic trends of the alcoholic serve this same purpose. Indeed, the interpersonal style of the addicted individual serves the purpose of avoiding intense and intimate interpersonal encounters.

The alcoholic utilizes a multiplicity of defensive interpersonal strategies in order to avoid interpersonal intimacy and onging interpersonal relatedness. The defensive style and defense mechanisms of the addicted person can be viewed as orally or pre-genitally overdetermined. The alcoholic utilizes these defensive strategies as a method for maintaining interpersonal distance. Depressive conflicts, paranoid trends, and the sadomasochistic behaviors of the alcoholic are maladaptive defensive operations which facilitate and maintain the global avoidance pathology of alcoholism. The pathological behavioral repertoire of the chemically dependent patient ultimately operates to drive people away. As discussed later in the text, addiction per se and the various pathological behaviors that invariably accompany the addiction process function like a semipermeable membrane. It is through the semipermeable membrane created by the chronic ingestion of alcohol that the alcoholic is able to maintain his or her tenuous world of interpersonal and intrapersonal relations (Forrest, 1979 & 1979a).

The alcoholic has been so narcissistically injured in his or her early life interpersonal relations that intense interpersonal intimacy, involvement and closeness are always potentially devastating and catastrophic matters. As such, the addicted patient primitively fears all interpersonal relations that demand closeness and ongoing intimacy. This is why the alcoholic verbalizes over and over again "leave me alone," "I'm a stranger within my own home." The paradox of this matter is that the addicted person desires and needs to be intimately and healthily involved with significant others. As a result of the tragic interpersonal historicity of the drinking alcoholic, the ability to love and experience genuine intimacy and human relatedness is lacking or pathologically distorted.

The alcoholic constructs his or her adjustment around the overutilization of denial, distortion and projection. This tripartite defense system is referred to as the avoidance defense system in Chapter Four. The alcoholic relies heavily upon a diversity of other defense mechanisms. As most clinicians know, denial is the defensive cornerstone of the addiction disorders. Frequently, rehabilitation personnel and psychotherapists tend to focus only upon the denial-oriented defensive strategies of the alcoholic. Distortion and projection are also primary defense mechanisms utilized by the alcoholic. Denial is the most primitive or regressive of these particular defense mechanisms. Although distortion and projection are likewise developmentally regressive defense mechanisms, they are nonetheless more adaptive than the denial defense mechanism. The alcoholic relies upon these ego-defense mechanisms in order to *avoid* human contact, intimacy and meaningful relatedness. These defense mechanisms are used in the service of the addiction process. In many respects, it is the defensive ego structure of the alcoholic that maintains the addiction process. Psychogenically, these defense mechanisms evolve as a result of the catastrophic interpersonal experiences of the alcoholic during the early developmental epochs of life. The alcoholic has, in fact, survived in life by overdeveloping and utilizing these very defense mechanisms. For this reason, the defensive operations of the alcoholic are very recalcitrant to the efforts of the psychotherapist. These defense mechanisms are genetic to the alcoholic character structure. Yet, successful treatment of the alcoholic always involves a modification of the avoidance defense system.

Within the confines of the therapeutic alliance, the therapist must actively and consistently confront the alcoholic's avoidance defense system (Forrest, 1982a; Bratter, 1982). Once the patient is able to establish a transference relationship with the therapist, he or she soon discovers that it is possible to give up or modify these overdetermined defenses. Ingesting alcohol can also be viewed as a defensive strategy that is utilized by the alcoholic in order to avoid intimate human contact. As mentioned earlier, the chronic ingestion of alcohol serves the interpersonal and intrapersonal purpose and function of a semipermeable membrane. The chronic alcoholic is able to filter, screen out, or block the impact of self-processes, human relatedness and contact by remaining intoxicated. The addicted patient avoids and denies full contact with the self by remaining intoxicated. Alcoholic persons vociferously deny, avoid and distort the reality of their own being and feelings vis-à-vis chronic intoxication.

The alcoholic is pathologically dependent. This is true in a variety of ways. Alcohol addiction is a disorder involving oral dependency. In an orally parasitic manner, the addicted individual attempts to attach self to others. This process entails a number of psychodynamic components. The alcoholic's primary functional security operation during the earliest developmental epochs involved the oral dynamism. Moreover, during these early months and years, the alcoholic is able to establish intimate and relatively anxiety-free interpersonal contact while feeding. This experiential framework creates a number of long-term interpersonal and intrapersonal dilemmas for the alcoholic. Alcoholic persons neurotically attempt to move toward and with significant others via the medium of intoxication. Ultimately, most alcoholics drive significant others away by this very process. The trap dimension of chronic alcoholism rests in the fact that the majority of alcoholic individuals are able to remain neurotically engaged with other human beings vis-à-vis the addiction process. The alcoholic hates and rejects the reality of his or her pathological dependence. A sizable segment of the alcoholic population acts out this dependency dilemma by attacking life in a very counter-dependent fashion. In reality, such an interpersonal stance is but an attempt to deny one's overdetermined dependency needs. The alcoholic consciously or pre-consciously resents being dependent upon significant others. More precisely, the addicted person resents being interpersonally dependent. This occurs as a result of the nature of the alcoholic's historic and chronic interpersonal relationships. The interpersonal and intrapersonal worlds of the alcoholic involve chronic pain, anger, conflict and an aggregate of other noxious affects and transactional realities.

The various dependency needs of the alcoholic have been inadequately managed by significant others during infancy and early childhood. It is almost as if significant others have denied the alcoholic his or her healthy need to be dependent! The alcoholic attempts, in a repetition-compulsion manner, to undo the dependency-oriented struggles of his or her early life historicity. Alcoholics fear their very powerful dependency needs, particularly as these needs relate to other people. The alcoholic actively chooses to be dependent upon the bottle rather than significant others. In this regard, the dependency-oriented pathology of the alcoholic is but another facet of the avoidance defense system. The alcoholic becomes dependent upon alcohol at the expense of learning how to be adaptively dependent upon significant others and people in general. The alcoholic is unconsciously enraged at *having* to choose substance dependency rather than healthy interpersonal dependency.

This issue is not without paradoxical dimensions. The alcoholic feels forced or compelled to choose alcohol addiction as a way of life. In terms of historic reality, the alcoholic seems to have an understandable rationale for actualizing the addiction choice. Chronic intoxication enables the alcoholic to partially perceive himself or herself as powerful, omnipotent and the antithesis of a weak, helpless, and dependent person. The alcoholic is consciously cognizant of the fact that imbibing alcoholic beverages makes it easier to socialize and remain at least superficially involved in the world of interpersonal relations. Therefore, alcohol facilitates neurotic interpersonal attachment. The alcoholic may perceive his or her addiction as a person-avoidance-oriented process. The more intensely the alcoholic attempts to deny his or her pervasive overdependency, the more interpersonally conflicted and enraged he or she becomes. The alcoholic actively punishes both self and significant others as a direct result of these dependency conflicts. The alcoholic continually tests the dependency tolerance of his or her spouse. Primitively, the alcoholic wishes to be dependently nurtured by a "good mother," an experience which he or she was denied during infancy and childhood. In the unconscious, this type of mothering experience would magically or ritually undo the alcoholic's interpersonal past. As the patient drives significant others away, he or she experiences an exacerbation of dependency conflicts. This results in a vicious circle involving interpersonal transactions having to do with parasitically attaching self to others, driving others away in the process, and finally further punishing self and significant others as a result of this very process. The dependency conflicts of the alcoholic, in an obfuscatory fashion, serve the addiction process by enabling the alcoholic to avoid adaptive and healthy interpersonal movements toward and with significant others. Thus, the dependency pathology of the addicted individual impedes or blocks the process of resolving and working through the matter of interpersonal intimacy.

The chronic alcoholic is very often a clearly hedonistic and narcissistic individual (Forrest, 1981). A primary task of the psychotherapist is that of helping the patient modify his or her narcissistic interpersonal style and character structure. This is a very difficult treatment task. Earlier, it was noted that the alcoholic parasitically attempts to attach self to others. Parasitic object attachments are also invariably narcissistic attachments. In the process of neurotically moving with and toward significant others, the alcoholic drives others away. This occurs as a result of the narcissistic nature of the alcoholic's interpersonal attachments. For the alcoholic, survival has been a lifelong matter of taking. While actively entrapped in the addiction process, the alcoholic is "out for self." Like Narcissus, the alcoholic is egotistically preoccupied with self. The pathologically narcissistic interpersonal style of the alcoholic is associated with a psychohistoric reality-based survival drive. Many alcoholics have survived in life as a result of their narcissistic pathology. This is an example of the paradoxically adaptive nature of the alcoholic adjustment mode. Following the establishment of even long-term sobriety, the clinical issue of narcissism often remains paramount relative to the interpersonal and intrapersonal adjustment of the alcoholic. While drinking, the narcissism of the alcoholic may be floridly uncontrollable and clearly destructive.

The drinking alcoholic (Forrest, 1983) is a manipulator par excellence. Drinking alcoholics are con artists, unreliable, irresponsible, immature and self-centered. The alcoholic is a master in the realm of using and manipulatively controlling others. After the alcoholic enters a rehabilitation or treatment program, it is quite common to observe a narcissistic conflict develop between the patient and the psychotherapist (Forrest, 1982a) or other staff members. Narcissistic struggles of this variety often involve the program physician and the patient. Alcoholic patients (Bratter, 1979 & 1982; Forrest, 1982a) confront, challenge and attack the narcissistic dimensions of the psychotherapist's character structure. Many alcoholic patients are quite adept at "proving" that therapists and treatment programs cannot help them! Patient-therapist narcissistic conflicts often account for the physician's uncomfortableness with alcoholics.

The sexual adjustment of the alcoholic (Forrest, 1982b) is often pathologically narcissistic. Indiscriminate sexual acting out upon the part of the alcoholic is always a reflection of narcissistic pathology. Alcoholic patients who do not act out sexually, in the form of having numerous affairs and one-night stands, can be narcissistically pathologic in their sexual relationship with a spouse. The behavioral manifestations of narcissistic symptomatology are varied. The alcoholic frequently demands immediate sexual gratification. The alcoholic may place any number of polymorphous sexual demands upon an unwilling partner and expect the partner to perform. Some alcoholics reject and deny the sexual needs of their spouse. In all of these sexual transactions, the alcoholic acts out his or her narcissistic character structure. The alcoholic can be a very selfish lover. Low desire, arousal problems and a basic rejection of sexual relations are often associated with alcoholism. The alcoholic is clearly narcissistic in a sexual sense.

Narcissistic pathology can be viewed as a defensive strategy that serves the purpose of avoiding meaningful and relevant human relatedness. The sexually acting out alcoholic literally "fucks" his or her unending list of sexual partners. This sexual adjustment style is a neurotic attempt to achieve in-depth, meaningful human contact and intimacy. The interpersonal style of the alcoholic is such that clinicians and psychotherapists have often confused the narcissistic acting out of these patients with that of sociopathy (Matuschka, 1978). This is a problem of differential diagnosis (Knauert, 1980 & 1982).

Narcissistic acting out precipitates an aggregate of depressive and guilt symptoms. Alcoholics continually struggle with feelings of depression and guilt. The superego structure of the alcoholic is overpunitive. The addicted patient vacillates between an interpersonal and intrapersonal adjustment style characterized by poorly controlled acting out and depression, intense self-hatred and self-punitive guilt. The acting out followed by depression and an intense guilt paradigm is basic to the alcoholic adjustment style. Drinking alcoholics respond to this vicious circle with further intoxication. The recovering alcoholic is faced with the difficult task of resolving and terminating acting out behaviors.

Many alcoholics remain dependent on intoxication in order to manage or cope with guilt associated with acting out. In reality, the alcoholic has ample reason to experience marked guilt feelings and depression following sobriety. Guilt feelings synergize the self-destructive trends of the alcoholic. Guilt can reinforce the self-destruction of continued intoxication. Guilt feelings are also associated with suicidal impulses and behaviors. The alcoholic perceives himself or herself as an unlovable, worthless, inadequate, and no good. Therefore, it is understandable that the alcoholic is set up to punish self. As children, alcoholics have felt extremely guilty about the various negative messages they have assimilated about themselves vis-à-vis significant others.

The therapist needs to openly convey to the alcoholic that he or she is not hopelessly unlovable, worthless and inadequate. However, it is extremely important to point out to the patient that he or she actively exacerbates and reinforces guilt conflicts via intoxication and the addiction process. When the patient achieves long-term sobriety and begins to live responsibly, extreme guilt and overpunitive superego functions progressively undergo a constructive change. The recovering alcoholic learns that he or she has fewer reality-determined reasons to feel guilty and depressed. Dealing with the guilt feelings of the alcoholic within the psychotherapy relationship teaches the patient to utilize guilt in a more rational and adaptive fashion. This process fosters responsible living and self-regulation.

Alcoholics feel intensively guilty over a surfeit of issues. Familial difficulties, poor academic performance, marital problems and perhaps multiple divorces, sexual conflicts, and alcoholism per se are but a few of the issues that the alcoholic feels guilty about. In short, the alcoholic experiences severe guilt over the matter of perceiving himself or herself as a gross failure in life. Some psychotherapists believe that the alcoholic is essentially refractory to the experience of internalized guilt. This position is clinically inaccurate. Such a position is usually constructed vis-à-vis the psychotherapist's lack of extensive clinical experience with alcoholic persons and generalized scotoma.

The behavioral repertoire of the alcoholic is obsessive-compulsive. Alcoholics become progressively more obsessive-compulsive. The alcoholic manifests an obsessive-compulsive character structure and personality. Intrapersonally and behaviorally, the alcoholic is an obsessive-compulsive. The alcoholic constantly ruminates about drinking. Alcoholics are obsessed with alcohol and intoxication. Every alcoholic is obsessed with many irrational fears. Obsessive ideation synergizes the compulsive characterological traits of the addicted person. The drinking compulsion of the alcoholic is synergized by obsessive ideation. By the same token, the drinking compulsion of the alcoholic reinforces irrational and obsessive self-dialogue. The compulsive features of the alcoholic evolve or are manifest prior to the development of the obsessive intrapersonal adjustment. Very early in life, the alcoholic adopts a compulsive adjustment style in order to defend the self from a world of pervasive and intense interpersonal anxiety. Compulsive motoric behaviors are a defense against intense anxiety. Obsessive ideation can likewise be viewed as a defense against various threatening affects that are associated with both internal security operations and interpersonal relations. In addition to utilizing compulsive defenses in order to bind intense interpersonal anxiety, the alcoholic controls himself or herself and the world by an overreliance upon this particular dynamism.

Alcoholics chronically struggle with the matter of control. To be anxious is to be out of control or potentially out of control. Alcoholic persons feel least anxious when they are able to perceive themselves as totally in control. Prototaxically, feelings of losing control and catastrophic anxiety are associated with the fear of death. Many alcoholics openly express a morbid fear of going crazy or losing their minds. The alcoholic is also intensely afraid of death and dying.

Characterologically, the alcoholic tends to be frugal, perfectionistic, rigid, and intransigent. A preoccupation with anality is not uncommon. One alcoholic male that I treated demanded that his wife fastidiously and meticulously keep their house clean. Another patient declared that he was "able to tell what kind of people he was dealing with by the condition of their bathrooms." In the case of the alcoholic, the compulsion to drink is such that the addicted person cannot drink one or two drinks. Consistently, the alcoholic drinks compulsively to the point of intoxication. It is difficult for the non-alcoholic to understand the alcoholic's compulsion to drink. Unfortunately, physicians and psychotherapists sometimes suggest to the chronic alcoholic that he or she "taper off" and only drink "two or three." Advice of this nature simply does not work. Messages of this variety are clearly iatrogenic. These messages can and do kill alcoholic patients (Forrest, 1979b). Even the recovering alcoholic selectively attends to drinking-oriented stimuli. Obsessively, alcoholics think about their favorite alcoholic beverages. They notice the liquor stores as they drive down the road, and the cold beer advertisements on television are consistently tempting.

Like the obsessive-compulsive personality, the alcoholic is constantly on guard against his or her drinking obsession and compulsion. This is most apparent with alcoholics who are seen in psychotherapy. Over and over again, the alcoholic vows to "never touch the stuff again." At the time the alcoholic makes this statement, he or she means it and is dedicated to total abstinence. Within a matter of hours or perhaps days, the alcoholic gives in to his or her compulsion and becomes drunk. This process is an unending one for many alcoholic persons and sometimes only terminates with death. Most alcoholics have attempted to quit drinking hundreds of times prior to entering therapy. Many alcoholics experience this same process as many as four or five times while in treatment. This is but one aspect of the working-through process in psychotherapy with alcoholics.

The alcoholic's attempts at sobriety are almost as ritualistic as the drinking process. Drinking alcoholics tend to frequent certain bars, drink only at home, or drink only vodka or another favorite alcoholic beverage and may engage in various other drinking rituals. The ritualism of the person who is attempting to remain abstinent is equally apparent. Attending Alcoholics Anonymous meetings each night of the week, seeing a psychotherapist once or twice a week on a regular basis, going to church, and other methods are employed by the alcoholic in defense of his or her sobriety. Jogging and meditation can become life-generating rituals or compulsions that help the alcoholic give up his or her negative addiction (Glasser, 1976; Forrest, 1979a). Positive addictions are, in fact, ritualistic compulsions. The alcoholic is driven by compulsion. Therefore, it is often necessary and perhaps easier to therapeutically push some alcoholics in the direction of developing a positive addiction as an alternative to alcohol addiction.

Alcohol is a magical substance. By ingesting this magical substance, the alcoholic becomes capable of accomplishing many magical things! Feeling less anxious and less depressed, feeling more powerful and masculine or feminine, being able to be more assertive, and a sense of temporary euphoria are but a few of the magical sources of gain that the alcoholic derives from intoxication. It is somewhat paradoxical that many "social drinkers" imbibe for many of these same reasons. Yet, the alcoholic is compulsively dependent upon the magic of alcohol and intoxication rather than the magic of reality and the world of meaningful interpersonal relations.

Throughout this text, it is suggested that the alcoholic chooses to be addicted. This is a cognitive and behavioral choice that the alcoholic makes on thousands of occasions. Each time the alcoholic drinks, he or she chooses to drink. Needless to say, a plethora of antecedent conditions shape the drinking choice. Alcoholism is a multivariately determined disorder; yet, every alcoholic is a unique individual. As a group, alcoholic persons differ in any number of ways. Vocational histories, personality characteristics, marital adjustments, race, educational backgrounds, family histories, intelligence, and pattern of consumption are but a few of the significant factors that contribute to the individuality and uniqueness of every alcoholic. In short, an alcoholic is always more than an alcoholic!

Alcoholism is a disorder of paradoxes. The alcoholic may lose his or her life as a result of choosing to be addicted; yet, every person who actualizes the addiction choice derives a wealth of secondary or, perhaps more accurately, *primary* gain from this adjustment style. Alcohol can make people feel better and dulls psychological and physical pain. As a result of intoxication, the alcoholic feels less insecure, less anxious, less depressed, and more in control of himself and others. However, the alcoholic (Pursch, 1979) ultimately makes himself or herself more agitated, depressed, and insecure as a result of chronic intoxication. The alcoholic omnisciently knows that his or her addiction works. Intoxication enables the alcoholic to remain functional. However, at some point, intoxication renders the alcoholic grossly dysfunctional.

SUMMARY

Interpersonal and intrapersonal processes are always fused; character structure, personality, and behavior represent the totality of this fusion. Alcohol addiction begins within the realm of interpersonal relations and is maintained by chronically parataxic interpersonal relationships. The unique and ongoing interpersonal and intrapersonal experiences of the alcoholic, in effect, cause or facilitate this particular symptom choice. Alcoholic persons have experienced chronic narcissistic need and entitlement deprivation during the epochs of infancy and childhood. Interpersonal experiences of this variety constitute the people-oriented historicity of the alcoholic. Approximately one-half of all alcoholic persons have been parented by an alcoholic. Growing up within an alcoholic family system constitutes a very powerful and prolonged interpersonal learning experience. The interpersonal and intrapersonal historicity of the alcoholic involves a form of long-term programming that often dictates the eventual actualization of the alcoholic adjustment style. The disturbed interpersonal relationships of the alcoholic facilitate self-system fragmentation, interpersonal anxiety, identity and role conflicts, depression, dependency, overdetermined orality, guilt and sadomasochistic struggles.

People can make people alcoholically sick, though some recovering alcoholics and psychotherapists reject this position.

However, people and significant others do shape and saliently reinforce the alcoholic's adjustment and behavioral repertoire. Every recovering alcoholic evidences adaptive growth and behavioral change as a function of new or different human relationships. Axiomatically, people can help facilitate behavioral change and adaptive personality growth.

Alcoholism is a baffling and complex disorder. Table I schematically depicts the complexity of alcoholism. Genetic factors and biophysiological variables may be the primary etiological components of this disorder. Research (Kaestner, Rosen and Appel, 1977) results "raise serious questions about the sufficiency of any univariate psychological hypothesis to account for the use of particular drugs or drug types." The interpersonal and intrapersonal aspects of alcohol addiction have not been adequately investigated.* In these respects, this text will be a significant contribution to the field of alcoholism.

---

*Alcoholics (Forrest 1978 & 1982b) manifest four essential characteristics: (1) their drinking is compulsive in nature and as such uncontrollable; (2) their drinking is most typically of long duration, or chronic; (3) their drinking results in intoxication; and (4) their patterns of drinking invariably result in severe interpersonal problems. The alcoholic is psychologically and physiologically addicted to alcohol. Alcoholism is a progressive disorder involving the total person.

Chapter Two

ALCOHOLISM AND THE PROBLEM OF NARCISSISM

INTRODUCTION

NARCISSISTICALLY oriented disorders and problems have been related to the psychopathology of virtually every psychiatric categorization of aberrant behavior. Schizophrenia, sociopathy, and depression are but a few of the major diagnostic categories that have incorporated the concept of pathological narcissism (Kernberg, 1975 & 1980; Hartocollis, 1977). Indeed, a number of clinicians and psychopathologists have made reference to each of these clinical groups as essentially narcissistic disorders. Unfortunately, the concepts of "narcissistic disorder" and "narcissistic personality" have come to encompass a multiplicity of definitions and meanings. Narcissistic personality refers to individuals with a diversity of behavioral symptoms and psychopathology (Masterson, 1981).

The present chapter elucidates the problem of narcissism as related specifically to the alcoholic. The origins and infantile roots of pathological narcissism basic to the alcoholic character structure and personality are discussed. A brief case history is included in this chapter. Through the development of our clinical understanding of the narcissistic and alloplastic adjustment modes, we can hope to create more effective treatment strategies specific to alcoholics and alcohol abusers. The alloplastic disorders are extremely difficult to modify within the context of the more traditional psychotherapies.

THE INFANTILE ORIGINS OF NARCISSISTIC DISTURBANCE

Orthodox psychoanalytical theory (Fenichel, 1945 & 1954) represents the first systematic investigation of personality development that elucidates the infantile origins of narcissism. Psychoanalytic theory and research conceptualizes the first three years of life as an extremely narcissistically oriented experience. This is particularly true of the initial six to eight months of human existence. During this developmental era of life, the infant is for all practical purposes an almost totally narcissistic being. The human infant is dependent upon significant others for the gratification of a multiplicity of life-sustaining, narcissistically oriented needs. Should significant others fail to meet the narcissistic needs and entitlements of the infant, death may occur. Partial fulfillment of these infantile narcissistic needs consistently results in the development of emotional problems and psychopathology. Indeed, many psychopathologists and personality theorists (Sullivan, 1953) have speculated that narcissistic injury is a major determinant or contributing factor in schizophrenia (Forrest, 1982d) and various other pathological adjustment dynamisms.

The concept of narcissistic need and entitlement deprivation is used extensively throughout this book. Narcissistic injury is used, as a concept, interchangeably with the concept of narcissistic need and entitlement deprivation. Most fundamentally, *narcissistic needs* refer to the life-sustaining needs of the human organism. Oxygen, food, appropriate temperature control, physical contact, and the maintenance of excretory functions are narcissistic needs. These needs of the infant and young child must be managed by significant others (mother, father and family system). Such needs are self-oriented, thus narcissistic and life-sustaining. *Narcissistic entitlement deprivation* refers to parental failure to provide those psychological and interpersonal processes that convey a basic sense of dignity, love, respect, worth, esteem, concern, and trust to the infant and child. As human beings, we are entitled to feel loved, worthwhile, adequate and respected within the context of our relationships, with significant others. Such needs are lifelong.

Narcissistic needs pertain to essentially physiological processes, while entitlement needs refer more to interpersonal and psychological processes. However, narcissistic needs and entitlement needs clearly include physiological and psychological components.

Narcissistic injury occurs when the narcissistic needs and entitlements of the evolving person are inadequately managed by significant others. Narcissistic need and entitlement deprivation most catastrophically affects the growth and development of the person under pervasive and chronic circumstances. Narcissistic need and entitlement deprivation is an interpersonal process. Throughout life, all people must consistently be able to manage their narcissistic needs and entitlements through relationships involving self and significant others.

Various forms of maladaptive behavior occur as a result of parental and/or significant others' overindulgence and prolonged gratification of the infant's narcissistic needs and entitlements. Pathological adjustment dynamisms are also related to parental and/or significant others' failure to adequately meet the infant's narcissistic needs. The mother-infant relationship and the total family constellation have been genetic to most theoretical assumptions specific to the development of emotional problems and psychopathology. Historically, personality theorists and clinicians have viewed the initial mother-infant relationship as being the prototypic basis for subsequent adjustment. Character structure and personality development are also affected by a complexity of subsequent developmental processes.

A very significant aspect of the early dyadic mother-infant relationship has to do with the mother's ability to effectively meet the narcissistic needs and entitlements of the infant. Effective and healthy management of the infant's narcissistic needs and entitlements is associated with the mother's ability to provide generalized need gratification levels which are not significantly overindulging or underindulging in nature. The schizophrenogenic mother and the "bad mother" prototypes are but a few of the clinical conceptualizations employed to describe mothers who are pathologically unable to meet the narcissistic needs and entitlements of the infant.

Oral fixation occurs as a result of chronic narcissistic injury. Various personality dynamisms reflect the manner in which the infant and child's narcissistic needs and entitlements have been managed by significant others. Pervasive narcissistic need and entitlement deprivation is associated with a character structure and life-style which is orally overdetermined. The narcissistically injured individual must, in a primitive, oral fashion, unendingly take from others. At the same time, these individuals are unable to give anything (emotionally or interpersonally) in return. Within this context, "give" and "take" refer to emotional or affective involvements and attachments. Healthy interpersonal relationships and healthy intrapersonal adjustments evolve as a result of mutually consistent emotional involvements and nurturing attachments.

Quite simply, the narcissistic personality structure evolves from a consistently deprivation-oriented infancy and early childhood experience.

A third possibility relating to the pathological maintenance of the infant's narcissistic needs and entitlements involves the mother's (significant others) inconsistent ability to respond to these primal demands of the infant. Inconsistency can assume any number of interaction possibilities. Perhaps the most basic pattern of inconsistency involves the mother's ability to meet the infant's narcissistic needs on one occasion and subsequently deny or reject these same needs on other occasions (Knauert, 1978). A good deal of clinical literature has been written about the many pathological ramifications of inconsistent parenting. A fundamental "red thread" in this literature has to do with the role of inconsistency in the development and maintenance of neurotic patterns of adjustment. It is theorized that inconsistent parenting facilitates the development of neurotic behavior. Inconsistent parenting encompasses the mother-infant relationship, the mother-infant-father relationship, the father-infant relationship, and the family system.

Other significant interpersonal transactions that feed into the development of narcissistically oriented intrapersonal conflicts have been illuminated in the literature (Kohut, 1977; Kernberg, 1980; Masterson, 1981). In summary: (1) the human organism must of survival necessity assume an initial stance with significant others and the phenomenal world that is almost totally narcissistic in orientation; (2) the inability of the infant to secure healthy narcissistic need and entitlement gratifications from significant others, particularly the mother, results in varying degrees and types of personality warp and psychopathology; and, most significantly, (3) failure upon the part of parents and significant others to meet the narcissistic needs and entitlements of the infant consistently results in later life alcoholic and alloplastic adjustments. The relationship between narcissistic injury and the development of the alcoholic character structure is quite complex.

NARCISSISM, INFANCY AND ALCOHOLISM

The alcoholic has experienced a deprivation oriented infancy and childhood. This is directly antithetical to the earlier discussed situation in which the infant's narcissistic needs and entitlements have been overindulged. In the case of the alcoholic, patterns of inconsistent parental gratification of the infant's and young child's narcissistic needs and entitlements do occur. However, these seemingly inconsistent patterns of infantile narcissistic and entitlement gratification break down upon close clinical scrutiny. Inconsistent patterns of infantile narcissistic need and entitlement gratification are juxtaposed to chronic and pervasive patterns of narcissistic injury. Inconsistent prototaxic experiences of the infant involving narcissistic injury do not appear to have a profoundly devastating long-term impact upon character structure and personality development.

The alcoholic has been subject to infantile and childhood experiences that were highly deprivation oriented (Forrest, 1979a). Deprivation includes physical or material matters. Deprivation also includes the global affective and interpersonal dimensions of the parent-child relationship. Indeed, the generalized emotional climate of the family constellation is often deprivation oriented.

This historic reality becomes apparent in the course of the psychotherapy relationship with the alcoholic patient. The parents of the alcoholic (Forrest, 1978 & 1979a) have not, for whatever reasons, been able to meet the pressing narcissistic needs and entitlements of the individual during the stages of infancy and childhood. This dilemma also occurs during the alcoholic's later stages of maturation and development. However, the catastrophic impact of this experiential reality is much more profound during the earliest eras of intrapersonal and interpersonal living. Alcoholics experience infancy and childhood as most painful and interpersonally hurtful eras. Child neglect, outright rejection and not being wanted by one or both parents, growing up in a foster home or with relatives, divorce or multiple divorces, object loss, and physical abuse and punishment are the basic experiential realities of the alcoholic's infancy and childhood (Ackerman, 1978). Indeed, one might marvel at the basic fact that the adult alcoholic has simply managed to survive in life.

A brief case history will elucidate the cogency of early life pervasive narcissistic need and entitlement deprivation in the etiology of chronic alcoholism.

> A thirty-two-year old male with a fourteen-year history of pathological drinking was referred for treatment to a military alcoholic and drug addict rehabilitation center. The patient was referred directly to this agency by the installation medical facility after having been medically treated ("detoxed") on an inpatient basis for some ten days. A number of relevant background experiences of this individual were deprivation related.
>
> The patient's biologic mother was allegedly some six months pregnant at the time of her marriage to the purported father, although the issue of "real father" was in question. The mother had given up two earlier children born out of wedlock. When the patient was two-and-one-half years old, his mother left home with another man. The patient was then parented by his grandparents. According to the patient, the grandfather was extremely "bad to drink." The grandparents retained custody of the patient until he was nine years old, at which time he became such a "burden" that he "had to be placed in an

> orphanage." This experience was subsequently followed by three adoptions of the patient into reasonably well-adjusted foster families. However, the patient appeared to have been unable to adjust to these foster family situations and was always returned to the orphanage. The patient stated during the initial intake interview that the only "real" home he had ever known was the Army.

This truncated case history includes only the patient's major life experiences which involved traumatic narcissistic injury. The concept of narcissistic need and entitlement deprivation also encompasses personal contact, "strokes," consensual validation, love, communication, and a multiplicity of other transactions that characterize healthy interpersonal relationships and generalized patterns of effective interpersonal living.

Within the psychotherapy relationship, it becomes relatively easy to experientially validate the many realities of narcissistic injury and the effects of chronic and pervasive narcissistic need and entitlement deprivation. Virtually every case history involving an alcoholic is essentially the same with regard to the matter of narcissistic injury. The extent of narcissistic injury may not, on the surface, appear to be as marked as that in the case study. In the absence of an extended psychotherapy relationship during later life or some other very potent, extended, facilitative interpersonal relationship, alcoholics are interpersonally and intrapersonally programmed and conditioned to actualize the alcoholic symptom choice. Chronic depression, anxiety, and hostility are also affects that evolve as a result of pervasive narcissistic need and entitlement deprivation.

The development of the alcoholic's narcissistic character structure is logical and predictable. Alcohol addiction and a narcissistic character structure are syntaxic. As a result of chronic infantile and childhood narcissistic injury, the alcoholic develops a character structure that is pathologically narcissistic (Forrest, 1979a). The alcoholic thinks, feels and behaves according to a plethora of narcissistic dictates. This adjustment style becomes a lifelong repetition compulsion involving various overdetermined methods for obtaining narcissistic need and entitlement gratifications. Grandiosity, megalomania, vanity, and self-centeredness describe the alcoholic's compulsive search for narcissistic supplies. Character behavior disorder or sociopathic adjustment dynamics are also associated with a deprivation oriented infancy and childhood. Indeed, most alcoholics are exploitative, manipulative and rather sociopathic. Individuals manifesting a long-term schizophrenic adjustment have experienced more intensive and pervasive early life narcissistic injury during infancy and childhood than the alcoholic.

The individual who eventually becomes addicted to alcohol and/or other addictive substances acts out a lifelong attempt to convince self and significant others that, in fact, she or he is worth loving. Alcoholics attempt to convince self and others that they deserve healthy narcissistic need and entitlement gratifications. The alcoholic conveys this message to significant others in a pathologically overdetermined manner. As a result, significant others reject or in other ways move away from the addicted person. At some point, an extremely narcissistic life-style becomes perhaps the only functional or workable coping style remaining for the alcoholic. This adjustment style becomes progressively more pathological and resistant to change. An overdetermined narcissistic character structure and adjustment style precipitates the progressive development of the pathology of self-centeredness. This process occurs and deters the potential for resolving narcissistic conflicts and pathology. As this particular character structure and adjustment style develops, the alcoholic's pathologic narcissism is continually reinforced. Immediate need gratification is the *modus vivendi* of the alcoholic. In essence, narcissistic disturbance constitutes the basis of the alcoholic's various interpersonal and intrapersonal living problems.

The children of alcoholics manifest very apparent psychopathology related to the matter of narcissistic need and entitlement deprivation. Overdetermined needs for attention and recognition, poor impulse control, low self-esteem, and self-centeredness are behavioral characteristics of the children of alcoholic parentage. This dynamic partially explains why the children of alcoholic parents so frequently become addicted to alcohol (Ackerman, 1978). It is very significant that this global experience with self and significant others may amount to a type of interpersonal programming that irreversibly sets up given individuals for the eventual actualization of the alcoholic symptom choice. Such individuals are continually and perhaps irreversibly reinforced into the alcoholic trap. Infantile and childhood narcissistic injury may not constitute the "necessary and sufficient conditions" prerequisite to developing alcoholism. However, the individual who experiences this specific emotional climate in combination with an alcoholic parent or parents is a far more likely candidate for developing alcohol addiction (Forrest, 1978). This applies to family constellation including an alcoholic stepparent or stepparents, alcoholic grandparents who assume primary parenting roles and similar familial systems that provide consistent and long-term alcoholic modeling.

It is very difficult to investigate and study the problem of alcoholism on a longitudinal basis (Emrick, 1974 & 1975). Therefore, clinical descriptions and evaluations of alcoholic individuals tend to be conducted after the person is fully engaged in the addiction process. Therapists sometimes have the opportunity to work with individuals who can accurately be diagnosed as problem drinkers or alcohol abusers. Such individuals are not floridly addicted to alcohol. Nonetheless, they do evidence the prodromal narcissistic symptomatology indicative of significant potential for the eventual development of chronic alcoholism (Forrest, 1978). In these cases, therapists also find a plethora of manifest narcissistic behaviors.

Case histories of the alcoholic personality (Blane, 1968) amount to little more than accounts of the narcissistic character structure basic to this disorder. The total behavioral repertoire of the alcoholic is in many respects limited to a self-orientation. Extramaritial affairs, failure to pay bills, child neglect and abuse, global interpersonal behaviors, and the alcoholic *modus operandi* are self-centered. The alcoholic's various acting out behaviors are narcissistically overdetermined.

Alcoholics are so caught up in the unending process of attempting to cope and deal with their various intrapersonal difficulties that they become progressively narcissistic. At some point, it becomes virtually impossible for the alcoholic to be non-self centered. This is most obviously the situation in the case of tissue-addicted individuals. These persons are narcissistically obsessed with alcohol and drinking. At this point, the alcoholic is simply not capable of significant interpersonal giving. The chronically intoxicated alcoholic attempts to feel good, experience pleasure and avoid a diversity of painful feelings associated with withdrawal. The alcoholic's basic narcissistic security operations are eventually centered around the matters of drinking and alcohol.

Alcoholic persons neurotically and narcissistically attempt to demonstrate to self and others a sense of basic worth as human beings. Indeed, the alcoholic life-style becomes a method for sustaining narcissistic self-validation and consensual validation. The overdetermined narcissism which is basic to alcohol addiction can be interpreted as a pathological methodology by which the addicted individual attempts to convey to self, significant others and the phenomenal world that he or she is important, valued and loved. This is the very antithesis of the experiential reality of the alcoholic's infancy and childhood. The alcoholic acts out in order to obtain narcissistically oriented needs and entitlements. At the same time, the alcoholic is pre-consciously or unconsciously attempting to magically undo the emotional hurt, pain and deprivation experienced during infancy and childhood. In this sense, the narcissism of the alcoholic (Forrest, 1979a) represents a method for ritually undoing the multifaceted narcissistic injuries of early life. The alcoholic attempts to undo the original causes of his or her massive feelings of unworth, inferiority, unlove and rejection.

These psychodynamic factors relate to the magical properties that have historically been ascribed to alcoholic beverages. In reality, alcohol does allow the alcoholic to transiently escape many of the intrapersonal and interpersonal difficulties of daily living. Thus, alcohol is magic for the alcoholic! This factor further reinforces the addiction process. Orality is a basic component of alcoholism and narcissism. The developmental relationships between orality, narcissism and alcoholism will now be examined.

ORALITY, NARCISSISM AND ALCOHOLISM

Alcoholism and symptomatic drinking behavior have been viewed as manifestations of oral fixation (Freud, 1953). In essence, the alcoholic has been referred to as (Fenichel, 1945) an "orally fixated" personality type. The various psychodynamically oriented "schools" of personality theory and psychotherapy have espoused this position. These explanations of alcoholic behavior are surprisingly superficial and fragmented. Rarely did Freud ever mention the alcoholic personality in his extensive writings. In fact, none of his lengthy case presentations involve the long-term psychoanalytic treatment of an alcoholic patient. The neo-Freudians and subsequent personality theorists have also avoided any in-depth explorations of the etiology and development of the alcoholic personality. The psychodynamic issues associated with orality, narcissism and alcoholism have not been adequately explored.

The oral phase of personality development has received extensive consideration in the clinical literature (Fenichel, 1945; Freud, 1953; Sullivan, 1953). Clearly, the oral phase of personality development has a crucial impact upon the later development and adjustment of every human being. A multiplicity of psychodynamic considerations surrounding this phase of personality development have a profound impact upon the future development of the human organism (Kernberg, 1975; Masterson, 1981). The precise extent and nature of the impact of the oral phase of personality development upon subsequent character structure, personality style and adjustment remains unclear. Yet, the oral dynamism does shape character structure and personality development. For the human organism, reality is first constructed and experienced through the medium of the mouth. During the initial weeks and months of life, the infant begins to differentiate between self, significant others and the external world through the sensory medium of the oral dynamism.

The infant first experiences and processes narcissistic need and entitlement deprivation vis-à-vis the oral dynamism. The breast and breast objects (physical and emotional contact repertoire) of the mother and significant others directly communicate to the (pre-alcoholic) infant a sense of intense anxiety, insecurity and unlove. This emotional climate creates a personal sense of non-well-being in the infant. The primal narcissism of the human infant is first expressed through the oral dynamism. Hence, it is at this most basic developmental stage of human existence that the individual begins to be interpersonally programmed for any number of later life adjustment difficulties and pathological states. The human infant is prototaxically and narcissistically preoccupied with the satisfactory maintenace of its own self-system. This is essential to physical and emotional survival. The infant is in the unique position of being almost totally dependent upon the mouth for the completion of this difficult and multifaceted task. Crying, screaming, eating, sulking, sleep, and gross bodily movements represent the basic communication repertoire of the human infant. Hunger, fright, anxiety, the need for physical contact, and indeed all the basic needs of the human infant are expressed via the mouth. The infantile oral dynamism provides the most primitive mode of human communication. Security and survival are contingent upon the infant's ability to elicit loving, comforting and need and tension-reduction-oriented helping behaviors upon the part of parents and significant others.

Most parents respond to these primitive infantile communications with the keenest sense of awareness and responsiveness. This seems to be particularly true with regard to the totally nurturant, symbiotic, mother-infant relationship. The healthy mother-infant relationship is characteristically very symbiotic. The mother and infant seem to respond to each other's narcissistic needs in an uncanny and almost unwitting fashion. This has not been the case with most, if not all, alcoholics seen in psychotherapy and treatment programs.

During the oral stage of development, the alcoholic has suffered consistent orally oriented narcissistic injury. This experience precipitates the eventual alcoholic symptom choice and facilitates a lifelong warp in basic character structure. The oral disturbance experienced at this time is quite diffuse and pervasive. Narcissistic injury is internalized, experienced and processed vis-à-vis the infant's oral dynamism. All infantile experiences and feelings are orally oriented. Infantile and childhood narcissistic need and entitlement deprivation relating explicitly to the oral dynamism also assumes a central role in the development of the narcissistic (Kernberg, 1976) and alcoholic character structures. The earliest and most primitive method for obtaining narcissistic need and entitlement gratifications is vis-à-vis the oral apparatus. For the human organism, the precursor to all forms of narcissistic need and entitlement gratification is fundamentally the oral orifice. It is through the mouth and its supporting biologic structures that the infant learns to experience pleasure and anxiety reduction. These processes are eventually associated with self-directed or self-regulated behavior. In the acts of suckling and other forms of oral anxiety-reducing behavior, the infant prototypically experiences self as an agent that can control and manipulate significant others and the external world. Aside from finding such experiences to be pleasurable, anxiety reducing, and rewarding, the infant rather quickly capitalizes upon the power inherent in this process. Clearly, the oral process is narcissistic and also fosters narcissism.

Once the narcissistic needs and entitlements of the prealcoholic infant have been consistently and traumatically deprived during the course of the oral stage of personality development (Forrest, 1979a), two very costly lifelong consequences appear to follow: (1) this early experiential process facilitates the development of an overdetermined oral narcissistic character structure; and (2) the method of choice for meeting or partially fulfilling the later life narcissistic needs of a pathological narcissistic character structure are always oral. Thus, the development of a prodromal alcoholic character structure is linked with the faulty parental management (particularly as related to the mother-infant dyad) of infantile narcissistic needs and entitlements in combination with the oral dynamism.

An infancy and childhood experience in which the oral and other more global narcissistic needs and entitlements of the organism are not satisfactorily met precipitates a compulsive and never-ending acting out of this original source of hurt, rejection and deprivation. Alcoholics continually seek pleasure, self-worth and personal esteem and relevance as human beings through narcissistic acting out. This dilemma is the example par excellence of a repetition compulsion. Personal-need gratification, often at the emotional and physical expense of others, "looking out for oneself," sexual hedonism, and a relative lack of concern and warmth for others characterize the alcoholic adjustment style.

Oral dependency conflicts are basic to the alcoholic character structure. For the alcoholic, alcohol is the symbolic equivalent of the "good" mother's milk. Narcissistic need and entitlement deprivation symbolically and sometimes concretely involves a deprivation of the mother's breast, physical contact and thus milk. In a broader sense, the mother's breast and milk can be viewed as the symbolic prototypes for subsequent interpersonal and intrapersonal security operations. Healthy parenting and mothering facilitate feelings of inner tranquility, lack of anxiety and apprehension, and a generalized feeling of personal well-being.

The alcoholic eventually discovers alcohol and its magical ability to superficially induce narcissistic gratification. Once the alcoholic experiences the transparent gains facilitated by alcohol ingestion, the developmental process of alcohol addiction is initiated. The alcoholic subsequently chooses to drink alcoholically on thousands of occasions. Alcoholism is an oral solution to both narcissistic injury and narcissistic gratification. Intoxication is a pathological form of narcissistic gratification.

Pathological dependency needs and conflicts are closely associated with both the oral dynamism and the matter of narcissism. Pathological dependency (Blane, 1968) is basic to the alcoholic character structure. The overdetermined dependency needs of the alcoholic are manifest in numerous ways. Some addicted individuals appear to have counter-dependent personalities (Forrest, 1978). In spite of surface appearances, these individuals are grossly dependent. Etiologically, the pathological dependency needs and conflicts of the alcoholic stem from infantile and childhood narcissistic need and entitlement deprivation. Dependency and dependency oriented needs and behaviors are genetic to the human organism. The oral dynamism is the primary instrument or apparatus by which dependency needs and behaviors are first expressed.

Dependent behaviors are syntaxic with the narcissistic nature of the human organism. Infantile narcissistic injury is closely related to the neglect and mismanagement of the infant's dependency needs. Narcissistic need and entitlement deprivation reinforces the development of an overdependent character structure. Counter-dependency conflicts and other distorted dependency trends also evolve as a result of chronic narcissistic injury. The narcissistic oral dependency need complex operates in a syntaxic manner which produces the alcoholic character structure and behavioral style. Narcissistic injury is a core dynamism in the etiological development of chronic alcoholism. The oral and dependency conflicts of the alcoholic are explored at length in subsequent chapters.

PSYCHOTHERAPEUTIC CONSIDERATIONS

Historically, psychotherapists and clinicians have been less than enthusiastic and optimistic about working with alcoholics (Bratter, 1979; Forrest, 1979c & 1982a). In large measure, this general sentiment is closely associated with the narcissistic character armoring of the alcoholic. The alcoholic is viewed as being poorly motivated for psychotherapy (Forrest, 1978a; Silverstein, 1980). Alcoholics act out while in treatment. Some therapists feel uncomfortable and threatened by alcoholics. In numerous other ways, this patient population has simply been perceived as not suitable or amenable to the armamentarium of most psychotherapists. Simple hospitalization and incarceration have been rather standard procedures for "treating" and administratively managing alcoholics. Such procedures can be clinically sound and appropriate. However, a plethora of other treatment strategies and modalities are required for the successful psychotherapy and rehabilitation of most alcoholics. These issues pertain to the generalized lack of psychotherapeutic success in treatment and rehabilitation efforts with alcoholics. Recidivism, the "revolving door," and agency dissonance are but a few of the clinical issues germane to the psychotherapy and rehabilitation of alcoholics (Forrest, 1978).

Alcoholic patients are pathologically narcissistic. Moreover, this reality is a major psychodynamic consideration throughout the course of all successful psychotherapy relationships with alcoholics. The therapeutic resolution of the alcoholic patient's pathologic narcissism constitutes a sine qua non of effective therapeutic work. Relatively effective psychotherapeutic treatment may produce partial abstinence or prolonged periods of total sobriety for many alcoholic patients. However, long-term sobriety, marked personality growth and behavioral change, serenity, and a "radically changed life-style" (Forrest, 1975) can only be accomplished through the effective psychotherapeutic resolution of the patient's narcissistic character armoring. This does not imply that the successful psychotherapy of alcoholism requires years of intensive work. The narcissistic pathology of most alcoholics can be significantly modified in the course of six to ten months of intensive therapy.

A successful therapeutic resolution of the alcoholic's pathologically narcissistic character structure is contingent upon the therapist's understanding of the relevance of this dynamism to the patient's historic life-style and adjustment. The therapist must focus the therapy relationship in the direction of exploring the present, as well as historic, meaning and personal relevance of the patient's narcissistically oriented behaviors and adjustment style. Needless to say, the development of an emotional climate characterized by empathy, trust, openness and warmth is a pre-condition to this form of patient self-exploration. The patient can learn to openly explore and modify the genetic origins of his or her narcissistic pathology.

The alcoholic's narcissistic adjustment style is neurotically ineffective, and the therapist must help the patient to understand this dilemma. The therapist also actively and consistently explores the role that alcohol has played in the patient's narcissism. Movement towards others becomes possible when the alcoholic begins to modify and terminate his or her manipulative behavior, con games, and narcissistically oriented interpersonal transactions. The drinking alcoholic continually drives away significant others. Alcoholics angrily attack other people. These interpersonal realities have been a historic source of extreme pain and hurt for most alcoholic individuals.

Within the psychotherapy relationship, the therapist must consistently confront (Forrest, 1982a) and help the patient deal with the various manifestations of his or her self-centered character structure. As the psychotherapy process begins to successfully unfold, the alcoholic begins to behave less narcissistically. Eventually, the alcoholic no longer drives others away vis-à-vis his or her overwhelmingly self-centered behavioral repertoire. At this point, a more healthy interpersonally adjustment style is set in motion, the patient begins to develop a more positive self-concept, the alcoholic's perceptions of others begin to change and significant others begin to feel and perceive the healthy change that the patient is making. These processes facilitate even greater growth and change. The synergistic effect of the successful psychotherapeutic (Forrest, 1983) process is well known to the psychotherapist.

Successful intensive psychotherapy with alcoholic patients encompasses a therapeutic resolution of the alcoholic "power fantasy" (Forrest, 1978). The psychopathology of the alcoholic's megalomania and power fantasy is psychogenically associated with narcissistic injury. The therapist helps the alcoholic face and deal with the specific or generalized elements of the power fantasy system. The patient struggles through the medium of power fantasy ideation to feel powerful, important, potent, and significant. Feelings of inadequacy, rejection, and worthlessness experienced during infancy and childhood are, in part, transcended or partially extinguished through the development of a compensatory power fantasy system. Long-term sobriety and bona fide characterological change are the products of a successful psychotherapeutic resolution of the alcoholic's power fantasy system. The narcissistic elements of the alcoholic's self-system frequently represent the nuclear neurotic core of this disorder. With some degree of regularity, individuals actively involved in Alcoholics Anonymous seem to be able to resolve the major elements of their narcissistic behavioral style. This working through of the alcoholic's pathologic narcissism seems to take place after a number of years of active participation in the A A program and an accompanied dedication to working the program.

Within the context of the patient-therapist relationship, the patient develops the capacity to openly share with the therapist all of his or her innermost feelings of inadequacy, impotence and inferiority. This aspect of the psychotherapeutic process extinguishes the patient's compulsion to neurotically overcompensate for these underlying feelings of insecurity. Thus, the alcoholic patient is able to give up his or her facade and neurotic overcompensation behaviors. The psychotherapy relationship helps the patient resolve various identity problems. The alcoholic becomes capable of giving up his or her parataxic fantasy ideation by openly exploring genuine feelings, behaviors and thought processes with the psychotherapist.

Successful resolution of the alcoholic power fantasy and the alcoholic's narcissistic character structure relates to the therapist's ability to help the patient consistently deal with many self-oriented existential and experiential realities. This treatment strategy helps the alcoholic patient gain an ability to know and understand who he or she is and, perhaps more importantly, to accept self. When this becomes possible, the patient no longer must depend upon the medium of a distorted narcissistic life-style in order to feel worthwhile and significant. At this therapeutic juncture, the alcoholic can begin to experience a meaningful and productive life. This is a very rewarding experience for the patient and the therapist!

Alcoholics are difficult to treat. For many therapists and counselors, these treatment difficulties are associated with the alcoholic's tendency to confront and challenge authority figures. Many therapists are extremely uncomfortable with the alcoholic's angry, confrontive behaviors (Forrest, 1982a). Alcoholics deny and avoid their many conflicts. Many alcoholics have a passive-aggressive personality style. All of these factors can be major obstacles to the psychotherapist's utilization of effective treatment techniques. When counselors and other treatment personnel understand the role and genesis of these confrontive, challenging, and passive-aggressive character traits of the alcoholic, therapy and rehabilitation efforts are significantly more successful and easier. Extensive clinical experience and ongoing professional supervision are essential to the therapist's ability to understand and effect a therapeutic resolution of the alcoholic symptom choice.

SUMMARY

This chapter elucidates the pathological and indeed catastrophic effects of an infancy and childhood experience in which the basic narcissistic needs and entitlements of the human organism are simply not met or fulfilled. It is theorized that such an experience in early living consistently facilitates the development of an overdetermined narcissistic character structure. Alcoholism is viewed as a narcissistic disturbance. This position is not new to the clinical literature. Schizophrenia, anaclitic depressions, and primary sociopathy are also etiologically associated with profound infantile and childhood narcissistic injury (Forrest, 1982d).

This chapter systematically delineates the various psychogenic interrelationships involving early deprivation of basic narcissistic needs and entitlements, the oral dynamism, dependency, and the later life alcoholic adjustment mode with its concomitant narcissistic character armoring. These clinical issues are considered at length in the following chapters. Alcoholic individuals manifest a plethora of clinical features that are not considered in this chapter. Nonetheless, narcissistic need and entitlement deprivation is a basic etiological factor in the development of the addictive character structure. Such a position is subject to caveats.

A brief section dealing with basic psychotherapeutic considerations specific to the problem of narcissism and the alcoholic patient is included in this chapter. This section is truncated. Much of the clinical material explored in this chapter pertains to the etiology and the treatment of all addictive disorders.

Chapter Three

ALCOHOLISM AND ANXIETY

INTRODUCTION

ANXIETY has long been associated with alcohol abuse and chronic alcohol addiction (Blane, 1968; Forrest, 1978 & 1982b). Indeed, it has been theorized that anxiety (Fann et al., 1980) causes alcoholism. The anxiety-based etiological theory of alcoholism has received considerable clinical support (Catanzaro, 1968; Forrest, 1978). Research evidence (Pattison, 1980) also consistently suggests that anxiety plays an important role in the development and maintenance of alcoholism. The problem of anxiety is central to alcohol abuse and alcoholism. The psychotherapeutic management and resolution of anxiety is essential to the successful treatment of alcoholics.

Interpersonal anxiety is a fundamental ingredient in the addiction process. Anxiety can be defined as the experience of interpersonal and/or intrapersonal apprehension or psychological discomfort. The source or sources of anxiety usually remain unknown to the anxious person. The origins of chronic anxiety tend to reside within the more primitive levels of human consciousness and awareness. However, the experience of acute anxiety can frequently be associated with rather specific target sources or precipitating factors. Within the explicit confines of the effective psychotherapeutic alliance, it is often possible for the patient and therapist to develop a rather precise understanding of the various sources of the patient's anxiety. The psychotherapeutic process uncovers the patient's preconscious and unconscious sources of anxiety. However, very few individuals become engaged in a psychotherapy relationship. As such, most individuals experience varying types and degrees of anxiety emitting from seemingly unknown sources. These factors explain the experience of "free-floating" anxiety.

The experience of anxiety results in a number of well-documented organismic responses (Mines and Yost, 1983). Elevated blood pressure, change in pulse, pupil dilation, respiratory change, change in galvanic skin response, and the total organismic "fight or flight" adaptation response are but a few of the physiological variables directly affected by the experience of acute or chronic anxiety. Physiologically, this pattern of organismic response to anxiety is much akin to a fear reaction. The detrimental effects of anxiety upon personality development and adjustment have long been recognized. Anxiety has been associated with virtually all forms of psychopathology.

This chapter explores (a) the etiological basis of anxiety in alcoholism, (b) the interpersonal and intrapersonal nature of anxiety, and (c) the role of pathological anxiety in the maintenance of alcoholism.

ALCOHOLISM, ANXIETY AND NARCISSISTIC INJURY

The alcoholic is chronically anxious (Forrest, 1978). Since birth, the alcoholic has experienced profound and potentially overwhelming feelings of anxiety. For the alcoholic, the experience of anxiety stems from pervasive narcissistic need and entitlement deprivation. The interpersonal and intrapersonal experiences of infancy are centered around the affect of anxiety. Birth represents the prototype of all subsequent anxiety experiences. The reality of infancy and childhood includes matters pertaining to eating, sleeping, stimulation, physical contact, temperature control, physical illness, and the maintenance of adequate interpersonal security operations. All of these processes are intimately linked with the experience of potentially profound, or overwhelming, levels of anxiety. During these developmental epochs, every human being is primitively confronted with the task of coping with a plethora of anxiety-producing realities.

Indeed, anxiety is an ever-present reality associated with being human. Interpersonal experiences shape each person's capacity for coping with anxiety. Interpersonal and intrapersonal factors in combination with genetic makeup interact to determine an individual's style of managing anxiety. These issues create the primary anxiety symptomatology of the alcoholic. The narcissistic injuries that the alcoholic has experienced during infancy, childhood and later developmental eras result in chronic and acute feelings of intense anxiety. Human beings experience anxiety when significant others fail to meet their narcissistic needs and entitlements.

The alcoholic experiences profound and near catastrophic levels of anxiety as a result of early life narcissistic injury. The mother or surrogate mother is the most important person in the world of the infant and young child. The mother of the alcoholic is unable to provide adequate infantile and childhood narcissistic need and entitlement gratifications. Commonly, the mother of the alcoholic rejects her infant. Foster home placements, giving the child up to parents or relatives, or abandonment have frequently been the fate of the alcoholic during the initial epochs of living. Characteristically, the mother of the alcoholic is anxious and conflicted. Many of these mothers are unable to tolerate intimate physical contact with their children. The mother of the alcoholic is emotionally ill-prepared to "mother" and parent. Some of these women experience marked anxiety associated with feeding or nursing. They may also be angry and poorly controlled in their interactions with the infant. Parental anger and rage may result in child abuse. Alcoholics tend to have experienced a great deal of verbal and physical abuse during childhood (Ackerman, 1978). These interpersonal realities facilitate the experience of intense anxiety.

Narcissistic entitlement deprivation is also a precursor to the experience of intense anxiety. The alcoholic senses and feels that he or she is unloved, unimportant and unwanted by parents and significant others. Parents have failed to communicate a sense of personal worth and dignity to the alcoholic. These parental and family transactions can be extremely anxiety producing. Parental management of the infant's narcissistic entitlements shape the self-system and self-concept of the evolving person. Consistent narcissistic entitlement deprivation facilitates the development of later life neurotic symptomatology.

Alcohol addiction develops as a function of the orally precipitated anxiety experiences of the infant and child. Anxiety is associated with orality in several ways. The orally oriented sources of infantile anxiety often stem from feeding disturbances related to the anxiety of the mother. Infantile oral anxiety can be precipitated by the lack of feeding or inconsistent patterns of feeding. The affective response of the infant and the global affective components surrounding the infant-mother dyad during feeding precipitate basic infantile oral-anxiety experiences. The anxiety that the infant experiences during feeding is prototaxically associated with narcissistic need and entitlement deprivation messages. The infant experiences intense anxiety due to disturbed feeding and disturbed orality. These primitive experiences convey to the infant a sense of being unloved, rejected, abandoned and worthless. If the mother and significant others fail to adequately provide for the infant's narcissistic needs and entitlements, death or schizophrenia may occur.

The initial oral experiences of the human infant are intensely intimate human encounters. The feeding experiences of mother and infant are interpersonal. For the infant, reality is almost singularly a matter of orality. The infant is also a totally oral-dependent being. The prototaxic oral experiences of feeling rejected, unwanted and neglected precipitate acute anxiety. The oral-dependency needs of the infant may be catastrophically threatened by a lack of feeding, inconsistent feeding patterns or as a result of intense anxiety surrounding feeding.

Anxiety experiences fused with orality create chronic, unresolved, interpersonal and intrapersonal anxiety. The primitive learning and neurological "programming" specific to disturbed mother-infant orality facilitates oral fixation and an overdetermined utilization of oral mechanisms to avoid anxiety. These processes are associated with the chronic anxiety problems of the alcoholic. The overdetermined infantile and childhood anxiety experiences of the alcoholic may result in central nervous system and neurological changes that result in chronic characterological anxiety.

It must be emphasized that the initial anxiety experiences of the infant are orally precipitated and interpersonally determined.

One distinguishing clinical characteristic of all alcoholics is that of chronic interpersonal anxiety (Forrest, 1978 & 1983). The process of being chronically anxious stems from the basic anxiety experiences of the infant with his or her mother and significant others. Developmentally, intense oral anxiety is very destructive in its impact upon character structure and personality makeup. The more pervasive and extended the orally based anxiety experiences of the infant, the more profound is the effect upon subsequent emotional adjustment and character structure.

Following the "oral stage" of personality development, matters pertaining to a disturbed orality continue to predominate the alcoholic's interpersonal and intrapersonal development. Thus, the orally precipitated anxiety experiences of the infant are significantly related to the intrapersonal and interpersonal adjustment of the evolving person as a child, adolescent and adult. The initial orally oriented anxiety experiences of the alcoholic are never left in the experiential past. Alcoholics continually bind anxiety through a variety of overdetermined orally oriented behaviors. Our culture seems to reinforce pathological orality. Overeating, preoccupation with eating, the consumption of alcoholic beverages, and smoking represent but a few of our culturally accepted and reinforced pathological oral behaviors (Harper, 1982). There are a number of culturally reinforced and yet pathological methods for orally controlling or binding anxiety; alcoholism is but one of these "methods." Depression and other affects are also associated with the oral dynamism. However, it is anxiety binding that primarily precipitates the oral pathology of chronic alcoholism, chain-smoking, bulemia and other eating disorders.

Much of the anxiety of the infant can, in fact, be controlled or extinguished via the oral dynamism. The acutely anxious or enraged infant quite typically becomes less anxious or enraged when a parent initiates feeding and/or physical contact. In a similar fashion, the alcoholic controls or significantly reduces his or her intrapersonal and interpersonal feelings of anxiety via the oral ingestion of alcohol. A diversity of threatening affects can be extinguished by intoxication. In this sense, alcoholic beverages acquire a magical property. The alcoholic learns to control or bind anxiety vis-à-vis alcohol ingestion. This process is similar to infantile feeding or nursing. The alcoholic progressively learns to bind anxiety feelings through the medium of alcohol. Intoxication serves the interpersonal function of keeping significant others removed from the self. Intoxication also serves the purpose of repressing the alcoholic's self-awareness of being anxious. Eventually, the alcoholic can only feel comfortable with significant others after reaching a state of intoxication or partial intoxication. Sobriety exacerbates the alcoholic's orally oriented sources of anxiety. The alcoholic experiences profound anxiety feelings associated with annihilation, rejection, and narcissistic injury. These feelings are initially experienced and processed within the context of the mother-infant relationship. Unconsciously, the adult alcoholic fears this same catastrophic anxiety experience in his or her relationships with significant others. In an obsessive-compulsive fashion, the alcoholic attempts to magically or ritually undo this interpersonal dilemma by moving towards others and significant others while intoxicated. Alcohol, like milk for the infant, partially extinguishes the interpersonal anxieties of the alcoholic (Forrest, 1983), thus facilitating a caricature of meaningful interpersonal engagement. The alcoholic neurotically binds interpersonal and intrapersonal anxiety vis-à-vis the orality of drinking and intoxication.

Juxtaposed to the alcoholic's pathologic initial and ongoing overdetermined oral binding of anxiety is the concomitant problem of inadequate ego development or self-system fragmentation. Inadequate ego development occurs as a function of orally oriented infantile and childhood anxiety experiences. The alcoholic experiences chronic anxiety associated with the matter of basic identity and manifests a less than adequately consolidated nuclear sense of self. An inadequately consolidated self-system precipitates acute anxiety relative to (a) the differentiation between self and significant others, and (b) the development of chronically inadequate ego boundaries. In the absence of an effective therapeutic experience, the alcoholic never resolves these sources of anxiety and chronic trepidation. These matters pertain to the ego structure and intrapersonal adjustment of *both* male and female alcoholics. Early life difficulties pertaining to adequately consolidating the self-system and differentiating effectively between self and significant others, especially as these matters relate to the mother-self relationship, facilitate long-term "blurring" of the ego boundaries (Kernberg, 1975; Forrest, 1978; Masterson, 1981). This process is always accompanied by intense and chronic internal anxiety. The alcoholic is constantly struggling with self-other differentiation problems. Alcoholics must also continually work at maintaining a functional degree of ego integration. Anxiety causes and maintains the intrapersonal and interpersonal pathology basic to these processes.

Alcohol serves an integrative ego function during the initial stages of the addiction process. The ingestion of alcoholic beverages significantly reduces or extinguishes the alcoholic's anxiety related to self-other differentiation, facilitates interpersonal engagement, and thus effects a neurotic solution to the problem of inadequate ego boundaries. Interpersonal movements toward and with others are very difficult for the alcoholic. Alcohol ingestion also provides a neurotic solution to these problems.

The vast majority of alcoholics treated in psychotherapy and rehabilitation programs do not experience overwhelming levels of anxiety after initiating and maintaining sobriety. However, movements toward and with significant others while sober precipitate increased feelings of anxiety. This is due to the pathology of self-other differentiation and a structural deficit of the ego or self-system. The alcoholic's recovery is contingent upon learning that sober interpersonal encounters involving closeness, intimacy, interpersonal relatedness, attachment, and ego involvement will not result in madness or ego defusion.

The pre-conscious and conscious fear of loss of gender identity is another psychodynamic issue pertaining to the anxiety-producing matters of self-other differentiation and self-system fragmentation. Gender-related anxiety is genetic to the alcoholic character structure. The alcoholic is chronically anxious relative to the matters of self-other differentiation and ego integration. Therefore, psychological investment of the self in others and interpersonal attachments pre-consciously and unconsciously equate with ego fusion and thus sexual fusion. Gender-identity pathology creates profound anxiety pertaining to matters of homosexuality and bisexuality. Alcoholics tend not to consciously understand this very powerful source of anxiety. Quite simply, much of the "Who am I?" dilemma of the alcoholic psychogenically centers around the basic question of "Am I really a man?" or "Am I really a woman?" These identity-oriented sources of anxiety stem directly from ego or self-system pathology. Self-system fragmentation by definition dictates the presence of chronic, diffuse, and potentially overwhelming levels of anxiety. Oral processes represent the most primitive method for binding anxiety stemming from defective ego integration. The pathological drinking behavior of the alcoholic thus represents a primitive psychological method for binding or controlling ego-threatening levels of anxiety. The alcoholic, like the infant, resorts to oral gratification when confronted with anxiety-producing stimuli. Alcoholism is a disorder of oral regression. Paradoxically, the alcoholic is able to derive ego strength and self-system integration vis-à-vis the addiction process.

Individuals who are addicted to other chemicals also experience chronic, near overwhelming levels of anxiety. Characterologically, these individuals are quite similar to the alcoholic. The overt behavioral style and character structure of most chemically dependent individuals closely parallels the alcoholic. Heroin addicts are behaviorally and characterologically similar to the alcoholic. Heroin addicts and other "hard" drug abusers are not as dependent upon the oral dynamism as an anxiety-binding method. However, all of the addictions involve the psychopathology of anxiety. Addicts attempt to bind anxiety through the use of substances external to the self. Addicted persons are unable to control anxiety through the medium of internal self-system resources.

Anxiety is always a crucial ingredient in the maintenance of the addiction process. Many variables can be related to the experience of chronic anxiety and/or intense anxiety. Anxiety and hyperactivity may be associated with metabolic problems, blood-sugar imbalance, genetic factors, or other biophysiological effectors of behavior. Biophysiological effectors of behavior may be related to hyperactivity and anxiety during the totality of an individual's life. Biophysiological variables also facilitate and maintain the addiction process. Human beings are biologically addictive.

The alcoholic experiences persistent and chronic anxiety. Developmental maturation does not result in anxiety reduction or resolution. As the alcoholic enters adolescence and adulthood, he or she becomes increasingly aware of very threatening levels of interpersonal and internal anxiety. The more inadequate, unloved, rejected, and inferior the alcoholic feels, the more anxious he or she becomes. The more aware the alcoholic becomes of having these feelings, the more anxious he or she becomes! Alcoholics make themselves anxious. It is very difficult for the alcoholic to experience a basic sense of comfortableness with self and others. The processes of maturation and aging provide for a greater number of successful interpersonal encounters and transactions while at the same time creating the conditions essential to more sensitive and critical self and other assessment. Thus, the alcoholic becomes increasingly prone to the experience of acute and conscious anxiety as he or she ages.

Prototaxic anxiety experiences are replaced by rational and internal anxiety experiences. Interpersonally determined anxiety eventually fuses with intrapersonally determined anxiety (Ellis, 1979). Eventually, the alcoholic is encapsulated in a world of chronic and profound anxiety. At some point, the alcoholic finds that drinking to control or partially extinguish anxiety no longer works. Chronic intoxication eventually synergizes the anxiety feelings and conflicts of the alcoholic. The alcoholic is interpersonally and intrapersonally trapped vis-à-vis alcoholism and anxiety. The alcoholic experiences overwhelming or near overwhelming anxiety as a result of the addiction process per se. Psychotic decompensation may actually be precipitated by the addiction process.

The chronic alcoholic is unable to resolve many developmental issues and conflicts relative to adolescence and adulthood. Alcoholics have failed to resolve and work through a plethora of developmental issues pertaining to infancy, childhood, the oedipal years, and latency. Further developmental deficits occur as a function of adolescent and adult intoxication. In reality, anxiety plays a crucial role in the alcoholic's pervasive developmental deficits and developmental arrest. Early life anxiety pertaining to internalized feelings of inadequacy, inferiority and worthlessness determine and reinforce the experience of anxiety pertaining to these same self-perceptions during adolescence and adulthood.

Chronic intoxication facilitates feelings of low self-esteem and low self-worth. Intoxication also results in behavioral inappropriateness. The more prolonged and intense the experience of intoxication, the more bizarre the individual becomes with regard to perceived (self and other) social or transactional behaviors. Thus, sobriety may precipitate intense anxiety feelings associated with reality and the "crazy" behaviors of the past. Many alcoholics consciously understand that giving up or terminating their addiction will result in acute anxiety feelings and internal turmoil. These individuals know that the process of attempting to deal with and resolve internal struggles pertaining to earlier developmental interactions with self and significant others will be anxiety provoking. In short, the deviant role behaviors of the alcoholic play an important part in his or her experience of marked interpersonal and intrapersonal anxiety. Anxiety caused by inappropriate or ineffective patterns of social interaction can also facilitate further intoxication. This is a matter that is synergized via a number of interacting processes. Perceiving oneself as inferior, inadequate, and inept as a result of social learning experiences with parents, parental surrogates, and significant others creates extensive social or interpersonal anxiety that dictates social alienation and social anxiety. Alcoholics tend to manifest poor or inadequate social skills. At some point in the addiction process, alcoholics drive themselves crazy as a result of their inappropriate behavioral transactions and the subsequent self-dialogue that accompanies these transactions (Forrest, 1979a & 1982a).

PSYCHOTHERAPEUTIC CONSIDERATIONS

The psychotherapeutic management of the alcoholic's anxiety is a paramount issue pertaining to the establishment and maintenance of long-term sobriety. Many alcoholics become acutely anxious after two or three weeks of total abstinence. The exacerbation of profound anxiety feelings following the establishment of total abstinence does not occur in every alcoholic patient. However, the effective clinical management of this affect is of the utmost importance in at least 70 percent of alcoholics becoming involved in rehabilitation programs and/or intensive psychotherapy. Acute alcohol withdrawal is frequently accompanied by potentially ego disorganizing levels of anxiety. At this time, the alcoholic is acutely anxious and verbalizes the fear of "losing my mind" or experiencing a "nervous breakdown."

It is appropriate (Wooddell, 1980) to provide psychotropic medication for patients experiencing borderline delirium tremens (DT's) or florid DT's. Acute alcohol withdrawal resulting in delirium tremens almost always results in catastrophic and disorganizing levels of anxiety. Appropriate medical management of acute alcohol withdrawal includes the utilization of such anti-anxiety agents as Librium® and Valium®. Physicians and therapists need to remember that alcoholic patients very quickly and easily become addicted to the minor tranquilizers and other addictive medications. Thus, it is imperative that the therapist utilize the therapeutic alliance to reduce patient anxiety rather than merely enabling the patient to switch addictions. The most potent source of the alcoholic's feelings of anxiety stem from his or her initial and prolonged parataxic interpersonal encounters. Therefore, the therapeutic alliance offers a significant and beneficial long-term method for helping the patient resolve anxiety. One very salient dimension of the corrective emotional experience (Forrest, 1978) offered via the medium of the psychotherapy relationship is that of allowing the patient the opportunity to affectively and cognitively integrate the experiences of human intimacy, relatedness, contact, warmth, concern and love. The patient learns vis-à-vis the psychotherapy experience that intimate interpersonal relationships are not by definition threatening, anxiety producing, and destructive. The alcoholic discovers in therapy that human intimacy does not result in annihilation, castration or the destruction of the self.

Short-term psychotherapy rarely effects a significant modification of the alcoholic's interpersonal and intrapersonal adjustment style. Brief therapy may help the patient establish short-term sobriety. However, the recalcitrant nature of the alcoholic's interpersonal and intrapersonal sources of anxiety dictate long-term psychotherapeutic engagement in order to achieve prolonged sobriety, behavior change and characterological change. If the alcoholic is unable to partially or significantly reduce internal distress and anxiety while sober and engaged in the treatment process, he or she can be expected to resume drinking. The armamentarium of the psychotherapist should include deep muscle relaxation, hypnosis, and other treatment strategies specifically designed to help the alcoholic patient modify and control anxiety (Byers, 1982). However, such treatment techniques are ancillary to the healing nature of the therapeutic alliance.

Anxiety (Freud, 1953) is a primitive response to death or impending annihilation of the self-system. Consistent with this position, the alcoholic experiences profound and chronic anxiety associated with death. The alcoholic experiences anxiety associated with the matter of his or her self-destruction via the addiction process. Alcoholics also experience intense existentially oriented anxiety. However, the alcoholic is unconsciously and preconsciously, if not consciously, acutely anxious with regard to his or her systematic attempt to destroy self. Alcoholics experience profound anxiety as a result of their apparent inability to modify, or somehow terminate, this vicious process of self-destruction. Alcoholics know that they are their own worst enemy. Yet, while actively entrapped in the addiction process, they remain totally impotent in the matter of reversing this process. On a daily basis, the drinking alcoholic experiences the physical and psychological pain of his or her suicidal intoxication. Death anxiety is associated with hangovers, marital conflicts, problems with the children, and legal involvements. All of these transactions (Scott, 1979) encompass self-inflicted or masochistic pain. These symbolic acts of self-destruction actually represent very concrete and direct attacks against the self. Every alcoholic experiences considerable anxiety related to the matter of going crazy. Fears of insanity are also symbolically related to death anxiety. In the unconscious, madness is but a step away from death. Craziness is a form of death.

SUMMARY

In this chapter, the concept of anxiety was defined as the experience of interpersonal and intrapersonal apprehension or psychological discomfort. Interpersonally determined anxiety plays a crucial role in the development and maintenance of the addiction disorders. The pathological anxiety of the alcoholic tends to be chronic and etiologically relates to the experience of pervasive early life narcissistic need and entitlement deprivation. Infantile and childhood narcissistic injury experiences precipitate profound and near catastrophic anxiety in the human organism. The early life anxiety responses of the infant are directly facilitated or precipitated by the mother and significant others. Thus, anxiety is interpersonally determined. The prototaxic anxiety experiences of the infant and child center around matters of feeding and orality. Later in life, the alcoholic attempts to bind or control ego-threatening levels of anxiety via the oral process of chronic alcohol ingestion. Alcohol is the later life equivalent of milk and other anxiety reducing, orally incorporated substances. Oral rage is often fused with oral anxiety. These processes are associated with the self-destructive aspects of chronic alcoholism.

The profound anxiety experiences of the infant and child dictate inadequate ego development. This becomes a developmental issue that is never fully resolved in the case of the alcoholic. Hence, the chronic anxiety of the alcoholic evolves from and creates self-system fragmentation. Self-system fragmentation is overtly manifest vis-à-vis identity confusion and gender conflict.

Anxiety also maintains the addiction process. The early life conflicts of the alcoholic involving anxiety facilitate long-term developmental psychopathology. During latency and adolescence, the alcoholic experiences progressively more intense feelings of anxiety. The alcoholic begins to cognitively recognize and understand anxiety feelings. During adolescence, the alcoholic typically learns (Forrest, 1982c) how effective alcohol is as an anti-anxiety agent. In this respect, the chronically anxious alcoholic is set up for engagement in the addiction process.

Chronic alcoholism can be viewed as a long-term process of self-medication. Self-medication via the ingestion of alcoholic beverages is aimed at extinguishing anxiety and other forms of psychological pain. During the later developmental stages of the addiction process, alcohol ingestion no longer effectively binds anxiety. At some point, continued alcohol ingestion actually synergizes the anxieties of the addicted individual. This poses a major dilemma for the alcoholic. Some alcoholics have utilized alcohol as an anti-anxiety agent for perhaps twenty or thirty years. These individuals are doubly confused when drinking begins to foster acute anxiety and disorganization.

Sobriety often exacerbates the alcoholic's feelings of stress and anxiety. The socially unacceptable and deviant role behaviors of the alcoholic contribute to internal feelings of anxiety associated with drinking. Many alcoholics experience anxiety after they enter treatment. Anxiety may be provoked by the patient's reality-oriented acceptance of prior alcohol-facilitated crazy behaviors.

The ability of the alcoholic to remain sober following rehabilitation or psychotherapeutic treatment is directly related to the matters of anxiety and anxiety reduction. Short-term psychotropic medication may help the alcoholic better cope with intense anxiety feelings facilitated by sobriety and treatment. Ultimately, the anxiety of the alcoholic is most effectively managed and resolved via the therapeutic alliance (Forrest, 1979b & 1983). Specific psychotherapeutic strategies may be employed by the therapist to help the alcoholic extinguish and resolve anxiety.

Prototaxically, anxiety serves the purpose of defending or warning the self-system of impending death. Alcoholics experience considerable anxiety specific to the matter of death. Alcoholics also experience anxiety related to the unconscious or pre-conscious, if not conscious, awareness that they are committing suicide vis-à-vis the addiction process. Every alcoholic is chronically anxious over the possibility of going crazy. The process of becoming mad is often primitively associated with death or symbolic death.

The alcoholic's experience of pathological anxiety can be associated with blood-sugar problems, metabolic disorder, and other more biophysiologically oriented processes. Nonetheless, the clinical issues discussed in this chapter elucidate the basic role of anxiety in the development and maintenance of alcoholism. The alcoholic must defend his or her self-system from the experience of overwhelming and disorganizing levels of anxiety. The defense mechanisms and anxiety binding and characterological dynamisms of the alcoholic are discussed in the next chapter.

Chapter Four

ALCOHOLISM AND THE AVOIDANCE DEFENSE SYSTEM

INTRODUCTION

ALCOHOL addiction and the other chemical dependencies evolve from a particular character structure. The addictive character structure is almost without exception the product of a deprivation-oriented infancy and childhood. The parents and significant others of the alcoholic are not able to consistently provide warm, nurturant, narcissistic need and entitlement gratifications for their offspring during the stages of infancy and childhood. In fact, such parents are often physically abusive, rejecting, excessively punitive, and neglectful of their children.

It is rather well-established (Ackerman, 1980; Wegscheider, 1981) that the parents of the alcoholic tend to have suffered similar parenting experiences during infancy and childhood. Frequently, the parents of the alcoholic are also alcoholic or abuse other chemical substances. Extended familial experiences of these varieties amount to a form of interpersonal and intrapersonal programming that may result in chronic alcoholism. Many individuals appear to be programmed to develop alcohol addiction. Perhaps this general set of living experiences creates the necessary, but not all inclusive, conditions for becoming an alcoholic.

The nuclear character structure of the alcoholic is closely associated with the avoidance defense system. This avoidance defense system is a product of the experience of pervasive infantile and childhood narcissistic need and entitlement deprivation. It is also psychogenic to the subsequent developmental process of becoming addicted to alcohol. The genesis and function of the alcoholic avoidance defense system will be explored in this chapter.

ORIGINS AND STRUCTURE OF THE AVOIDANCE DEFENSE SYSTEM

The problem of denial is well known to clinicians and psychotherapists involved in the treatment of alcoholics and substance abusers. The research and clinical literature (Forrest, 1978a & 1982d; Knauert, 1979; Emrick, 1979) indicates that pathological denial is central to the maintenance of the addiction process. Denial is one of the most primitive defense mechanisms. Significant efforts have been directed at elucidating the relevance of denial as a defense mechanism of the alcoholic (Blane, 1968). However, very little has been done in the area of exploring the psychogenic roots of the denial-oriented character structure of the alcoholic. Denial has frequently been espoused to be the primary component of the alcoholic's personality makeup and behavioral style. In reality, denial is but one significant element of a system of avoidance defenses basic to the alcoholic character structure.

The avoidance defense system of the alcoholic poses one of the most difficult barriers to our psychotherapeutic and rehabilitation efforts with this clinical population. Most typically, psychotherapists have attempted to resolve or significantly modify the addicted individual's denial defenses as a precursor to the implementation of effective ongoing treatment strategies. A major task that needs to be accomplished early in the psychotherapy of alcoholism is that of focusing upon the reality of the patient's addiction (Forrest, 1982a). The clinical methodology for accomplishing this fundamental treatment task may vary somewhat from patient to patient and between therapists. Nonetheless, the therapist attempts to facilitate the patient's ability to meaningfully internalize the reality of being addicted to alcohol. Initially, most alcoholics vehemently reject the various efforts of the therapist that are employed to confront them with the reality of their chemical dependence. These therapist-patient interactions cogently demonstrate the manner in which avoidance defenses characterize the total adjustment style of the alcoholic.

The denial of alcoholism is non-reality oriented. Therapists also have difficulty focusing upon the other glaring katagogic trends of the alcoholic that relate to the more generalized matter of avoidance defenses. Indeed, the denial-oriented defensive parameters of the alcoholic character structure may actually foster death. Many alcoholics are totally unable to evidence an ego-integrated acceptance of being addicted and thus actualize subsequent life-sustaining behavioral changes (Forrest, 1979b). In view of these clinical realities, psychotherapists are continually confronted with the basic importance of the avoidance defense system in maintaining the ego structure and self-system integrity of the alcoholic. The avoidance defense system constitutes the paradoxical cement of the alcoholic character structure and self-system.

Attempting to delineate the precise origins of the alcoholic avoidance defense system is very difficult. Clinical speculation and inference must be applied to the process of attempting to understand the etiology of the avoidance defense system. Extensive clinical work with alcoholic persons helps elucidate the evolution, role and function of the avoidance defense system in the developmental processes of alcoholism and alcohol abuse.

For the alcoholic, infancy and early childhood have been without exception very hurtful and painful eras of existence. Indeed, the interpersonal and intrapersonal experiences of infancy and childhood have involved extensive emotional and physical deprivation in the case of alcoholic persons. The alcoholic's fundamental infantile and childhood narcissistic need and entitlement gratifications have not been satisfactorily managed by parents and significant others. The alcoholic has felt rejected, unwanted, abandoned and unloved within the context of early life experiences with significant others. The mother, parental imagoes and significant others of the alcoholic have failed to meet his or her basic narcissistic needs and narcissistic entitlements. This interpersonal and intrapersonal historicity is basic to the development of the alcoholic character structure.

The development and maintenance of a rather specific defense system is genetic to the developmental process of alcoholism. In the absence of the evolution of this particular defense system, the primary psychopathology of alcoholism does not become an actualized reality. Less definitively stated, the probability of progressing through the various developmental stages of alcoholism is significantly reduced in the absence of developing an avoidance defense system. These are very recondite and perplexing clinical issues. A rigid and fixated avoidance defense system can be associated with schizophrenia and marked thought disorder psychopathology. In this sense, the avoidance defense system of the alcoholic is more functional and adaptive than the defensive structure of the schizophrenic. Most schizophrenics have experienced more intense and more profound narcissistic injury than the alcoholic. The character structure and adjustment style of the alcoholic are similar to the schizophrenic (Forrest, 1982d).

The avoidance defense system of the alcoholic evolves from a highly deprivation-oriented infancy and childhood. This defense system is essential to the psychological, if not physical, survival of the organism. Unfortunately, the avoidance defense system tends to be continually reinforced throughout the remainder of the alcoholic's life. Thus, the character structure of the alcoholic is an internal trap. The avoidance defense system is genetic to the alcoholic character structure and evolves from infantile, childhood and lifelong narcissistic injury.

Infantile and childhood narcissistic need and entitlement deprivation is an element of the early referential process that is cognitively incomprehensible to the infant and young child. However, the feeling or affective components of this type of early life interpersonal and intrapersonal reality potently construct the rudiments of a self-system and ego structure that perpetually strives to transcend or *avoid* this painful reality. Initially, the undifferentiated self (Kernberg, 1975, Bowen, 1978; Masterson, 1981) is the sole referent for processing feelings of unworth, unlove, abandonment, rejection and deprivation. Narcissistic injury is an interpersonal and intrapersonal process. Yet, the alcoholic is initially hurt and damaged vis-à-vis relationships with significant others. During the earliest developmental eras of life, it is parents and significant others that have communicated to the alcoholic a perpetual sense of non-well-being. Paradoxically, the healthiest and most adaptive defensive responses of the infant involve avoiding and denying the experience of narcissistic injury. The early life denial and avoidance defenses of the alcoholic have been reflexive and prototaxic in nature. This is due to the primitive and unsophisticated cognitive, perceptual, and central nervous system development of the organism at this time. Nonetheless, the affective set that develops from the initial experiences of narcissistic injury is strongly reinforced during subsequent anal, oedipal, phallic and adolescent stages of development. Alcoholics seen in psychotherapy can often vividly recall the many developmental realities of chronic narcissistic injury.

Many alcoholic patients report in therapy that they remember asking themselves over and over again during latency, "What's wrong with me?" or "What is it about me that makes my parents dislike me so much?" Indeed, this type of self-questioning is very much a part of the alcoholic's reported conscious awareness of self during the subsequent stages of adolescence. Alcoholics chronically attempt to avoid, deny and repress their feelings and experiences involving profound narcissistic injury. These efforts to deny and avoid the painful realities of the past do not work. The avoidance defense system constitutes a neurotic solution to the alcoholic's history of narcissistic need and entitlement deprivation. The avoidance defense system is grossly pathological and yet paradoxically life sustaining. The alcoholic's overdetermined defense system is set in motion shortly after birth.

The avoidance defense system of the alcoholic is essentially tripartite in nature. As mentioned earlier, denial is the most commonly understood defense mechanism basic to the alcoholic character structure. The avoidance defense system of the alcoholic is constructed vis-à-vis two other primary defense mechanisms. These defense mechanisms have not been extensively explored in the alcoholism literature. Distortion and projection are the other two defense mechanisms that constitute the primary core of the alcoholic's avoidance defense system. While other defense mechanisms may be central to the character structure and behavioral style of the alcoholic, they are clearly of secondary clinical relevance to the development and maintenance of the alcoholic adjustment mode.

The actual psychogenesis of the avoidance defense system begins with the overdetermined development of the denial defense mechanism. As such, this component of the alcoholic character structure is the most primitive and thus the least amenable to therapeutic and rehabilitation modification. Denial represents a methodology by which reality input can be totally blocked from conscious awareness. In the absence of conceptual and cognitive sophistication, the infant reflexively employs the denial defense mechanism in order to counteract a variety of primal sources of trepidation and anxiety. The overdetermined utilization of this defensive maneuver upon the part of a forty-year-old alcoholic is associated with denying and blocking out the experiences of infantile and childhood narcissistic injury. Denial is subsequently learned, reinforced, and overlearned for forty years! These factors explain the resistance and therapeutic problems associated with the therapist's attempts to change or modify this particular aspect of the alcoholic character structure. Interpersonally and intrapersonally, the alcoholic learns and continuously overlearns to deny feelings of rejection, abandonment, hurt, and unworth. For the alcoholic, part of the magic of childhood rests with the ability to simply deny the experience of narcissistic injury. In many respects, infancy and early childhood are unique eras with regards to the denial defense mechanism. In effect, the reality distortions of these eras are permitted, accepted, and even actively reinforced by significant others. This is a comfortable situation for the young child. Thus, the utilization of the denial defense mechanism is interpersonally and intrapersonally reinforced during infancy and childhood. In short, the denial defense mechanism evolves during the earliest developmental eras of human life. This defensive dynamism is created in the service of defending the infant and child from intense interpersonally determined anxiety. The denial defense mechanism also helps control or bind feelings of internal anxiety.

Rejection, physical and emotional deprivation, and pervasive narcissistic injury result in the infant's prototaxic fear of annihilation by parents and/or significant others. Parents and significant others play very important roles in facilitating the infant's feelings of anxiety, fear and terror. Thus, parents, parental imagoes, and significant others constitute major reinforcement contingencies that serve to create, enhance and maintain the alcoholic's denial defense mechanism. In order to psychologically and physically survive, the alcoholic has learned to deny overwhelming and catastrophic feelings of rejection, worthlessness, inadequacy and anxiety. Thus, in a neurotically adaptive fashion, denial plays a major role in the maintenance of the alcoholic self-system.

The distortion defense mechanism is the second primary defensive component of the alcoholic avoidance defense system. The distortion defense mechanism is less primitive than the denial defense mechanism. Distortion-oriented defenses evolve during the eras of infancy and childhood. The distortion defense mechanism also defends the self from threatening and anxiety-producing interpersonal feedback. Distortion is a defense against interactions and feelings that communicate a sense of being unwanted, unloved, and worthless. Such feedback must be distorted in order to maintain ego fusion and self-system integration. The prototaxic cognitive and affective operations of the young child encompass a primitive awareness and understanding of the experience of narcissistic injury. Infants and children reactively internalize and process their various experiences with significant others. The alcoholic's distortion defense mechanism may be operative and functional by the age of two-and-one-half years. However, the pathologically affective, productive, and reinforcing utilization of this defense mechanism comes about during the anal phase of personality development. Roughly speaking, it is when the child has reached the age of three or four that parents accurately observe and report the appearance of distortion tactics. Typical verbal reflections of the child's distortion defenses include, "I didn't hear you, Mommie." or "I only ate one cookie." The distortion defense mechanism is utilized to bend or reconstruct reality input so that it is less damaging, anxiety producing, or threatening to the ego. Distortion defenses do not grossly deny or block out reality. Our interpersonal and intrapersonal skills, cognitive sophistication, and expertise in the utilization of the distortion defense mechanism change with age and experience in living. Denial and distortion serves the explicit purpose of keeping painful or anxiety-producing stimuli external to the self. Denial is a defense mechanism that more totally blocks threatening feedback or stimuli from conscious awareness. The distortion defense mechanism is akin to a filtering process. Distortion enables the developing person to learn to attend to feedback that can be tolerated by the ego while altering feedback that is grossly ego alien and anxiety producing.

In terms of psychological economy, it is generally less costly to overutilize the distortion defense mechanism than the denial defense mechanism. This principle of defense mechanism economy becomes progressively more operational as the individual moves from infancy to childhood through adulthood. Gross denial of reality and primitive distortions are difficult to maintain in the face of the individual's ongoing interpersonal transactions. Significant others and even persons tangential to the self continuously provide reality-oriented feedback. Developmentally, the alcoholic manifests ever-increasingly sophisticated styles of distorting reality specific to the goal of maintaining a reasonably well-integrated and anxiety-free self-system.

When the alcoholic reaches the psychotherapist's office (Forrest, 1982a; Bratter, 1982), he or she manifests a plethora of denial and distortion-determined symptoms. Indeed, the world of the drinking alcoholic is characterized by pervasive distortion and denial. All of the defense mechanisms serve the alcoholic *modus operandi*. Denial and distortion defense mechanisms maintain the alcoholic's self-system. The alcoholic distorts and denies communications, feelings and all ego-alien feedback. Reality-oriented data and feedback can be anxiety producing and ego dystonic. The alcoholic states, "I only had two drinks," when in fact he or she may have had ten or more drinks; "I had to work late," and "Drinking had nothing to do with the fact that I lost my job" also reflects the distortion defense. These verbal distortion defense tactics serve the purposes of providing the alcoholic with a rationale for further intoxication and drinking as well as a defense against the realistic processing of feedback and input specific to the self.

A life-style constructed around the overdetermined utilization of the avoidance defense system is difficult and stressful. The alcoholic continually struggles and works at maintaining these defenses. A sudden collapse of the avoidance defense system will potentially result in personality disorganization and ego defusion. Depersonalization, acute anxiety and panic, acute and pervasive identity confusion, and profound personality disorganization can be associated with a decompensation of the alcoholic's massive avoidance defense system. Typically, the process of personality disorganization following a collapse of the alcoholic's avoidance defense system is a short-lived experience. The potential for developing a more healthy personality structure can also be initiated by this process. The massive avoidance defense system of the alcoholic must collapse or become dysfunctional prior to the initiation of long-term sobriety and thus basic characterological change.

Projection is the third basic defense mechanism of the alcoholic avoidance defense system. The projection defense mechanism also develops during early childhood. The projection-oriented defenses of the alcoholic stem from the experience of narcissistic injury. Projection follows the evolution of the denial and distortion defense mechanisms. The projection defense mechanism represents the most psychologically sophisticated and developmentally least primitive component of the alcoholic's tripartite avoidance defense system. The projection defense mechanism is usually operational by age three or four. At this time, children begin to blame or project negative situational causality upon peers, a parent, or significant others. The early verbal vicissitudes of the projection defense mechanism include: "Johnny broke my truck," "Mommie said 'Yes,' " and "They made me do it." Basic to the functional utility of the projection defense mechanism is the externalization of threatening feedback and data directed at the self. The denial and distortion defense mechanisms serve this same purpose. However, the projection defense mechanism additionally serves the purpose of directing anxiety and causality at a particular target person, group or circumscribed situation. In utilizing the denial defense mechanism, the alcoholic blocks out or rejects from consciousness painful interpersonal or intrapersonal feedback; utilization of the distortion defense mechanism allows for reality input, but at the point at which input becomes significantly anxiety producing or ego alien, the individual begins to filter and screen out feedback according to its positive and negative valence in the maintenance of the self-system; the projection defense mechanism actively involves the transference or projection of damaging, painful, or anxiety producing feedback to another object or target person.

The overdetermined utilization of the projection defense mechanism enables the alcoholic to blame the spouse, children, employer and various other sources for his or her alcoholism and other problems. The alcoholic verbally projects blame on others: "The old lady is the source of all my problems," "If it weren't for him, I wouldn't need to drink," and "That SOB caused it." The drinking alcoholic literally projects blame on every person and target that is external to the self. The alcoholic utilizes the projection defense mechanism in an overdetermined fashion. Projection is reflexively employed by the alcoholic to cope with all interpersonal transactions and intrapersonal operations that precipitate significant feelings of anxiety, trepidation or dissonance within the self-system.

Life becomes progressively more difficult for the drinking alcoholic. The psychological survival of the alcoholic is in many respects paradoxically contingent upon the functional maintenance of the projection defense mechanism. This dilemma also pertains to the denial and distortion defenses. However, projection constitutes the explicit defensive process by which the alcoholic is able to cathect feedback and data that are catastrophically threatening to the self-system onto objects or significant others external to the self. In these respects, projection maintains the addiction process. The projection defense mechanism is crucial to the maintenance of the alcoholic self-system during the middle and later stages of alcoholism (Forrest, 1978). The psychological level of sophistication basic to the projection defense mechanism is such that this strategy of avoidance, as a function of basic reality operations, is often more readily utilized by the adult alcoholic than the denial and distortion defense mechanisms.

Most adults are quite sensitive to gross forms of reality distortion and denial. Therefore, it is easier and more appropriate for the alcoholic to project inadequacies and sources of threat upon others or situational factors. It can be economically easier for the alcoholic to project rather than deny and distort. The projection defenses of the alcoholic also serve the unique purpose of binding or controlling the paranoid dimensions of the self-system. This issue will be explored at length later in the book.

As indicated earlier, the alcoholic avoidance defense system is essentially tripartite in nature. However, it should also be emphasized that the alcoholic utilizes all of the various defense mechanisms for avoidance purposes. Pathological reliance upon the denial, distortion, and projection defense mechanisms simply preempt the alcoholic's dependence and employment of the other defense mechanisms. The avoidance defense system is genetic to the alcoholic character structure. Rationalization, reaction formation, repression, suppression, and the other defense mechanisms are generally secondary to the maintenance of the alcoholic self-system and the alcoholic character structure.

The primary gain afforded the alcoholic by the avoidance defense system is that of avoidance. The alcoholic avoids self, significant others and the phenomenal world vis-à-vis the avoidance defense system. The process of alcoholism can be viewed as serving the purpose of a semipermeable membrane. The precarious and vulnerable state of the alcoholic's self-system is such that alcohol serves the explicit purpose of establishing and maintaining a barrier or filtering device for anxiety-producing incoming data and stimuli. The ingestion of alcohol distorts intrapersonal and interpersonal feedback and fosters denial, distortion, and projection. Intoxication also synergizes the process of selective self-other inattention.

PSYCHOTHERAPEUTIC CONSIDERATIONS

Psychotherapists have long recognized that the successful treatment of alcoholics begins with a resolution or modification of the patient's denial. Indeed, therapists tend to believe (Forrest, 1978 & 1983) that the key to therapeutic success with alcoholics involves helping the patient overcome denial. Alcoholics notoriously deny that they cannot control their drinking. They also deny being alcoholic.

The psychotherapist needs to help the alcoholic modify his or her avoidance defense system. Successful treatment of the alcoholic is contingent upon far more than the resolution of the denial defense mechanism. The alcoholic must radically alter his or her denial, distortion and projection defenses. A great deal of the interpersonal and intrapersonal psychopathology of alcoholism is associated with the avoidance defense system.

The therapeutic relationship involves intimacy, attachment and interpersonal relatedness. Early in the treatment process, it is important for the psychotherapist to supportively reinforce the alcoholic's commitment to the therapeutic alliance. Within the context of a working therapeutic alliance, the alcoholic can begin to trust another human being and develop the capacity for interpersonal intimacy. This process fosters a resolution of the avoidance defense system. The therapist needs to consistently confront and supportively challenge the alcoholic's avoidance defenses. Sobriety and an extended commitment to the psychotherapeutic process are prerequisites to the alcoholic patient's ability to significantly modify his or her avoidance defense system.

Within the confines of a productive therapeutic alliance, the therapist and patient need to openly explore the patient's early life experiences with parents and significant others. The therapist must also consistently explore the patient's fears of rejection, abandonment, annihilation and possibly engulfment. A productive therapeutic relationship is antithetical to the alcoholic patient's infantile and childhood experiences involving pervasive narcissistic injury. It is important for the therapist to actively explore the patient's distancing and avoidance behaviors. After several weeks of treatment, the therapeutic focus is shifted to the patient's current, as well as historic, avoidance of feelings, emotions and self.

SUMMARY

In summary, the psychogenesis of the alcoholic's avoidance defense system stems from an overdetermined need to avoid an intrapersonal awareness and ego integration of the experience of infantile and childhood narcissistic need and entitlement deprivation. This process generalizes and involves the intrapersonal and interpersonal adjustment style of the alcoholic during subsequent developmental stages. The avoidance defense system is an elaborate, relatively sophisticated, and chemically based methodology for avoiding and repressing a plethora of unresolved early life conflicts. The alcoholic's self-system is very brittle and fragile. Avoiding all sources of anxiety and threat, keeping feelings and emotions external to the self, and simply avoiding intimate contact with self and others becomes the all-encompassing *modus vivendi* of the addicted individual.

The alcoholic continuously overlearns to avoid and externalize all potential sources of self-threat and anxiety. Many alcoholics do not establish close interpersonal relationships; some are loners. The avoidance defense system creates and maintains relationship pathology. Quite simply, the alcoholic is a person who avoids others. Alcoholics avoid intrapersonal and interpersonal contact, intimacy and closeness.

Alcoholism is a disorder of avoidance. Denial, distortion and projection form the nuclear core of the alcoholic avoidance defense system. This avoidance defense system is genetic to the alcoholic character structure. The alcoholic avoidance defense system (a) evolves from the experience of pervasive early life narcissistic need and entitlement deprivation, (b) functions in the service of defending the ego or self-system from profound and potentially catastrophic levels of anxiety, and (c) is both ego syntonic and yet paradoxically entropic in nature. The avoidance defense system also binds or controls anxiety.

The modification of this aspect of the alcoholic self-system is psychotherapeutically complex and difficult. However, the therapeutic modification of the alcoholic's avoidance defense system is prerequisite to the establishment of long-term sobriety and concomitant characterological change. Long-term sobriety, personality growth and behavioral change become realities for alcoholics who are able to persist in successful psychotherapy relationships. Basic trust, meaningful human relationships, contact and intimacy are accomplished following significant modification and resolution of the avoidance defense system.

Chapter Five

ALCOHOLISM, ORALITY AND DEPENDENCY

INTRODUCTION

CHRONIC alcohol addiction has been viewed as a disorder encompassing primary oral- and dependence-oriented psychopathology (Menninger, 1938; Fenichel. 1945; Freud, 1953). These issues were discussed briefly in Chapters Two and Three. The clinical literature dealing with alcoholism and the addictions has touched superficially upon orality and dependence as these matters relate to addiction symptomatology. Orality and dependence are genetic components of the alcoholic character structure and personality. Psychoanalysts (Fenichel, 1945; Blum and Blum, 1969) have long maintained that the alcoholic is orally fixated. Psychoanalytic theory (Fenichel, 1954) suggests that the personality development of the alcoholic is essentially pre-genital. According to analytic theory, oral fixation determines the symptomatic drinking behavior of the alcoholic. Psychoanalytic theory (Forrest, 1983) also emphasizes the role of pathological dependence in the etiology of chronic alcoholism.

Modern "schools" of psychotherapy and counseling (Glasser, 1965; Ellis, 1979) have tended to avoid in-depth etiological theories of deviant or pathological behavior. Rogers (1952) indicates that a poor or inadequate self-concept is the basis for symptomatic behavior. Glasser (1965 & 1976) explains symptomatic behavior as evolving from the individual's inability to secure adequate amounts of love and feelings of self-worth. Existential theory (Yalom, 1981) speculates that man has become the product of a neurotic society. The transactional analysts view faulty behavior as the product of an improper balance of learned or neurologically programmed ego states (Harris, 1969). Rational-emotive therapists (Ellis, 1976 & 1979) stress the role of irrational learning and irrational self-dialogue in the development and maintenance of ineffective behavior. The behavior therapists (Wolpe, 1958; Sobel and Sobel, 1976; Wellman, 1979) view behavior pathology as the direct result of relatively unique, ineffective, prolonged, social learning experiences. Behavior therapists have avoided psychodynamic explanations of maladjustment.

None of these models or theories of psychotherapy and personality incorporate significant clinical experience with alcoholics. The Freudians and neo-Freudians have avoided any significant clinical work with alcoholics. While the therapies and personality approaches of the late sixties and seventies (reality therapy, transactional analysis, behavior therapy, and rational-emotive therapy) have moved in the direction of both treating and explaining the addictions, they have only tangentially become involved in these clinical areas. Recently, behavioral strategies of treatment have been applied to the addictions (Wellman, 1979). However, the behaviorists have contributed very little, if any, new etiologically oriented data dealing with alcoholism and the addictions.

It is important for the psychotherapist to understand the major psychodynamic components of chronic alcoholism. An important therapist ingredient in the process of effective psychotherapy with alcoholics is that of comprehending the role of past and present psychodynamic issues specific to the creation and maintenance of addictive behaviors. The patient's interpersonal and intrapersonal pasts are precursors to present character structure and symptomatic behaviors. The etiology of the alcoholic's oral and dependency pathology is discussed in this chapter. Oral-dependency pathology is basic to the alcoholic character structure. These processes reinforce and maintain the addiction process.

THE VICISSITUDES OF ORALITY AND DEPENDENCE

Our initial interpersonal encounters in life are oral. Oral processes sustain life. The infant is totally dependent upon significant others for the maintenance of numerous life-support functions. The mother's management of the infant's oral processes profoundly effects characterological development.

American society is orally oriented and orally preoccupied. It is pathologically significant that between ten and eleven million Americans are alcoholic. Alcoholics may be programmed for chemical addiction vis-à-vis their relatively unique lifelong interpersonal encounters. The mother's ineffective and pathologic management of the oral dynamism also plays a very important role in precipitating the alcoholic symptom choice.

As pointed out in Chapters Three and Four, the alcoholic has experienced profound anxiety pertaining to matters of mother-infant physical contact, feeding, elimination, and generalized narcissistic injury. These issues are prototaxically fused with the mother's inadequate management of the oral dynamism. Narcissistic injury is experienced orally by the infant.

Oral anxiety is a crucial ingredient in alcoholism. The initial orality of the infant-mother dyad is an extremely anxiety producing matter for both parties. The mother or mother surrogate first conveys anxiety to the infant via the feeding process. It is the primitive oral experiences of the infant that precipitate the internalization and subsequent acting out of anxiety. The infant responds to the mother's anxiety associated with physical contact, global "mothering" skills and feeding by becoming anxious. The anxiety-oriented oral experiences of the infant involving feeding generalize and contribute to the development of a chronic sense of non-well being. Thus, a poor or negative self-concept, feelings of inadequacy, unlove, and rejection are always steeped in anxiety.

The experience of mother-infant anxiety pertaining to oral processes is interpersonally determined. The infant learns to be anxious as a result of the anxiety of the mother and significant others. One very important hallmark of the alcoholic is that of being chronically anxious within the realm of interpersonal relations. Prototaxically, the interpersonal anxiety of the alcoholic derives from the transactions with the mother involving feeding and other oral matters.

A crucial factor in the etiology of the oral pathology of alcoholism is that of binding anxiety via oral processes. While the infant first experiences and internalizes profound anxiety orally, he or she also first learns to bind or reduce anxiety through oral behaviors. Screaming, yelling, crying and feeding are infantile oral methods for anxiety reduction. Thus, the infant employs these oral behaviors in order to bind or reduce the experience of anxiety so basic to his or her primitive interpersonal and intrapersonal worlds. The infant experiences intense anxiety associated with the act of feeding. However, the infant also primitively discovers that the ingestion of milk, or other appropriate substances, significantly reduces anxiety. Even the most inadequate or ineffective feeding procedures of the mother result in some degree of anxiety reduction upon the part of the infant and possibly the mother. In a very prototaxic fashion, the infant learns to bind anxiety in a variety of oral ways. All human beings must accomplish this fundamental task. Yet, this process remains neurotically overdetermined and unresolved in the case of the alcoholic. The alcoholic learns very early in life to overdepend upon oral procedures in order to bind ego-threatening levels of anxiety. Overdetermined oral-anxiety binding is a primary factor in the etiology and maintenance of the addiction process. Alcoholics respond to anxiety and stress in a plethora of orally overdetermined ways.

The defensive ego operations of the alcoholic are orally oriented and orally fixated. Verbal or oral attacks against others, projection, the ingestion of alcohol, denial, smoking heavily, and eating problems are but a few of the orally overdetermined methods of anxiety binding that are chronically and pathologically employed by the alcoholic. These ego-defensive strategies are quite primitive. Nonetheless, they can be surprisingly durable and functional. Most alcoholics continue to manifest a rather obvious oral character structure after achieving sobriety. However, very few recovering alcoholics evidence thought disturbance or gross self-system fragmentation subsequent to attaining sobriety. In spite of the regressive nature of the alcoholic's oral character structure, decompensation and long-term thought disturbance are not common among this clinical population.

The alcoholic experiences oral rejection during infancy and childhood. However, the infantile and childhood deprivation experiences of the alcoholic have not been total or complete, but rather inconsistent. The infantile narcissistic need and entitlement deprivation experiences of the alcoholic have been inconsistent. The infant experiences brief periods of adequate or near-adequate mothering. These intervals of adequate mothering may be limited to the infant's oral ingestion of milk, which significantly reduces anxiety. Orally induced anxiety reduction or need gratification primitively means to the infant that life can be tolerated vis-à-vis orality. In part, this relates to the very persistent nature of alcoholism, smoking, overeating, drug addiction, and oral disorders. Ultimately, the alcoholic defends his or her self-system from death and anxiety via the overdetermined oral processes of infancy. These various factors support and reinforce the alcoholic's pathologically overdetermined oral character structure.

The adult alcoholic is able to bind anxiety by chronically ingesting alcohol in much the same way he or she did by ingesting milk as an infant. Thus, alcoholic beverages symbolize the "good" mother's milk. However, alcoholic beverages also symbolize the "bad" mother's milk. The early life experiential world of the alcoholic has been dichotomously good and bad with regard to self-mother-significant other transactions. The infant's experiences of badness and goodness are symbiotically fused with the mother object as well as orally processed and determined. Initially in life, the infant is completely fused with the mother object. The self is then primitively differentiated from the breast and eventually the mother, as a unitary object, via the oral process.

The oral pathology of adult alcoholics involves the incorporation of early life "bad" ego introjects. Bad ego introjects are evidenced symbolically and concretely through the medium of oral rage. Oral rage is basic to the adjustment style of every alcoholic. The infant orally internalizes anxiety and physical and psychological deprivation experiences. Adult alcoholics continue to orally internalize painful affective experiences. The internalization of negative experiences and affects is very oral during infancy and childhood. The "adult" alcoholic drinks in order to "stomach" hurtful, threatening, anxiety-producing feelings and experiences (Matuschka, 1979). Alcoholic individuals also drink in order to stomach their pasts. As an infant and child, the alcoholic orally experienced and internalized anxiety and other painful stimuli. As an adult, the alcoholic continues this pathological oral transaction with self. The alcoholic is compelled and driven to orally destroy himself or herself. Alcoholics primitively believe that they are worthless, inadequate, and not deserving of human love, concern, and dignity. Unconsciously, the alcoholic believes that he or she deserves to be punished and destroyed. This unconscious dictate also requires that the alcoholic orally destroy himself or herself.

Unconsciously, the alcoholic wishes to vent his or her rage against the mother object and significant others. During infancy and childhood, the alcoholic must internalize the consistent experiences of narcissistic injury. These experiences are pathologically incorporated within the self-system. Thus, the alcoholic prototaxically believes that he or she is worthless and unlovable. Yet, the alcoholic is profoundly enraged as a result of being forced to internalize these very negative affects. As an infant and child, the alcoholic was not able to act out or retaliate effectively against his or her mother and significant others over these matters. The futile attempts of the infant to attack his or her mother and mother imagoes via such behaviors as "nipple attack" are impotent and destined to failure. However, the residual effect of these processes involving oral rage shapes the alcoholic character structure.

Interpersonal violence is orally experienced and internalized by the infant. Likewise, the initial retaliatory rage of the infant against the mother and significant others is cathected orally. The alcoholic eventually drinks to destroy himself or herself. The alcoholic also drinks to destroy those closest to the self. Alcoholism is by definition (Forrest, 1978 & 1980) a violent disorder. The rage, anger, and resentments of the alcoholic are orally directed at self and others. Chronic oral ingestion of alcohol results in a partial or total destruction of the self. Chronic alcoholism results in the total psychological destruction of the self.

Most primitively, the oral rage of the alcoholic evolves from the mother-infant relationship. People who are emotionally attached to the alcoholic become the symbolic extensions of the mother object. Therefore, these people become the primary recipients of the alcoholic's oral rage. The wife of the male alcoholic is the most direct mother symbol and she is frequently attacked by the alcoholic. The alcoholic discharges profuse oral rage in a plethora of ways. Verbal attacks and confrontations (Forrest, 1982a), type of work choices, physical aggression and perhaps violent acting out, psychosomatic symptoms, automobile accidents, and chronic heavy smoking are but a few of the pathological methods that the alcoholic utilizes for rage reduction. The mother-infant relationship precipitated oral rage of the male alcoholic creates lifelong conflicts and problems relative to courtship, marriage, and all forms of male-female relating. Unconsciously, the male alcoholic wishes to mutilate, destroy, or murder all females. All women are symbolic substitutes for the male alcoholic's mother. In essense, the male alcoholic attempts a talion murder of the mother object vis-à-vis all relationships with women. The alcoholic is also profusely angry and mad at the world.

There is a rationale for the anger, rage, and resentment of the alcoholic. Comprehending the psychopathology of alcoholism is an exercise in understanding paradoxes! The alcoholic learns in an overdetermined fashion to rely upon the oral ingestion of alcohol in order to bind anxiety and other negative affects. Yet, this neurotic solution must ultimately fail. At various developmental junctures, the addiction process works relatively well. Drinking may actually help the alcoholic control rage and anxiety. However, the alcoholic internally commits suicide by drinking. Externally and socially, the alcoholic may become socially deviant and behaviorally inappropriate as a result of intoxication. Internally, intoxication facilitates some degree of tension reduction and psychological relief. The alcoholic becomes intrapersonally and interpersonally trapped.

The alcoholic self-system is a fragmented composite of good and bad mother ego introjects. This is a matter of primary clinical significance. The ego pathology of the alcoholic is similar to that of the borderline personality (Kernburg, 1975 & 1980; Masterson, 1981). The narcissistic and alloplastic disorders evolve from early deprivation experiences involving primarily the mother and significant others.

The alcoholic manifests a more primitive oral character structure than the borderline personality or the narcissistic personality. The primitive oral disturbance of the alcoholic represents an attempt to establish some functional degree of synthesis between good and bad ego introjects. The ego structure of the alcoholic is surprisingly resilient. However, the alcoholic manifests a chronic blurring of the ego boundaries. Many clinicians have interpreted this to mean that the alcoholic manifests significant identity distortion or primary identity pathology. This clinical observation is essentially correct. However, the basic identity conflicts of the alcoholic stem from more regressive psychopathology associated with ego development and self-system fragmentation. The vast majority of alcoholics do not suffer from thought-disturbance symptomatology or primary object sexual deviation (Forrest, 1982b). Every alcoholic does experience significant difficulty with regard to the issue of gender identity. The male alcoholic suffers from a less than adequately consolidated nuclear sense of maleness (see Chap. 7). Likewise, the female alcoholic (Wilsnack, 1982) experiences chronic and marked anxiety over matters pertaining to her femininity.

Early life narcissistic need and entitlement deprivation experiences create self-system fragmentation. The ego of the alcoholic manifests a chronic structural weakness. Moreover, this structural weakness of the alcoholic ego evolves from the internalization of dichotomous good and bad ego introjects during infancy and childhood.

Continuous internalization of bipolar ego introjects during these developmental epochs results in an ego structure characterized by chronic and primitive splitting (Kernburg, 1976). Splitting is accompanied by rather intense, chronic anxiety. During infancy and early childhood, the alcoholic has attempted to orally bind anxiety associated with the splitting process. Thus, the alcoholic has also attempted to orally extinguish the splitting process. Perhaps inconsistency is the only consistency within the alcoholic's intrapersonal and interpersonal worlds! Eventually, the alcoholic attempts to synthesize his or her bipolar ego structure via the oral process of alcoholism. In a rather strange and yet logical fashion, the addicted individual learns to rely upon alcohol as a solution to ego deficit and self-system fragmentation. Alcohol ingestion orally extinguishes the alcoholic's anxiety related to the matter of inadequate ego boundaries while at the same time providing at least a functional degree of integration of good and bad ego introjects. Chronic alcoholism represents the example par excellence of an oral solution to self-system fragmentation. Questions having to do with "Am I really a person?", "Am I really a man?", or "Am I really a woman?" primitively relate to the matter of splitting and ego structure. The alcoholic experiences chronic conflict over these identity-oriented issues. Alcoholism becomes a primitive oral solution and defense in the service of the ego.

Alcoholism is by definition a chronic adjustment of pathological dependence. The oral dynamism represents the most primitive of human processes. Human beings are also extremely dependent organisms. Dependency needs begin prior to birth. In-uterine life involves total dependence. During infancy, the human continues to be near totally dependent. A state of essential dependency continues throughout life.

Human beings are most dependent upon the maintenance of life-support systems that meet basic biophysiological needs. These lifelong dependency needs include adequate food, oxygen, water, and proper temperature control. Human beings are also very dependent upon other people. Dependency relationships begin vis-à-vis the infant-mother dyad. As noted earlier, human beings are totally dependent in an interpersonal sense prior to birth. Birth represents the most prototaxic biophysiological rupture of a dependency relationship. Following birth, human beings continue this state of total interpersonal dependence primarily through the medium of the oral relationship with the mother object or a surrogate mother object.

The early life fusion of oral and dependency needs plays a very important etiological role in alcoholism. The overdetermined dependence and oral needs of the alcoholic are psychogenically and functionally linked. Dependency occurs prior to orality. However, interpersonal dependence begins with orality.

The catastrophic early life interpersonal experiences of the alcoholic create an eventual lifelong disturbance having to do with overdependence. Intense early life feelings and experiences of rejection, unwant, physical and psychological abuse, and unlove create the alcoholic's overdetermined need to be dependent. Pathologic dependence defends the self-system from anxiety and the threat of personal annihilation produced by narcissistic injury. By remaining pathologically dependent, the alcoholic attempts to ritually, or magically, undo the narcissistic injuries of the past. The alcoholic also becomes anxious in the absence of a multiplicity of suppliers for his or her unending dependency needs. Alcoholics have never learned how to function independently. The pathologic dependency needs of the alcoholic result in a chronic oral search for essentially a healthy mother-infant feeding relationship. Terminating overdetermined dependency behaviors facilitates the experience of marked anxiety. Yet, the experience of terminating alcoholic dependence is akin to giving up the mothering of infancy. The alcoholic partially understands his or her dependency-oriented conflicts. To remain orally dependent, or alcoholic, synergizes the process of making oneself chronically anxious over the matter of being pathologically dependent!

The process of becoming and remaining dependent upon alcohol is anxiety producing. However, the alcoholic learns that he or she is assured of some degree of relief by ingesting alcohol. Remaining dependent upon alcohol at least partially guarantees the alcoholic that he or she will not be totally annihilated by significant others. In order to terminate his or her profound dependence upon alcohol, the addicted individual must become dependent upon people rather than alcohol. This is a very threatening matter for the alcoholic. Chronic intoxication is the alcoholic's solution to dependency-oriented interpersonal problems. Rather than becoming adaptively dependent upon significant others and people in general, the alcoholic becomes pathologically dependent upon alcohol.

Having been taught to feel inadequate, inferior, and insecure, the alcoholic rather logically learns to be pathologically dependent upon sources external to the self for feelings of adequacy and self-fulfillment. A lifelong dilemma of the alcoholic is that of never being able to secure these so badly needed external and internal sources of need gratification. The alcoholic is unable to meet his or her intrapersonal and interpersonal dependency needs. Human beings are highly dependent upon their interpersonal and social skills in order to meet internal needs for approval, success, recognition, and feelings of self-worth. In the event that an individual is unable to obtain adequate amounts of positive feedback and "strokes" from significant others, the person tends to seek out ineffective or neurotic solutions to the pain and hurt experienced as a result of this inability to be successful in relationships with others (Matuschka, 1980). Alcoholics chronically fail in their relationships with people. The alcoholic subsequently seeks out non-person-oriented solutions in order to reduce the pain and anxiety surrounding interpersonal failure. This is a method for securing some degree of future security and anxiety reduction in relationships with significant others and self. Thus, the alcoholic is set up to become highly dependent upon solutions external to the self for basic need and dependency gratification.

Intoxication results in a rather pleasurable non-person-oriented solution for most, if not all, of the interpersonal and intrapersonal difficulties of the alcoholic. The alcoholic has been searching for this solution for many years. The drinking solution is initially inexpensive, easily actualized, socially acceptable, and initially has few negative side effects. As such, it is only a matter of time until the alcoholic becomes psychologically and physiologically dependent upon intoxication as an external, non-person-oriented solution to his or her various interpersonal and intrapersonal conflicts.

The drinking solution is relatively easy and quick. Within a matter of minutes, the alcoholic can secure a significant degree of tension reduction. This powerful solution is also pleasurable. Most people are dependent upon more rational and adaptive solutions to their needs for pleasure and pain reduction. Most people are able to secure these need gratifications via their network of interpersonal relations. This is the exact method of need gratification that is most difficult for the alcoholic to actualize. The alcoholic has historically been very unsuccessful in the matter of establishing and maintaining effective interpersonal relationships.

Alcoholics have maladaptively learned, time and again, that it is simply not worth the time, risk, work, and effort to utilize people-oriented solutions to personal conflicts (Forrest, 1982a).

The alcoholic resents his or her overdetermined dependency needs and chronically rebels against being dependent. The addiction process involves a perpetual rebellion against being dependent. By remaining intoxicated, the alcoholic pathologically attempts to convey to the world that he or she is powerful and potent. The alcoholic attempts to be the antithesis of a chronically infantile and dependent personality type. Alcoholics attempt to neurotically convince self that they are not passive, inadequate and dependent. Many people perceive the alcoholic as aggressive, assertive, and independent. Indeed, many alcoholics appear to be assertive and independent. However, alcoholism is but a fragile defense against gross dependence. The inconoclastic attitudes of the alcoholic are a defense against intense dependency needs. By proceeding from work to the bar, the alcoholic defiantly demonstrates to the spouse that he or she is not dependent upon the marriage or the family (Wegscheider, 1981). Telling the boss or employer to "go to hell" indicates to some people that the alcoholic is a very independent person. The alcoholic acts out in order to convey the message to self and others that he or she is independent.

Every alcoholic is extremely dependent. Yet, every alcoholic manifests dependency pathology in a relatively unique manner. Marked oral dependence vis-à-vis the ingestion of alcoholic beverages can even be viewed as a relatively unique and individual matter. Alcoholics are orally dependent upon the ingestion of alcohol. However, select individuals choose to drink whiskey. Others choose to drink only vodka or perhaps beer. Some alcoholics consume after-shave lotion or rubbing alcohol. The dependency pathology of the alcoholic is multifaceted and exists on a rather broad continuum.

Some alcoholics appear to manifest a counter-dependent adjustment style (Forrest 1978; Knauert, 1979). The counter-dependent alcoholic vehemently rejects and denies his or her dependency-oriented conflicts. The counter-dependent alcoholic tends to be overly aggressive and assertive. Frequently, these individuals have a history of aggressive acting out, wrecking automobiles, being involved in multiple marriages and numerous affairs, and other life-style transactions that connotate distorted independence. The counter-dependent alcoholic behaves in accord with the reaction formation defense mechanism. The generalized demeanor of the counter-dependent alcoholic conveys the messages "I can manage anything" or "There isn't anything that I can't handle by myself." On the surface, this may appear to be true.

Nevertheless, the counter-dependent alcoholic is alcohol dependent. In spite of appearances, the oral dependence of the alcoholic remains a reality. Counter-dependent alcoholics may mask their profound dependence upon alcohol for longer periods of time than the more passive-dependent alcoholic. People who are very close to the counter-dependent alcoholic seem to attend primarily to his or her non-drinking behaviors. These individuals fail to realize or appreciate the alcoholic's very real chemical dependence. Psychotherapists can also fail to adequately focus upon the alcoholic's drinking behaviors. Therapists sometimes attend to the patient's acting out pathology (Forrest, 1979b) at the expense of dealing with the addiction process per se. Treatment efforts focusing specifically upon the alcoholic's acting out symptomatology are most appropriate during the middle and later stages of the psychotherapy process (Forrest, 1983).

Overdetermined dependency needs always encompass a desire to be mothered. The alcoholic has experienced grossly inadequate mothering during at least infancy and childhood. Mothering begins with a primary mother object and eventually includes a father and significant others. The overdetermined dependency conflicts of the alcoholic are clearly evidenced within the realm of male-female relationships and more particularly within the context of marriage. The alcoholic tends to select a spouse (Forrest, 1978 & 1983) who will tolerate and actively reinforce his or her inordinate dependency needs. Both spouses within an alcoholic family system tend to be pathologically dependent (Paolino and McCrady, 1977; Wegscheider, 1981). Many alcoholic males attempt to deny their dependency needs by becoming involved in numerous extramarital affairs. This issue can also be acted out vis-à-vis three or four unsuccessful marriages. Another solution is to never marry, thus avoiding the possibility of becoming highly dependent upon a spouse. Typically, the overdetermined dependency needs of the alcoholic are manifest within the confines of an extended symbiotic marital relationship with one spouse or perhaps two spouses.

The alcoholic is pathologically dependent upon a spouse for a number of reasons. Being a diffusely dependent individual, it logically follows that the alcoholic should establish a few, or at least one, dependent interpersonal attachment. Interpersonal attachment and thus interpersonal dependence is a most difficult matter for the alcoholic. However, the majority of alcoholics are able to establish an interpersonal attachment with a spouse. Such marital attachments are in many respects quite akin to mother-son or father-daughter relationships. For the alcoholic, dependency pathology within marriage is a matter of being mothered and finding a surrogate mother or father rather than being married to a mature, relatively independent significant other. The spouse of the alcoholic (Ackerman, 1978; Forrest, 1980) frequently assumes family responsibility for childrearing and paying bills. The wife of the alcoholic may assume responsibility for the entire family. Pragmatically, spouses of alcoholics are in many respects forced into these familial roles. These unhealthy family roles do foster family survival.

Many alcoholic males act out their marked dependency needs via the selection of a heavy, if not obese, large-breasted spouse. There are exceptions to this generalization. However, such cases do floridly point out the relationship between oral and dependency needs and the alcoholic character structure. It should also be pointed out that many alcoholic marriages begin while the addicted individual is drinking heavily. For the alcoholic, intense interpersonal attachments are possible primarily as a result of heavy drinking. In the absence of heavy drinking, many alcoholics are not capable of sustaining interpersonal dependence or actualizing marriage. However, the interpersonal and intrapersonal attachments and dependence of the alcoholic marriage are superficial facades when drinking is involved. Some alcoholics achieve the goal of marriage as a matter of convenience. They are profusely taken care of by a spouse and "permitted" to continuously drink.

The dependence of marriage provides the alcoholic with an enhanced sense of adequately defined self. The marital relationship provides the alcoholic with a sense of "maleness" or "femaleness." For the alcoholic, one significant reinforcer of continued marital attachment is that of neurotic identity consolidation (Bowen, 1978). Being married and having a family provides concrete evidence to self and significant others that one is male or female. This factor facilitates marital persistence. Divorce or being without a spouse equates with being homosexual or less than adequately "male" or "female" in the pre-conscious of the alcoholic. In this sense, the alcoholic becomes increasingly dependent upon a dysfunctional marital relationship as a source of ego strength. The alcoholic marital relationship becomes progressively more pathological as the addiction process unfolds. The alcoholic marriage is a regressive symbiotic dependency relationship.

Dependency conflicts are genetic to the character structure of the alcoholic and often the non-addicted spouse. The pathology of dependence becomes increasingly apparent within the confines of the alcoholic family system. Dependency pathology within the alcoholic marriage provides both partners with an enhanced sense of security and independent identity. The non-addicted spouse persists in these disturbed marital and family relationships in order to bind identity-determined sources of anxiety.

As indicated earlier, both oral and dependency-oriented conflicts play crucial roles in the initiation and subsequent maintenance of the addiction process. The chronically intoxicated alcoholic is unable to work through or resolve these conflicts. Prolonged intoxication reinforces and regressively exacerbates the pathological oral and dependency needs of the alcoholic.

PSYCHOTHERAPEUTIC CONSIDERATIONS

The overdetermined oral and dependency needs of the alcoholic persist in spite of successful psychotherapy or rehabilitation experiences. The character structure of the alcoholic is steeped in the pathology of these particular dynamisms. Effective psychotherapy effects a partial resolution of these dimensions of the alcoholic character structure and behavioral style. Alcoholics who have been successfully treated in psychotherapy continue to manifest overdetermined oral and dependence needs. Chain-smoking, overeating or marked weight gain, and the continual oral ingestion of fluids (most typically coffee) are but a few of the more apparent indices of the persistence of marked oral and dependence needs in the recovering or recovered alcoholic. Heavy smoking, weight gain, and drinking perhaps fifteen or twenty cups of coffee a day are relatively healthy alternatives to chronic intoxication.

Effective psychotherapy can facilitate the development of positive compulsions and addictions (Glasser, 1976; Forrest, 1979a). This is ubiquitously true. Instead of continuously drinking alcoholic beverages, in therapy the alcoholic talks almost continuously about drinking. This situation also applies to alcoholics who become actively involved in the Alcoholics Anonymous community. The recovering alcoholic drinks coffee on a continual basis rather than alcohol. Frequently, recovering alcoholics compulsively attach themselves to other recovering alcoholics. Psychotherapy relationships, Alcoholics Anonymous, and even jogging or meditation are positive addictions. These addictions can be extremely positive with regard to their overall "effect" upon the individual. Positive addictions may involve any number of other ritualistic, almost obsessive-compulsive behavioral patterns that promote physiological and psychological well-being. Positive addictions are alternatives to such negative addictions as alcoholism and drug dependence (Glasser, 1976; Forrest, 1979a).

The overdetermined oral and dependency features of the alcoholic character structure persist for life. As effective psychotherapists (McGahee, 1978), we merely alter these characterological dynamisms in a relative, but more adaptive sense. The sober alcoholic continues to bind anxiety orally. The counter-dependent alcoholic, although this concept is by definition erroneous, continues to be orally assertive and aggressive following treatment.

SUMMARY

The significant clinical aspects of the oral and dependency conflicts of alcoholics were discussed in this chapter. Alcoholics have been narcissistically injured during the epochs of infancy and childhood. Narcissistic injury is initially experienced and processed orally. Narcissistic injury is also interpersonally determined. Initially in life, the alcoholic has been orally rejected. Interpersonal messages that mean "you are unwanted," "unloved," and "inadequate" are prototaxically processed via the oral dynamism. Paradoxically, anxiety and other negative affects that accompany these messages tend to be orally reduced or controlled by the infant. Suckling, eating, and other oral processes serve the explicit purpose of binding anxiety. These relatively unique early life experiences condition the alcoholic to bind and control his or her chronic feelings of anxiety through an overdetermined orality. The alcoholic controls his or her various interpersonal and intrapersonal insecurities by ingesting alcohol. The overdetermined oral needs of the alcoholic thus facilitate and maintain the addiction process. Alcoholism is an oral solution to the alcoholic's various interpersonal and intrapersonal conflicts.

Chronic alcoholism can also be viewed as an oral attack against the self (Menninger, 1938). The rage, anger, and resentment of the addicted individual become orally directed at self and significant others. Self-system fragmentation is basic to the alcoholic character structure. The alcoholic attempts to orally destroy the primitive "bad" ego introjects within his or her self-system. Unfortunately, a total destruction of the self may be the end result of this process.

The sober or recovering alcoholic continues to be orally overdetermined. Smoking, eating, continual ingestion of coffee and other beverages, and even a preference for oral-genital forms of sexual expression (Forrest, 1982b) often characterize the oral orientation of the recovering alcoholic. The alcoholic manifests an oral character structure. This factor is associated with the alcoholic's ever-present capacity for massive regression.

The dependency pathology of the alcoholic is fused with the oral dynamism. Alcoholics are dependent upon external, oral solutions to their more basic problems stemming around the matter of interpersonal dependence. Alcoholism is a neurotic substitute for healthy interpersonal dependence. Conditioning and learning experiences that foster feelings of inadequacy and inferiority also reinforce dependency. Every addict (Forrest, 1980; Bratter, 1982) is pervasively dependent. Chronic alcoholism can be viewed as a defensive strategy employed by the alcoholic to deny very profound dependency needs. Particularly when intoxicated, the alcoholic behaviorally attempts to reject his or her dependency needs. The counter-dependent alcoholic's most vociferous attempts to deny being dependent are extremely superficial. The dependency-oriented struggles of the alcoholic are always manifest in an individual fashion. Alcoholic marital relationships are constructed around the overdetermined dependency needs of both spouses. The overdetermined oral and dependency needs of the alcoholic tend to relate to his or her selection of a particular spouse.

The oral and dependency needs of the alcoholic are relatively refractory to psychotherapeutic modification. Following successful psychotherapeutic treatment, the alcoholic typically continues to be orally and dependency fixated. Psychotherapeutically precipitated characterological change is always a relative matter. The psychotherapist needs to employ treatment strategies that are designed to decathect the alcoholic's overdetermined oral and dependence needs.

Chapter Six

ALCOHOLISM, DEPRESSION AND ORAL RAGE

INTRODUCTION

ALCOHOLICS manifest chronic depressive symptoms. At the point of psychotherapeutic or rehabilitation engagement, the alcoholic is clinically depressed (Forrest, 1982a). Many alcoholics seem to manifest endogenous depression. Alcoholics are often in the midst of a major life crisis when they enter treatment. Many of these individuals are experiencing a reactive depression (Della-Giustina and Forrest, 1979). Alcoholics experience depressive symptoms (Knauert, 1979 Bratter, 1982) as a result of divorce, job loss, gross psychological decompensation, and detoxification. These are but a few of the crisis-oriented situations that can precipitate a reactive depression. Indeed, it is little wonder that the alcoholic is significantly depressed at the time of entering psychotherapy or a rehabilitation program!

Clinical research (Hoffman, Jackson and Skinner, 1975; Beckman, 1975; Forrest, 1978; Wegscheider, 1981) consistently indicates that the alcoholic is depressed. However, the depression and depressive trends of the alcoholic have not been adequately investigated. Descriptions and definitions of depression are also frequently inadequate. Etiological accounts of the depression of the alcoholic are generally non-existing.

The oral and depressive psychopathology of the alcoholic has been briefly elucidated by a number of analytically oriented psychotherapists and clinicians. The depressive disorders have been associated with orality and oral fixation (Cameron, 1963; Gaylin, 1968; Kernberg, 1980). Chronic alcoholism is viewed by the Freudians and neo-Freudians as essentially relating to oral fixation and an overdetermined oral character structure. The oral character type (Fenichel, 1945) is prone to depression and depressive trends. Blane (1968) briefly associates alcoholism, dependence, depression and orality. To date, very little clinical material has been written about the depression and depressive trends of the alcoholic.

Alcoholism is a violent disorder. Menninger (1938) described alcoholism as a "focal suicide." The alcoholic suicidally and orally destroys himself or herself vis-à-vis the ingestion of alcoholic beverages. Alcohol addiction results in the destruction of the self. Each year more than 13,000 alcoholic Americans die from cirrhosis of the liver. Alcoholics also destroy themselves psychologically via the addiction process. The destructive nature of alcoholism is well documented (Forrest, 1978 & 1982; Scott, 1979). Alcoholic or intoxicated individuals commit acts of suicide, homicide, family violence, and are involved in fatal automobile accidents far more frequently than non-drinking or non-alcoholic persons. Roughly 50 percent of all fatal automobile accidents involve intoxicated drivers. Alcoholic Indians (Forrest, 1976) and alcoholic military personnel (Forrest, 1978) frequently experience psychological difficulties pertaining to the control of hostility and aggression. These alcoholic groups (Forrest, 1976 & 1978) also manifest depression.

The depression and depressive trends of the alcoholic are associated with orally oriented symptomatology specific to the alcoholic character structure. Pathological aggression and hostility are also associated with the alcoholic's depression and overdetermined orality. This chapter discusses these various clinical issues. Depression, orality, and rage are characterological features of the alcoholic. These characterological features facilitate and maintain the addiction process. The interrelatedness and fusion of the alcoholic's characterological depression, orality and rage are also discussed in this chapter.

DEPRESSION AND DEPRESSIVE SYMPTOMATOLOGY

Depression is a mood disturbance. The depressive disorders vary considerably with regard to behavioral and affective symptomatology. Generally, depression is a reaction to loss or threatened loss, failure, or personal discouragement. Neurotic depressions are characterized by self-depreciation, dejection, and overdetermined reassurrance needs (Cameron, 1963). The depressed individual continuously expresses feelings of inferiority, hopelessness, and worthlessness. Neurotically depressed individuals are constantly tired, without energy, uninterested in people and activities, and negative in worldly perspective. The fantasy ideation of the depressed person centers around matters of personal unworthiness and despair. Somatic symptoms often accompany the neurotic depression. Cameron (1963) defines the neurotic depressive reactions as "mood disorders in which tension and anxiety are expressed in the form of dejection and self-depreciation, somatic disturbance, and repetitive complaints of feeling inferior, hopeless and worthless." Guilt also plays a prominent role in neurotic depression. In addition, the depressed person is often angry.

Psychotic-depressive reactions (Della-Giustina and Forrest, 1979) constitute another clinical category of depression. The psychotic-depressive reaction is a mood disorder in which dejection, guilt and organized delusions of self-depreciation dominate the individual's internal adjustment. The psychotically depressed attempt to shut out as much of their environment as possible. The psychotically depressed person (Jacobson, 1971) withdraws into deep preoccupation. Feelings of dejection, self-depreciation and self-condemnation reach delusional proportions. Attempts by significant others to reassure or contradict the severely depressed individual's expressed sense of worthlessness may result in an actual exacerbation of the depression. Such is not the case in the neurotic-depressive reactions. Guilt associated with psychotic depression is acutely conscious and the depressed patient is interested in very little else. Suicidal ideas, and indeed "successful" suicides, evolve from the murderous self-hate that is basic to all psychotic-depressive reactions.

Psychotic depressions, as well as even the more neurotically oriented depressions, have been further classified (Della-Giustina and Forrest, 1979) as "agitated depression" and "retarded depression." The agitated, psychotically depressed patient becomes increasingly anxious and overactive, reaching the point of being so restless and tense that he or she is incapable of sitting still or resting for more than a few minutes at a time. Such patients may talk continuously about their fears and despair. The individual who is experiencing an agitated depression is extremely apprehensive, pacing back and forth, crying, picking at his or her body, and sometimes demanding cruel punishment. The patient who is in a retarded depression appears stunned, having a bent back, arms hanging limp, eyes fixed on the ground, and he may hold his head in his hands and stare at the floor for extended periods of time. Motorically, the patient is slowed down. His or her speech is slow and repetitious. Sentences tend to frequently trail off unfinished. Such patients are inevitably hospitalized. Typically, the appetite disappears, problems with constipation appear, sleep decreases to a few hours a night, and the patient loses significant weight. Males usually become impotent. Women become frigid and experience menstrual difficulties. The retarded-psychotic depression has also been referred to as a depressive stupor, as these patients become almost completely unresponsive and often require tube feeding in order to maintain life. Following recovery from a depressive stupor (Cameron, 1963), it is rather common for the patient to report that during this illness he or she was completely engulfed in an intrapersonal world of nihilistic delusions.

It is important to briefly delineate the clinical characteristics of the reactive depressions and the endogenous depressions. These varieties of depression are often associated with alcoholism. Reactive depressions and endogenous depressions are most typically classified within the neurotic depression rubric. Object loss, resulting in reactive depression, involves not only loved ones but, as importantly, the emotional support that these significant others have provided the individual. Reactive depression can be associated with a specific event. These depressions are understandable to the patient and significant others. The depressive symptomatology of the reactive depression is classically of short-term duration. Death, divorce, and separation precipitate reactive depressions. In the case of most persons, these depressions go into remission within a matter of a few months. A traumatic object loss, such as the death of a spouse, results in a normal mourning process (reactive depression) that is essential to the establishment of a new and healthy emotional adjustment style upon the part of the surviving person.

Endogenous depressions (Jacobson, 1971) are mood disturbances involving long-term or chronic, flat and "dampened" affect. The endogenously depressed individual frequently reports that he or she "always been down in the dumps" and that "things have never excited me much." Chronic feelings of inferiority, worthlessness, and hopelessness are central to the self-perceptions of the endogenously depressed person. Everyone has relatively good and bad days in the sense of being depressive. The endogenously depressed individual (Della-Giustina and Forrest, 1979) is almost always "down." These persons consistently function in a depressive fashion. Interpersonally, they display flat affect, their wordly involvement can be described as bland, and they are generally incapable of sustaining elevated affect. The endogenously depressed individual may or may not recognize his or her affective disturbance. This particular depressive adjustment style can be seen as an adaptive adjustment in that it prevents the occurrence of a more regressive depression. However, all of the depressive adjustment styles are clearly pathological and maladaptive.

THE VICISSITUDES OF ALCOHOLISM, DEPRESSION AND ORAL RAGE

Depression is basic to the alcoholic adjustment style and the alcoholic character structure (Forrest, 1978; Knauert, 1980). Alcoholics manifest various forms of depressive symptomatology. The alcoholic's depressive struggles occur prior to the acutalization of the alcoholic symptom choice.

Alcoholics have experienced pervasive and chronic early life narcissistic need and entitlement deprivation. This process entropically facilitates the depressive symptom structure of the alcoholic. Klein (1968) has delineated the etiology of infantile and childhood depressions. Parental loss or other significant object losses, parental rejection, and disturbed mother-infant relationships precipitate early life depressions or anaclitic depressions. In addition to creating intense interpersonal and intrapersonal anxiety, infantile and childhood deprivation experiences facilitate long-term depressive characterological features.

Depression is a prototaxic response to the experience of early life narcissistic injury. However, infantile and childhood depression is an adjustment response that follows and is generally secondary to anxiety. In the case of the alcoholic, depression is always associated with anxiety and other pathologic affective states. Alcoholics have had many depressing infantile and childhood experiences. Indeed, the life-style of the alcoholic is consistently depressive. Early life narcissistic injury first precipitates intense anxiety (an adaptive organismic response) that is followed by depression. Anxiety and depression are mutually inclusive affects. Narcissistic injury causes both depression and anxiety. Intimate interpersonal encounters that convey to the individual that he or she is somehow unwanted, inadequate, inferior, unloved, and basically "not good" result in depressive characterological trends and chronic depression. Alcoholics have been interpersonally and intrapersonally programmed to be depressed. Chronic and intense deprivation experiences are depression-oriented experiences. Being hurt and depressed during the initial epochs of human living dictates the reappearance of this same adjustment pathology during subsequent developmental stages.

As adolescents and adults, alcoholics behave in various self-defeating ways that actually precipitate feelings of depression. Much of the experience of depression has to do with having been a long-term failure. This is one major dilemma of the alcoholic. Early life depressions are often associated with parental and familial experiences. However, this situation changes when the child begins to socialize and interact with other children. At this time, the depressed child often becomes more depressed. Low self-esteem and a negative self-concept facilitate interpersonal and intrapersonal transactions that reinforce depression. In essence, the alcoholic perpetually makes himself or herself depressed during the various developmental stages of life.

Initially in life, affect is associated with orality. The infant's first anxiety and depressive experiences are orally internalized. Narcissistic injury experiences are prototypically experienced vis-à-vis the oral dynamism. Thus, infantile depression is first internalized orally. Rage accompanies the internalization of grossly negative infantile affective states. The infant experiences rage in combination with anxiety and depression.

A paradigm involving depression, orality, and rage facilitates the addiction process. The depression and depressive trends of the alcoholic vary considerably with regard to affective intensity and overt behavioral effect upon the individual. The majority of alcoholics have endogenous types of depression dating to infancy and childhood. However, many alcoholics do not appear to evidence behavioral patterns associated with overt depression. Even these individuals have struggled with chronic depressive trends. Such individuals have not been grossly crippled by the depressive process. They have been able to function in spite of being depressed. Paradoxically, many alcoholics mask depression by drinking alcoholic beverages. Alcohol is a central nervous system depressant. Yet, the alcoholic can learn to utilize alcohol as an antidepressant.

Most alcoholics have been unhappy during childhood. Flat or blunted affect, social withdrawal, self-preoccupation, and the other clinical symptoms of depression are central to the childhood adjustments of many alcoholics. The symptoms of depression are frequently first identified when the child enters school. Social isolation, inadequate and disturbed peer relationships, academic difficulties, frequent crying and flat affect are some of the cardinal features of depression that may be identified and recognized by teachers and school personnel. Unfortunately, the school socialization process sometimes operates to disengage children manifesting these psychological "symptoms" and thereby reinforces depression and other adjustment pathology. Children who enter school depressed often become even more depressed as a result of the nature of the educational socialization process. Feelings of inadequacy, inferiority, and a general psychological sense of non-well being can contribute to the child's academic demise.

Although many alcoholics clearly have average or above average intelligence, as a group they have encountered academic difficulties as early as the second or third grade. In fact, many alcoholics drop out of school prior to high school graduation. However, other alcoholics are able to complete advanced college degrees. At any rate, the educational system effectively disengages many alcoholics. Academic failure, interpersonal conflicts, intrapersonal pathology, and familial conflicts are but a few of the significant variables that operate in combination to disengage alcoholics from the socialization process provided by our educational system.

The failure inherent in all socialization transactions synergizes and reinforces the depressive conflicts of many alcoholics. Interpersonal failure facilitates depression. Failure experiences generalize and are intimately associated with transactions that involve personal feelings of rejection, disapproval, inadequacy, and "not belonging." Feelings of hurt and pain (and thus depression) are associated with alcohol addiction.

Adolescence compounds the depressive conflicts of the prealcoholic. Chronic interpersonal rejection and failure, academic difficulties, and family problems continue during adolescence. In the case of alcoholics, the particular maturational and developmental struggles associated with this developmental epoch are of clinical significance. Peer relationships, dating, a plethora of matters pertaining to sexuality and identity, and the issues of establishing one's independence and autonomy are major developmental tasks that need to be resolved and worked through during adolescence. The alcoholic has been marginally successful in mastering and resolving the various developmental tasks of adolescence. Alcoholics experience intensified interpersonal conflicts during adolescence. Direct peer rejection, conflicts with school personnel and authority figures, an inability to simply get along, an inability to date or develop meaningful opposite sex relationships, and even being known as a troublemaker within the confines of the church are characteristic of the alcoholic's adolescent adjustment pathology.

Most alcoholics do not manifest an overt clinical depression at this developmental juncture. However, many alcoholics do begin to act out aggressively during adolescence. Alcoholics are impulsive (Ellis, 1979; Forrest, 1980 & 1982a) and have a low frustration tolerance. They are prone to pathological acting out. The alcoholic's acting out behaviors are a defense against intense anxiety and profound depression. Indeed, the acting out dimensions of the alcoholic character structure are associated with the avoidance defense system. The avoidance defense system and acting out function to defend the alcoholic's self-system from defusion vis-à-vis a combination of potentially overwhelming negative affects and cognitions.

Physical aggression, verbal attacks, an angry interpersonal demeanor, and a "know-it-all" attitude characterize the adolescent *modus vivendi* of many alcoholics. This adjustment style enables the individual to deny his or her powerful feelings of inadequacy, inferiority, and impotence. These behaviors are also a defense against depression. A small segment of the alcoholic population experiences an overt depression during adolescence. These individuals withdraw and detach themselves from others. They manifest an overt depression and frequently make a conscious decision to drink alcoholically in order to neurotically control depression.

The alcoholic neurotically attempts to escape his or her feelings of depression throughout life. Certainly, the intoxicated alcoholic remains vexed with depression. Adolescence and adulthood are developmental eras that are characterized by heightened self and other awareness. In these respects, the basic process of aging consistently places more difficult emotional demands upon the alcoholic.

During adolescence (Forrest, 1978), many alcoholics consciously realize that they are in essence loners. This is a sad and painful realization. This process is also a depressing reality. Such adolescents find that they have virtually no friends or close interpersonal ties. Moreover, they are aware of the fact that peers actually avoid them. In some cases, the "loner syndrome" is transcended by superficial aggressive and/or sexual acting out. The physically aggressive male and the sexually promiscuous female are able to gain a degree of peer relatedness and status that neurotically defends them from the experience of being a loner. However, acting out symptomatology only masks inadequacy and the depressive trends associated with this interpersonal style. Some alcoholics are able to establish relatively functional interpersonal ties with other loners during this developmental stage. These interpersonal relationships are superficial and often constructed around drinking. Most alcoholics can recall that they had one or two adolescent "drinking buddies." These "birds of a feather" constructed their relationships around the common denominator of drinking and intoxication. Many alcoholics in this social rubric also vividly recall being "down," "blue," or depressed during adolescence. They remember that their few friends were also depressed.

Acute interpersonal rejection can precipitate clinical depression. As an adolescent, the alcoholic typically does not manifest overwhelming depression but rather struggles to deal with pervasive feelings of depression. The alcoholic becomes even more confused over not knowing how to effectively manage or modify depressive feelings. Family separation is a familial matter (Wegscheider, 1981) which reinforces the depressive trends of the prealcoholic adolescent. Alcoholics are ambivalent about their family relationships. The parents or surrogate parents of the alcoholic are also pathologically ambivalent about family separation. The alcoholic experiences depression within the confines of the family system. Adolescence (Bowen, 1978) facilitates the reality of impending family separation. The adolescent and his or her parents and other family members react to the reality of family separation with a sense of loss and ambivalence. Parents may want the adolescent to leave the family system and "make it on his or her own." At the same time, parents want the adolescent to remain within the family system. Unconsciously, these parents want to somehow magically undo their inadequate parenting and thus guarantee a later successful separation from the family. These family systems tend to be pathologically symbiotic. This factor reinforces persistence within the family system. Some alcoholics report that they were extremely anxious over the matter of leaving home as they "knew" they were going to "have a lot of trouble" after leaving. However, most "couldn't wait to get away from the old man and old lady." Attitudes and perceptions such as these reflect ambivalent conflicts. Adolescent children within an alcoholic family system experience a threatening exacerbation of oedipal sexual conflicts associated with the matter of family separation.

The emotional climate within the family of the alcoholic has often been extremely depressive. It is during adolescence that many alcoholics become painfully aware of this reality. Family depression has been central to the affective life of many alcoholic persons. The alcoholic's family constellation can be depressed. A wide variety of living problems, to include an addicted parent or parents, can be associated with the depression of possibly all family members involved in these family systems. Alcoholics manifest an adjustment style that is closely associated with the adjustments of their parents and family of origin.

Invariably, the adult life of the alcoholic includes many depressive experiences. First of all, the addiction process is depressive oriented. The incipient alcoholic is depressed. The addiction process creates depression. Many alcoholics enter adulthood depressed. Marriage, vocational engagement, and parenting are the basic developmental tasks that need to be accomplished during adulthood. Alcoholics eventually experience difficulties within each of these realms. Some alcoholics do not encounter major conflicts in any of these realms until they reach the age of forty or later. Many alcoholics vehemently deny problems associated with their drinking for the duration of their lives. These individuals sometimes deny to the point of death. However, most alcoholics have experienced marked difficulties in each of these areas. Furthermore, they consciously recognize these difficulties and will verbally admit them.

The alcoholic often experiences depression during adulthood as a result of his or her inability to successfully manage these very important developmental tasks. It is understandable that the alcoholic is not able to effectively manage the various sources of stress associated with parenting. Marital disharmony and divorce are seven times greater in alcohol abusers than the general population (Schafi, Lavely, and Jaffe, 1975). Many alcoholic persons (Paolino and McCrady, 1977; Wegscheider, 1981) are unable to find or secure a marriage partner. Vocationally, the alcoholic experiences a multitude of difficulties. Some alcoholics are unable to simply hold a job. Alcoholics are prone to frequent job changing. Research (Gade and Goodman, 1975) suggests that the vocational preferences of the children of alcoholics are influenced and related to the alcoholism of the addicted parent. Parenting is an exceedingly difficult task for the alcoholic and his or her spouse. Inadequate parenting skills are probably associated with the high incidence of alcoholism and chemical dependency in the children of alcoholics (Forrest, 1980; Wegscheider, 1981). In short, the alcoholic is consistently a poor and ineffectual parental model. Many alcoholics are painfully aware of this reality. They attempt to be a "good" parent. The recovered or recovering alcoholic very quickly realizes his or her dearth of effective and appropriate parenting skills and often attempts to change this situation. A drinking, alcoholic parent cannot provide the parenting skills, guidance and modeling essential to the psychological growth and emotional well-being of children.

The entire family system becomes pathologically depressed as the alcoholic family member progresses into the latter stages of the addiction process (Forrest, 1978). The initial stages of the addiction process may create depression in family members. Marital conflict, separations, and divorce facilitate family depression. Losing a job, being fired, or not being promoted depresses the alcoholic. These transactions also create feelings of anger and depression in the spouse and children of the alcoholic. Hangovers, chronic physical symptoms associated with long-term heavy drinking or alcohol addiction, and nutritional factors all synergize the depression of the alcoholic. The alcoholic consistently reinforces his or her depressive trends. The ongoing process of compounding depression is basic to the alcoholic trap. Alcoholics victimize themselves from within. Social withdrawal, isolation, interpersonal disengagement and intrapersonal conflicts reinforce the depression of the alcoholic and other family members.

Guilt is intricately related to the alcoholic's depression. Alcoholics feel chronically guilty. Alcoholics have been conditioned to feel guilty. Some have felt guilty about being a psychological and financial burden to their parents. The alcoholic has been conditioned to perceive himself or herself as inadequate and worthless. This process fosters guilt feelings. Yet, the parents of the alcoholic frequently expect their children to be exceptional or "super" people. When alcoholics fail to measure up to unrealistic parental expectations, they experience intense guilt. Chronic interpersonal failures, academic failures, vocational failures, marital failure, and failure as a parent create a profound sense of personal guilt.

Guilt is always secondary or tertiary to the depression of the alcoholic. Guilt reinforces depression, thus compounding the depression of the alcoholic. The masochistic trends of the alcoholic are also related to guilt. Unconsciously, if not pre-consciously and consciously, the alcoholic believes he or she deserves to be punished as a result of marked guilt feelings associated with chronic failures and personal shortcomings. Alcoholics masochistically punish themselves in order to atone for personal guilt. Invariably, the alcoholic also sadistically attempts to punish others for their role in his or her misery. Transactions of this variety ultimately result in further self-hate, self-punishment, guilt, and depression. Depression can be seen as a masochistic expression of self-hate. A vicious circle of depression, guilt, sadomasochism, and compounded depression is central to the global adjustment style of many alcoholics.

Many alcoholics have experienced a multitude of lifelong difficulties pertaining to religious or spiritual matters. Guilt usually plays a significant role in the religious conflicts of the alcoholic. As children, many alcoholics have been taught to be "God-fearing." They have been told that they will be punished by God for their many sins and transgressions. As human beings, they evidence shortcomings and fail to live up to the rigorous religious doctrines in which they have been indoctrinated. This process also facilitates intense guilt feelings. Guilt associated with religious matters thus synergizes depression. Commonly, the alcoholic has rejected religion for these very reasons. In order to somehow integrate his or her dichotomous religious training and life experiences, the alcoholic typically continues to perfunctorily maintain some form of spiritual involvement. Alcoholics Anonymous can help the alcoholic work through conflicts pertaining to guilt, depression and religion.

Oral rage is basic to chronic alcoholism and depression. Oral rage is a basic component of the alcoholic character structure. Karl Abraham (Gaylin, 1968) emphasized that "those who go into depression will be those who have an early narcissistic injury and an oral predisposition." It was his belief that primary narcissistic injury occurred prior to the resolution of the oedipal complex and that later life brought a repetition of this disappointment in the case of individuals becoming symptomatically depressed. The alcoholic has experienced chronic and pervasive early life narcissistic need and entitlement deprivation. Every alcoholic is orally fixated. Persons who are predisposed to depression have an intense need for narcissistic gratifications. These individuals have an overdetermined and pathological need to be loved and approved of by significant others. The depression of the alcoholic is a struggle from within. Furthermore, depression can be a defense against oral rage. The alcoholic attempts to deny life by remaining intoxicated. Alcoholics also neurotically deny depression, anger and rage vis-à-vis the oral ingestion of alcoholic beverages.

Rage is initially experienced, processed and cathected orally. The alcoholic experiences intense rage intially (during infancy and childhood) as a result of being narcissistically injured by significant others. Characterologically, oral rage is fused with depression. Alcohol addiction is an oral disturbance. Alcoholism is always a process that is steeped in violence and rage.

The oral rage of the alcoholic evolves as a result of early infantile oral disturbances involving primarily the mother. As indicated earlier, narcissistic need and entitlement deprivation experiences are first processed by the human infant via the oral dynamism. Abandonment, rejection, neglect, unwant, and unlove are initially experienced orally. The most prototaxic organismic responses to interpersonal feedback of this variety involve anxiety, hurt, depression and rage. Narcissistic need and entitlement deprivation experiences cause the individual to feel anxious, hurt, depressed and extremely angry. Infants and young children may overtly manifest only a primary anxiety response to extremely psychonoxious interpersonal encounters. However, a sense of personal rejection, hurt, depression and rage always occurs prior to or with the experience of intense internal anxiety.

Very early in life, the person who has been the victim of intense narcissistic injury evidences rage. Specifically, the rage of the infant is expressed as a total organismic response. Rage is also initially experienced and cathected orally. Oral rage involves the total aggressive and behavioral repertoire of the infant. Crying, screaming, and biting are infantile methods of cathecting rage orally. The initial infantile object and primary target of oral rage cathexis is the mother or surrogate mother. Infants and young children who have experienced pervasive narcissistic need and entitlement deprivation are enraged. They cathect oral rage toward significant others.

Rage is also orally directed at the self. As an infant and child, the alcoholic impotently attempts to "get even with" or retaliates against his or her mother and significant others. Rage is initially cathected against those closest to the self. However, rage is also masochistically directed against the self. The narcissistically injured infant attempts to orally destroy parental objects. As a child, the alcoholic begins to direct oral rage against the self because he or she primitively believes that self deserves to be punished, if not psychologically and physically destroyed. This fragmented component of the self-system accounts for the chronic sadomasochistic behavior of every alcoholic. Furthermore, this issue explains the alcoholic's oral rage. The aggressive, hostile and violent behaviors of the alcoholic are manifest in various and sundry ways. However, the oral cathexis of rage is the most violent expression of this process with regard to the destruction of self and significant others.

The infantile oral process of feeding and the ingestion of milk is accompanied by a reduction of anxiety and other negative affects. These processes can also create anxiety and other unpleasant affective states. However, anxiety and rage reduction are effected vis-à-vis the oral dynamism. As such, the alcoholic in choosing to be addicted (every alcoholic makes this choice on literally hundreds or perhaps thousands of occasions) acts out a rather specific repetition compulsion that has been determined during the earliest of developmental epochs. Orally ingesting alcohol, like ingesting milk during infancy, is a process that is utilized by the alcoholic to control threatening affective states. Alcohol can facilitate or inhibit the acting out of rage-oriented behaviors. The drinking alcoholic is involved in a process of orally destroying the self. Some alcoholics act out violently against others only when they are intoxicated. Paradoxically, other alcoholics are extremely aggressive, angry and hostile *while sober*. After drinking, these individuals become comparatively soft spoken, docile and quite congenial.

The oral rage of the alcoholic is in many respects cannibalistic. Aside from the matter of cannibalizing the self, alcoholic individuals symbolically act out their cannibalistic trends through the verbal destruction of those closest to them. The spouse and family members of the alcoholic feel as though they are being orally destroyed by the alcoholic. The wife of an alcoholic verbalized in psychotherapy, "I've always felt as if my husband could, at any moment, chew me up and spit me out." This patient was also able to recall cannibalistic dreams involving her alcoholic husband. The alcoholic complains, "bitches," and is a chronic complainer and whiner (Ellis, 1979). Nothing is ever "right." Verbal assaults against spouse, family and friends are basic to the *modus operandi* of the alcoholic. Many alcoholics verbalize that they can "never keep my mouth shut." Likewise, the drinking alcoholic always manages to "put his foot in his mouth." The alcoholic cannibalistically destroys those closest to self. As the addiction process unfolds, the alcoholic terminates or destroys virtually all of his or her interpersonal relationships. In numerous respects, the interpersonal demise of the alcoholic is oral and cannibalistic. The cannibalistic trends of the alcoholic originate during infancy and are specifically associated with rage and the feeding process. The most primitive form of retaliation for narcissistic injury specific to this developmental epoch is the oral incorporation (cannibalizing) of the "bad" mother. The alcoholic's anger, confrontations, resentment, and verbal demeaning of his non-addicted spouse can be viewed as a caricature of this original attempt to orally destroy the mother object.

Problems with anger, rage and resentment are basic to the intrapersonal and interpersonal adjustments of every alcoholic. Orality is closely associated with rage reduction. The destructive dimensions of the alcoholic's oral rage are pervasive. Destruction of the self, destruction of significant others, and chronic interpersonal failure vis-à-vis the addiction process are all realities that are associated with the alcoholic's characterological oral rage.

Rage and orality are key psychodynamic factors in the alcoholic's depression. Alcoholics are literally mad at the world. Pregenital characterological features are also central to depression and chronic alcoholism. Oral dynamics are related to depression and alcohol addiction. Overdetermined anal and oedipal characterological trends are also associated with alcoholism and depression. The chronic depressive features of the alcoholic are manifest in regressive pre-genital strivings and also in obsessive-compulsive symptomatology. Rage, anger and resentment are affective components that defend the alcoholic from very potent and near overwhelming feelings of depression. The global symptomatology of the alcoholism is a compromise or neurotic solution to pervasive interpersonal and intrapersonal conflicts. The oral rage of the alcoholic can be viewed as a defense against depression.

It is not uncommon (Knauert, 1982) for the alcoholic to manifest a short-term psychotic depression following the establishment of sobriety. Individuals who have been chronically intoxicated for as long as twenty or thirty years often manifest extreme symptomatology following the establishment of sobriety. Fortunately, most of these individuals are able to maintain their sobriety and sanity in the event that they are able to establish a therapeutic alliance during the initial weeks of sobriety. The depression that these individuals manifest following sobriety is an essential ingredient in their addictive makeup. By remaining intoxicated for years, the alcoholic has been able to deny, control or neurotically put off his or her depression. Depression usually follows sobriety. The addiction process masks or controls depression.

Ethyl alcohol (Pursch, 1981) is a mood elevator as well as a mood depressor. Alcoholics learn how to use alcohol to modify various uncomfortable feelings. When used properly, ethyl alcohol serves the purpose of an antidepressant medication. The alcoholic learns rather early in the addiction process that the ingestion of alcoholic beverages will significantly elevate his or her mood. Ingesting alcohol also allows some endogenously depressed alcoholics to externalize oral rage. Thus, alcohol parad pharmacologically defends the self-system from depressio

Oral rage is a projection-oriented defensive strategy. The holic projects his anger, depression and anxiety upon the enviro ment and significant others. The oral rage of the alcoholic is a secondary component of the avoidance defense system that functions to keep feelings, intrapersonal awareness and interpersonal matters external or tangential to the self. Being angry and hostile at others is a method for managing (avoiding) personal hurt and narcissistic injury. Rage is a defense against depression and anxiety as well. The alcoholic who becomes markedly depressed following residential treatment is invariably anxious.

PSYCHOTHERAPEUTIC CONSIDERATIONS

The effective psychotherapeutic management of the alcoholic's depression can prevent an exacerbation of rage-oriented conflicts. Therapists who work with alcoholics need to focus directly upon the relationships between depression, anger, rage and hostility (Knauert, 1978; Forrest, 1979a & 1983). As long as the alcoholic continues to be orally enraged, he or she will also continue to remain intoxicated and engaged in the process of destroying self and significant others. The alcoholic katagogically persists in denying his or her depression by remaining intoxicated and orally enraged. Some alcoholics need to get "sicker" in order to get better within the confines of the psychotherapeutic encounter. For the alcoholic, getting sicker means becoming depressed and learning how to overcome depression within the psychotherapy relationship (Forrest, 1980 & 1982a).

The sadistic component of the alcoholic character structure is pathologically manifest via oral rage. While the chronic depressive trends of the alcoholic can be associated with this sadistic characterological component, depression is both psychodynamically more adaptive and psychotherapeutically more amenable to modification than the oral rage associated with depression. Therefore, the psychotherapist needs to deal with the hurt and depression of the alcoholic patient as well as specific rage-oriented target behaviors. Depression synergizes the sadistic predisposition of the

.mportant for the therapist to focus ion per se in order to curtail suicidal :xperiences guilt over the matter of be- quently becomes even more depressed. the patient's superego then potentially nihilate the ego. These factors pernicious- at one-fourth of all suicide victims have a alcohol in their bloodstream (Schafi, Lavely and Jatic, e alcoholic becomes increasingly guilty as a result of feeling g. lty and being depressed! This vicious circle results in the internalization of oral aggression and rage. At some point, the alcoholic begins to feel hopelessly trapped from within. Some alcoholics parataxically attempt to escape profound feelings of guilt and depression by venting rage directly against significant others or even insignificant others. One-half of all homicides in this country (Banks, 1982) are committed by people who are under the influence of alcohol. Alcohol is a common denominator in many suicides and homicides. These behaviors are also associated with depression and rage. The bete noire is truly within in the case of the drinking alcoholic! The alcoholic is internally enraged and depressed.

Alcoholics are sometimes diagnosed or labeled by therapists as manic-depressives, dypsomaniacs and cyclothymics. The cyclothymic personality makeup has been characterized as occurring in the extroverted individual (Kister, 1964). Such individuals are apparently warm, friendly, superficially gregarious and competitive. However, such individuals are subject to frequently alternating moods of elation and sadness, generally precipitated by internal factors rather than external situations. The cyclothymic pattern can result in a chronic euphoric or depressed state without resulting in gross reality disturbance. The cyclothymic individual very rarely requires hospitalization for mood swings. In actuality, very few alcoholics are diagnosed as cyclothymic personality types. The cyclothymic personality pattern rarely precedes a manic-depressive psychosis. Most cyclothymic personalities do not decompensate into the more regressive psychoses. Manic-depressive reactions, which are almost always associated with chronic depression and, less frequently, chronic hypomania can be viewed as radical affective exaggerations of the cyclothymic personality. Dypsomania is but another term used to describe pathological mood changes.

The alcoholic (Knauert, 1982) has infrequently been labeled a manic-depressive or cyclothymic personality type. Psychotherapists respond primarily to the alcoholic's depression or depressive features in making these diagnoses. Psychotherapists have also been reluctant to view alcoholism as anything but a secondary symptom (Forrest, 1978). Historically, the alcoholic has been diagnosed as a manic-depressive, psychoneurotic, acting out neurotic, and a character-behavior disorder or sociopath. If the psychotherapist focuses upon the non-drinking-oriented behavioral symptomatology of the alcoholic, he or she will see a plethora of other symptoms. This therapeutic focus can reinforce the patient's alcoholism. Alcoholics placate therapists who assume this therapeutic stance, and consequently, treatment fails.

Once the alcoholic is engaged in the psychotherapeutic process (Sena, 1980), it is important for the therapist to focus upon the patient's affect, emotional lability, and "borderline" manic-depressive trends. Neophyte counselors and therapists (Forrest, 1978b) often fail to recognize that a few weeks or months of total abstinence facilitates increasing internal distress for the patient. Initially, sobriety is a very rewarding and reinforcing experience for the alcoholic. However, as time goes by and the alcoholic remains abstinent, he or she often finds that life becomes increasingly intolerable. The therapist and patient discover many of the reasons why the alcoholic has chosen to be alcoholic *following* the establishment of sobriety. Alcoholics who are able to remain totally abstinent for six to eight months while actively engaged in psychotherapy have an excellent probability of remaining sober (Forrest, 1979a). The sober management of depression, anxiety and rage is extremely inportant in this regard. Patients who become sober only to subsequently find themselves experiencing overwhelming feelings of depression, anxiety and rage have ample reason (or an excellent "excuse") to resume the addiction process. Many alcoholics feel flooded with negative feelings after the initial experience of sobering up.

SUMMARY

The interdependent and pathological relationships between alcoholism, depression, and oral rage were explored in this chapter. Chronic or endogenous depression is central to the alcoholic character structure. Alcoholic individuals drink alcoholically as a defense against depression and other negative affects. Pervasive narcissistic injury creates the alcoholic's depressive trends and characterological warp. Although not addressing himself to the alcoholic personality, Fenichel (1945) quite lucidly states this essential position:

> The formulation can now be made that the disposition for the development of depressions consists in oral fixations which determine the reaction to narcissistic shocks. The experiences that cause the oral fixations may occur long before the decisive narcissistic shocks; or the narcissistic injury may create a depressive disposition because it occurs early enough to still be met by an orally oriented ego. It may also occur that certain narcissistic shocks, because they are connected with death and reaction to death, always involve oral introjection of the dead person, create the decisive oral fixation. Regarding the factors that create oral fixations in the first place, the same holds true as for other fixations; the determinants are extraordinary satisfactions, extraordinary frustrations, or combinations of both, especially combinations of oral satisfaction with some reassuring guarantee of security; actually traumatic experiences in the nursing period can be found more often in subsequent manic-depressive patients than in schizophrenics.

In her brilliant work on the topic of anaclitic depression, Rene Spitz (1968) emphasizes the role of object loss and narcissistic injury in the etiological development of these disorders: "There is one factor which all cases that developed the syndrome (anaclitic depression) had in common. In all of them, the mother was removed from the child somewhere between the sixth and eighth month for a practically unbroken period of three months, during which the child either did not see its mother at all, or at best once a week." Spitz also noted oral symptomatology and anal-sadistic trends in anaclitically depressed children.

Early life narcissistic injury creates depression (Jacobson, 1971) and intense anger or rage. The alcoholic experiences prolonged or chronic narcissistic injury. Infantile and childhood experiences become reinforced during subsequent developmental epochs. Overdetermined orality is central to the depressive adjustment styles. The alcoholic's overdetermined orality is furthermore fused with rage. The alcoholic's oral rage is initially associated with and cathected against the mother or surrogate mother. Alcoholics have been psychologically and almost physically destroyed or annihilated by their mothers and significant others. Depression, rage and anxiety are basic to the alcoholic symptom choice. These affects play a crucial role in the causation and maintenance of the addiction process.

Catastrophic pain and hurt, literally inflicted upon the infant by significant others, dictates the development of depressive symptomatology combined with an overdetermined need to orally retaliate. A primitive sense of self-hatred accompanies this process. The oral rage of the alcoholic is invariably directed at significant others and the external world. Oral rage is also directed against the self. The alcoholic's masochistic attack against the self is of paramount clinical importance, as this process can and does end in self-destruction. Many alcoholic persons (Banks, 1982) drink themselves to death. The oral rage of the alcoholic is cathected against every member of the alcoholic family system. The resentment, anger, hostility and oral rage of the alcoholic can be viewed as a defense against profound feelings of depression and anxiety.

Guilt is a core ingredient in the depressive struggles of the alcoholic. Guilt operates to synergize both the depressive symptomatology of the alcoholic and the addiction process per se. Most alcoholics have been taught to feel guilty about many things quite early in life. Religious matters and sexuality are often associated with the alcoholic's guilt conflicts.

The overdetermined guilt conflicts of the alcoholic derive from the experience of chronic narcissistic injury. Alcoholics feel guilty as a result of being so inadequate and worthless in the eyes of parents and significant others. The alcoholic also experiences guilt over the singular issue of drinking and his or her alcoholism. Guilt can be a masochistically oriented affective process that operates to push the alcoholic into an even deeper depression. Alcoholic family systems reinforce the alcoholic's low self-esteem and guilt feelings by continually discussing his or her inability to control drinking and aggression (Sternberg, 1976; Martin, 1980). In a talion fashion, those closest to the alcoholic continually reinforce and exacerbate feelings of guilt as a means of getting even with the addicted person for the hurt and pain that he or she has inflicted upon them.

Psychotherapists sometimes scotomize the role of affective disturbance in the maintenance of the addiction process. It is very important for the therapist to continually explore the alcoholic's self-defeating depression, guilt and oral rage. The psychotherapist must also emphasize to the patient that he or she can behave differently. The therapist needs to focus on the concrete here and now with the patient. By doing so, the patient becomes capable of behaving more rationally and adaptively.

One of the many caveats pertaining to the psychotherapy of alcoholism involves differential diagnosis (Wanberg, 1979; Knauert, 1982). Many clinicians have inaccurately labeled the alcoholic a character–behavior disorder, an acting out neurotic, or a borderline personality. The depressive conflicts of the alcoholic were differentially elucidated in this chapter. Few alcoholics have a history of manic-depressive mood disturbance, although every alcoholic suffers from chronically exaggerated "ups and downs." Depression, in juxtaposition with oral rage and the other topics of this text, constitutes a total gestalten, which encompasses the characterological pathology of the alcoholic.

Chapter Seven

ALCOHOLISM AND IDENTITY

INTRODUCTION

THE alcoholic manifests serious identity pathology. Clinical and research literature dealing with alcoholism and identity (Blane, 1968; Forrest, 1978 & 1983; Armor, Polich and Stambul, 1978) indicates that the alcoholic experiences various identity conflicts as well as role confusion. Unfortunately, clinicians have failed to adequately define the concept of "identity conflict." It seems as though most clinicians and psychotherapists agree that alcoholics experience significant problems in the area of identity. However, the identity problems of the alcoholic have not been adequately elucidated. Identity conflict also means many different things to different clinicians.

It is important to adequately describe and define the concept of identity. Identity has been defined in various ways. Erickson (1959 & 1963) has written extensively about identity. Identity can be thought of as the degree or extent to which a person knows and understands himself or herself. Such an awareness of self obviously focuses mainly upon conscious awareness. Identity also includes a pre-conscious and even unconscious awareness of self. Biological and social maturation fosters the development of identity and self-awareness. Eventually, identity includes an awareness of one's personality traits, values, vocational goals, and other more esoteric matters pertaining to the self. Identity encompasses the basic question, "Who am I?" Most people are able to establish a rather consistent and consolidated identity by the time of late adolescence or early adulthood. However, identity is always evolving and never statically determined or fixed. Identity is never static. The human being continuously changes, grows and evolves until the point of death. Every developmental epoch potentially affects and changes an individual's basic identity.

Adolescence is a particular developmental era that significantly alters identity. One of the paradoxes of identity is that an extensive and accurate awareness of self does not guarantee healthy or asymptomatic adjustment! Thus, the adolescent who suddenly becomes very cognizant of his or her emergent sexuality may be threatened over this changing identity awareness and manifest transient or long-term behavioral pathology as a result. However, a crucial ingredient in healthy adjustment is always "knowing who I am" in an identity-oriented sense. The optimally adjusted individual consistently has a firm grasp of who he or she is. Such individuals manifest excellent ego strength.

Identity involves holistic perceptions of the self. Biophysiological and psychological development processes esemplastically shape and determine a person's identity. Basically, identity is also a hypothesis about the self. Like all hypotheses, the self-hypothesis may prove untenable when tested against reality. Most typically, an individual's hypothesized identity is confirmed by reality vis-à-vis the process of interpersonal consensual validation. This process reinforces and consolidates the self-system. Random factors can also affect the development of identity. Identity can be profoundly affected by such variables as race, community and life circumstances, over which the individual has little, if any, influence. Genetic factors determine gender (Ellis, 1963). Gender is the basic structure of identity.

Aside from a biological identity, all people have numerous perceived psychological identities. Significant others and casual aquaintances perceive each person differently at different times and according to situational contexts. People perceive themselves differently within even short intervals of time and within different role-demanding situations. As such, identity may be viewed internally as somewhat fluid. In view of these factors, it is understandable why the concept of identity is difficult to define. The identity symptomatology and identity-based psychopathology of the alcoholic does not exist sui generis!

This chapter encompasses an exploration of the identity-oriented conflicts of the alcoholic. An etiologically oriented discussion of the identity pathology of the addicted person is presented throughout the chapter. A brief clinical case study is included in this chapter.

IDENTITY PATHOLOGY AND ALCOHOLISM

The identity-based symptomatology of the alcoholic is associated with infantile and childhood narcissistic injury. The impact of disturbed interpersonal encounters during these earliest developmental stages always affects adjustment during subsequent developmental epochs. Thus, the alcoholic character structure always includes a residual pathological core that evolves from one developmental epoch to another. There is a nuclear core to the alcoholic character structure that is essentially refractory to change or radical modification.

Clinicians appear to share a number of common viewpoints relative to self-concept formation and the establishment of identity (Rogers, 1952; Glasser, 1965; Ellis, 1979; Forrest, 1983). Learning to differentiate between self and others (Bowen, 1978) is a basic task that must be accomplished in order to establish identity. The process of self-other differentiation initially involves the infant-mother dyad or infant-surrogate mother dyad. During childhood and for the remainder of life, this process includes the tasks of effectively differentiating between self and significant others, self and others, and self and the phenomenal world. Basic identity is established within the context of interpersonal relationships. The infant's prototaxic relationship with a mother object facilitates a sense of "me" and enables the evolving person to differentiate between mother and self. Identity always involves a plethora of interpersonal processes. However, the mother-infant relationship (Kernburg, 1975; Masterson, 1981) most primitively and profoundly shapes the self. Interpersonal processes continue to maintain the sense of selfhood. Interpersonal and intrapersonal processes associated with later developmental eras also shape and determine identity. The process of aging builds upon the infantile and childhood experiences that so profoundly affect and create basic identity.

The development of the ego or self-system begins with the process of breast-self differentiation. Prototaxic thinking characterizes the initial months of the infant's life. Prototaxic is a Greek term which means *first arrangement*. The infant's experiential world is prototaxically experienced and processed. The communication repertoire of the infant is limited to primitive reflexive actions. The infant's cognitive, perceptual and motor development is primitive. In relation to the breast and as a function of basic oral processes, the infant begins to form a most rudimentary awareness of self as distinct from mother.

Sullivan (1953 & 1956) characterized the first few months of an infant's life as a time when there is no differentiation between self, object and the people comprising the infant's interpersonal world. However, the infant begins to differentiate between self and the mother vis-à-vis the mother's nipple. Soon the mother's nipple (or a substitute for the mother's actual nipple) is differentiated from self. Sullivan theorized that the infant perceives the nipple as (1) an emotionally comfortable nipple ("good nipple") or (2) an anxiety-producing nipple ("bad nipple"). When the mother is comfortable in her relationship with the infant, not anxious, and is relaxed, affectionate, caring and loving, the infant perceives the nipple as "good" or comfortable. The mother conveys her basic feelings toward the infant via physical contact, voice, and her general manner before, during and after the feeding process. When the mother interacts with the infant in a fashion that is characterized by anxiety, irritability, revulsion and perhaps even hostile rejection, the infant experiences intense anxiety. Thus, the mother becomes the "bad nipple." During the fourth to sixth month of life, the infant begins to more accurately differentiate between self and mother. In Sullivan's terminology, the "good nipple" becomes the "good mother" and the "bad nipple" becomes the anxiety-producing mother or the "bad mother." These relatively amorphous precepts remain separate until about the end of the first year. They are fused between the twelfth and sixteenth months into a nuclear conceptualization of "mother."

As a result of the mother-infant relationship, the infant (during the latter half of infancy) evokes three concepts (Sullivan, 1953) of self: (1) the "good me," (2) the anxious me or "bad me," and (3) the panic-ridden me or "not me." The mother's relatively anxiety-free, warm care conveys a sense of respect, love and value to the infant. Thus, the infant feels loved, valued, worthwhile and respected. The infant relates to self as "good me." When the infant is cared for by his or her mother and significant others in a predominantly anxious, hostile and rejecting fashion, he or she perceives self as worthless, inferior and inadequate. Thus, the infant develops an anxiety-ridden ("bad me") self. The Sullivanian "panic-ridden-me" concept describes infants who have experienced extreme anxiety within the mother-infant relationship. These infants have been treated with extreme hostility and rejection. They feel markedly repulsive, worthless, inadequate, inferior and it is out of these feelings that the individual develops a sense of the panic-ridden me ("not me").

The panic-ridden me is associated with schizophrenia and gross personality disorganization. These three concepts of "me" exist in varying degrees in all persons from childhood throughout adulthood. The relationships between the three me's never remain static. However, a relatively stable equilibrium with the "good me" (emotionally comfortable me) predominating occurs in most people. In addition to the roles of the mother, father and significant others in the development of the infant's ego or self-system, the person significantly "affects" his or her interpersonal and intrapersonal worlds. The simple gender of the infant, physical characteristics of the infant, or perhaps the fact that the infant is hyperkinetic all have a very significant effect upon the mother and significant others comprising the infant's interpersonal world. Clinicians (Fenichel, 1945; Freud, 1953) tend to have overlooked these realities. The infant can have a negative interpersonal and intrapersonal impact upon the mother and significant others, which may unfortunately prove to be the actual demise of the infant. These issues are quite recondite.

The alcoholic's infantile and childhood experiences involving narcissistic injury facilitate the development of the Sullivanian "bad me" identity. Alcoholics consistently verbalize that their mothers and family systems were unpleasant, stressed and anxious. The feeding process in combination with the anxious mother's nipple and other physical and interpersonal constituents of the mother-infant dyad convey to the infant a basic sense of non-well-being. These factors result in identity disturbance and identity-based psychopathology. Marked interpersonal disturbance within the mother-infant dyad precludes the experience of basic consensual validation. It is always "in reference" to significant others that human beings develop an adequately consolidated nuclear sense of "me-ness." Infants and young children need consistent interpersonal experiences with a warm, loving, caring, nurturant mother in order to begin the process of effectively differentiating a consolidated nuclear sense of self.

Healthy or optimal adjustment is contingent upon consistent and nurturant consensual validation experiences. Consensual validation is the process by which "a person arrives at a healthy *consensus* with one or more people about some aspect of his feelings, thoughts, and interpersonal relationships, and this consensus is validated by repeated experiences which emphasize its soundness" (Chapman, 1976). Consensual validation initially occurs within the context of the mother-infant relationship. This process involves the evolving abilities of the infant to differentiate between self and the mother's nipple, between self and the mother, and eventually between self and significant others. The process of self-other differentiation is very prototaxic during infancy and early childhood. Intense and potentially catastrophic anxiety impedes the process of healthy self-other differentiation.

Healthy consensual validation cannot take place within the context of an intense dyadic interpersonal relationship that is characterized by rejection, hate, anger, detachment, anxiety and marked emotional "uncomfortableness." An experiential world constructed vis-à-vis interpersonal relationships that produce extreme anxiety, panic and "not me" feelings is the antithesis of an experiential world characterized by consistent consensual validation. The self-system or ego structure of individuals subjected to consistent anxiety producing "not me" experiences is pathologically fragmented. It is essential that the evolving person be able to establish a healthy and adequate identity during the first three years of life. Early life self-system fragmentation is the basis for chronic identity-based conflicts and psychopathology. Identity conflicts of the "*Who am I*?" variety are more basically and fundamentally associated with ego pathology and self-system fragmentation.

The alcoholic has experienced a disturbed mother-infant relationship. This process creates a structural weakness in the ego or self-system. Ego deficit globally and chronically affects the behavior and adjustment of the alcoholic. The alcoholic's ego pathology also plays a very important role in the actualization of the alcoholic symptom choice. Identity conflicts are very difficult to resolve when the rudiments of an adequately consolidated self-system have never been established. A diversity of other tangential symptoms are also associated with self-system fragmentation. A structurally weak and inadequate ego structure or self-system results in persistent blurring of the ego boundaries (Kernburg, 1976; Masterson, 1981). Ego deficit impairs the process of self-other differentiation. A blurring of the ego boundaries precipitates chronic anxiety and identity confusion. Ego deficit can also be associated with thought-disorder pathology or florid schizophrenia. The chronic alcoholic is not schizophrenic. However, the ego structure of the alcoholic includes a structural weakness that is akin to that of the schizophrenic. The structural weakness of the alcoholic ego rests at a far more adaptive point on the adjustment continuum than that of the schizophrenic. Alcoholic persons very seldom evidence a schizophrenic adjustment prior to the onset of their alcoholism.

Approximately 8 to 12 percent of alcoholics are psychotic after establishing sobriety. Many alcoholics (Knauert, 1980) manifest thought-disorder *symptoms* during the processes of sobering up and the initial two or three months of recovery. The etiological common denominator in alcoholism and schizophrenia is narcissistic injury. Pathological-distancing mechanisms are basic to both of these adjustment styles. The inability to tolerate interpersonal intimacy, the need for detachment, aloofness, and a plethora of other relationship difficulties characterize both of these pathological conditions. Identity distortion and confusion is also central to alcoholism and schizophrenia.

Ego deficit or self-system fragmentation results in chronic and intense anxiety within the realm of virtually all interpersonal relations. Anxiety is associated with the alcoholic's intrapersonal process. The alcoholic has failed to develop the rudiments of an adequate ego structure or self-system. Yet, most of these individuals are not perceived as grossly disturbed by parents and school personnel. However, at the time of puberty and early adolescence, many alcoholics are identified as symptomatic by parents, teachers, or other school personnel. Moreover, many alcoholics are able to recall that adolescence was a time when they began to feel uncomfortable around others and experience marked interpersonal conflicts. Most alcoholics initiate their drinking careers during adolescence. At this time, the increasingly complex interpersonal demands of living became a very real threat to the ego integrity of the alcoholic. The alcoholic turns to alcohol as a coping device or defensive strategy. The chronic ingestion of alcohol can be viewed as a pathological defensive strategy in the service of the ego. The alcoholic becomes progressively more dependent and addicted. Psychologically, the alcoholic makes himself or herself dependent upon alcohol. Terminating alcoholism or a chemical dependency primitively equates with various loss of control phenomena. The alcoholic fears insanity or madness and ultimately death as consequences of giving up his or her addiction.

During adolescence, the alcoholic begins to act out his or her ego deficit. Many alcoholics evidence serious adolescent adjustment problems. In general, the structural weakness of the alcoholic's ego results in two malignant interpersonal adjustments during adolescence. The alcoholic can experience intense and conscious anxiety within the realm of interpersonal relations and subsequently begin to evidence an adjustment style that is aimed at moving away from others. In contrast to this alternative, the alcoholic can assume an aggressive, overly assertive pseudo-movement toward, with, or against significant others. These overdetermined interpersonal trends become obvious with the onset of adolescence. However, the prodromal ego pathology of the alcoholic is overtly manifest during earlier developmental stages.

Each year thousands of adolescents are identified and treated as alcoholics (Forrest, 1983). The developmental drinking histories of most alcoholics begin sometime during the adolescent years. Alcoholism is like a mosaic. One aspect of this mosaic involves drinking in order to maintain ego integration. During the adolescent years, many alcoholics begin to consciously fear fragmentation and personality disorganization. This matter is associated with the "normal" identity conflicts that are brought to the fore at this time. This process synergizes an adolescent identity crisis. The alcoholic acts out his or her identity problems in order to prevent ego defusion. As noted earlier, this task can be accomplished by interpersonal detachment and withdrawal or by an overdetermined pseudo-movement toward or possibly against others. Some alcoholics feel like isolates or loners during adolescence. Others attempt to be involved with peers and friends, but many of these individuals are quick to point out in retrospect that they neurotically drove others away from them.

During adolescence, male alcoholics act out their ego pathology vis-à-vis aggressively moving against others far more frequently than do female alcoholics. In an overdetermined fashion, the alcoholic attempts to convince self, significant others, and indeed the "world" that he is, in fact, a man. Physical aggression, poorly controlled violence, fast driving, sexual escapades, and a "devil may care" attitude typifies the *modus vivendi* of many adolescent males who eventually manifest alcoholism. These behaviors and scurrilous and iconoclastic attitudes are in the defense of a masculine identity. The male alcoholic feels inadequate as a person and a "man." Developmentally, this issue remains neurotically unresolved.

Women alcoholics struggle with the questions, "Am I really a person?" and "Am I really a woman?" Many women alcoholics first experience conscious anxiety associated with identity at the time of adolescence. Identity pathology and self-system fragmentation are extremely anxiety producing and threatening realities for both male and female alcoholics. Within the confines of the psychotherapeutic relationship, male alcoholics tend to be most threatened and intensely anxious about identity conflicts.

Women drink alcoholically (Wilsnack, 1973 & 1982) in order to feel feminine. Female alcoholics are concerned about their adequacy as women. Drinking may offer these women a temporary escape from sex-role conflicts. On a conscious level, alcoholic women are no less feminine than non-alcoholic women. However, alcoholic women experience significant conflicts about their adequacy as women stemming from the existence of masculine traits in the unconscious levels of their personality. Wilsnack (1973) found "78 percent of the alcoholic women, but only 35 percent of the non-alcoholic women, who were married had suffered some kind of obstetrical or gynecological disorder." The alcoholic's problems included difficulties in conception, repeated miscarriages, and permanent infertility (26 percent of alcoholic wives were unable to have children, as contrasted with 4 percent of non-alcoholic wives). Every alcoholic woman is anxious about her femininity, but this issue seems to be of less acute clinical importance in the treatment of female alcoholics than in the therapeutic management of male alcoholics (Forrest, 1980d).

Male alcoholics consciously fear being less than adequately masculine. Male and female alcoholics are extremely anxious over the issue of being adequately male or female. Alcoholics believe and feel as though they have never been adequate in any respect. The alcoholic's identity problems begin with ego deficit, become identity conflicts, and subsequently involve sexuality (Forrest, 1982b), masculinity and femininity. The final step in this paradigm is that of being confused about the possibility of being homosexual.

The alcoholic's identity conflicts become increasingly intrapersonally oriented following adolescence. Conscious intrapersonal conflicts make the process of daily living more difficult. The identity conflicts of the alcoholic have historically been associated with the issue of homosexuality. This is particularly true in reference to male alcoholics. Historically, clinicians have tended to view the male alcoholic as a latent homosexual. A small percentage of the alcoholic population (male and female) is exclusively homosexual in sexual preference and sexual object choice (Forrest, 1982b). Karl Menninger (1938) states, "It is almost axiomatic that alcoholics, in spite of a great show of heterosexual activity, have secretly a great fear of women and of heterosexuality in general, apparently regarding it as fraught with much danger." This statement is made in reference to the male alcoholic. Menninger goes on to point out that the homosexuality of many alcoholics is expressed only when they are drunk. Menninger (1938) views alcohol addiction not as a disease but rather as "a suicidal flight from disease, a disastrous attempt at the self-cure of an unseen inner conflict." Stekel (1952) emphasizes that one dimension of the alcoholic paraphilia is a strong unconscious homosexual striving. Research data indicates "in view of the prevalent view that alcoholism is related to homosexual strivings, it is interesting that none of the 46 patients studied was completely homosexual, and only one engaged in more homosexual than heterosexual activity" (Cameron, 1963). Recently (Blum and Blum, 1969; Steiner, 1971; Sternberg, 1976; Forrest, 1982b), psychotherapists have given less and less credence to the notion that the alcoholic is "latently" homosexual. In fact, homosexuality is not consistently discussed in the alcoholism research literature (Hoffman, Jackson, and Skinner, 1975; Emrick, 1975; Armor, Polich and Stambul, 1978).

The alcoholic-homosexual controversy continues to be poorly understood and subject to divergent viewpoints. As a group, clinicians have consistently associated the identity conflicts of the alcoholic with homosexuality or latent homosexuality. This position applies to male and female alcoholics. More women are being identified and treated as alcoholics. Likewise, more women with alcoholism and homosexual conflicts are seeking out treatment.

One salient reason for the clinical association between alcoholism and homosexuality is the characterological and personality similarities between these two diagnostic groups. Some homosexuals and alcoholics appear to have very little in common. However, descriptions of the personality of the homosexual (Bergler, 1956) are similar to descriptions of the alcoholic personality structure (Blane, 1968; Forrest, 1980). According to Bergler, the personality of the homosexual involves a mixture of the following elements:

> (1) masochistic provocation and injustice-collecting; (2) defensive malice; (3) flippancy covering depression and guilt; (4) hypernarcissism and hypersuperciliousness; (5) refusal to acknowledge accepted standards in non-sexual matters, on the assumption that the right to cut moral corners is due homosexuals as compensation for their 'suffering', and (6) general unreliability, also of a more or less psychopathic nature. The most interesting feature of this sextet of traits is its universality. Regardless of the level of intelligence, culture, background or education, all homosexuals possess it.

In addition to these personality characteristics, many homosexuals are anxious and depressed. Homosexuality is frequently associated with family disturbance. The homosexual is also the victim of an overwhelming obsessive-compulsive disorder: homosexuality! Many homosexuals and alcoholics continually struggle against their compulsions and obsessions.

Obviously, there are other psychopathological features common to these disorders. The personality and behavioral similarities that have been discussed partially explain why clinicians have indicated that alcoholics are "latently" homosexual. Yet, it is important to emphasize that very few alcoholics are homosexual.

Menninger (1938) indicates that the alcoholic shows a great deal of heterosexual activity. Male and female alcoholics do put a great deal of neurotic energy into their heterosexual activities. Male alcoholics are generally more neurotic than female alcoholics in their efforts to be sexually adequate. Overdetermined and destructive sexual acting out is an important hallmark (Forrest, 1982b) of male and female alcoholics. Consciously, the drinking alcoholic seldom recognizes the overdetermined nature of his or her "flight into heterosexuality." The alcoholic's sexual acting out and promiscuous sexual behaviors represent a pathological method for partially resolving identity conflicts. Thus, the sexual acting out of the alcoholic can be viewed as a defense against bisexuality and homosexuality. Some alcoholics compulsively seek out a person of the opposite sex for the sole purpose of having sexual relations. As one male alcoholic patient explained this process: "It seems like I've always got to find another woman to screw." One affair after another, seducing a neighbor's wife, numerous marriages, or the seduction of an adolescent daughter are behaviors that can be associated with the alcoholic's overdetermined sexual acting out. It should be pointed out that many promiscuous alcoholics are members of subcultures that actively reinforce sexual acting out behaviors. Within such a subculture or reference group, one's measure as a *man* or woman is often overtly or covertly determined by the number of seductions or affairs the person completes. The sexual frame of reference of the male alcoholic is akin to that of the late adolescent. This process often becomes more dysfunctional when the alcoholic reaches the later stages of the addiction process (Forrest, 1978). The sexual acting out behaviors of many women alcoholics (Forrest, 1982b) are similar to those of male alcoholics.

As mentioned earlier, the male alcoholic frequently appears to be more anxious over the matter of identity than the female alcoholic. This factor often drives the male alcoholic into a destructive pattern of heterosexual acting out. However, the sexual acting out style of both male and female alcoholics is invariably destructive at the core. A great deal of secondary gain is derived from the process of overdetermined sexual acting out. The male alcoholic's compulsive "flight into heterosexuality" is frequently more pronounced than that of the female alcoholic. There are two reasons for this. These factors also explain the male alcoholic's intense and pronounced anxiety associated with the matter of gender identity. First of all, the woman alcoholic evolves from a homosexual relationship with her mother. This is a biologically determined fact of life. During the initial months and years of life, the female experiences homosexuality within the confines of the most intense and profound of all human encounters. This is such an elementary and basic fact of human living that therapists have overlooked the psychological significance of this process. Certainly, the mother-female infant (child) relationship is not bizarrely homosexual, deviant or perverted. A warm, nurturant and loving involvement between the mother and infant daughter is a basic psychological prerequisite for the well-being and healthy adjustment of the daughter. An intimate relationship between a mother and daughter teaches both parties to live comfortably with their sexual identities.

Alcoholic women have experienced a serious disturbance within the context of their relationships with their mothers. The mother of the woman alcoholic is extremely anxious and uncomfortable in the mothering relationship. Many women alcoholics describe their mothers as cold, distant, controlling, tense, aloof and weak. Alcoholic women have often had an alcoholic father.

Identity confusion and sexual conflicts play an important role in the mother's (i.e. mother of the woman alcoholic) inability to establish an intimate and loving relationship with their daughters. Intimate relationships are globally demanding. Loving, intense, intimate relationships require a great deal of giving of the self. Within the context of all intimate relationships, one source of anxiety and fear is that of giving up or losing oneself in the relationship. In short, intimacy demands ego fusion with a significant other. This process of ego fusion can be extremely anxiety producing. Ego fusion with a daughter is very anxiety producing for the mother who manifests ego deficit. This loss of self or blurring of the ego boundaries within the context of an intense and intimate human relationship involves a sexual dimension. Loving always requires a significant degree of ego fusion. The process of loving can also involve physical or sexual fusion. Connotatively and inferentially, sexual fusion is basic to the process of loving. Thus, mothers who question their adequacy and identity as women experience (pre-consciously, if not consciously) considerable anxiety over their "homosexualized" relationships with their daughters. These women experience the partial equivalent of this response in heterosexually eroticized relationships with their sons. These processes can contribute to the identity pathology of male and female alcoholics.

Every male must establish a basic identity vis-à-vis the mother-son relationship. Identity is also consolidated within the parameters of the family constellation. Identity consolidation is a lifelong process. Women are "given" their basic identities in the sense that their gender is the same as the mother object. The male must learn to differentiate between self and mother *as a woman*. This is a form of self-other differentiation which demands continual work. All women must learn to effectively differentiate between self and mother, but the sexual "oneness" or fusion within the mother-female infant (child) relationship more readily and easily facilitates the development of a nuclear psychological and sexual sense of "me." In addition, the homosexual nature of the mother-daughter relationship creates the basis for a lack of catastrophic anxiety in the realms of bisexuality and homosexuality. This situation pertains to disturbed, healthy or relatively healthy mother-daughter relationships. The life process of the male, as a result of the additional ego demand of gender differentiation, chronically involves the matter of working through or developmentally managing the process of manliness. The developmental life process of the woman encompasses this same process. However, women evolve from a relationship framework that qualitatively makes this process both potentially easier and more complete at any developmental juncture. Males are, therefore, prone to the experience of identity-determined anxiety to an extent that exceeds that of women. Many biologists and embryologists would more than obsequiously support this position by pointing out that all human beings begin the life process as females!

It is clinically significant that males are generally more inclined than females to continually strive to prove or demonstrate the fact of their biological identity. This phenomenon is in part culturally determined. Likewise, physiologic and hormonal factors may potentiate this process. Yet, the fact remains that men strive in an overdetermined fashion to prove or demonstrate their manhood. Males, more so than females, seem to have historically chosen a predominance of violent and aggressive ways to demonstrate their identity. Within the framework of modern American society, very few women are enamored with the sport of football to the extent of breaking their legs, arms and bodies on a weekly basis while engaging in this "sport!" By the same token, fewer females spend their weekends glued to the television set watching men act out against each other via sports of controlled violence. Competitiveness among women and *with* men is relatively new in our culture. In sum, a number of very potent culturally related variables potentially reinforce and exacerbate the ego pathology of male and female alcoholics.

In recent years, our culture has become rather obsessed with the issue of identity. In order to be a "man," one must drink a particular brand of beer, drive a certain type of car, be aggressive and athletic, sexually attractive and young. The "real woman" is sensuous, attractive, wears a certain brand of hose, makeup and clothes, and she is slender and youthful, regardless of her age! These culturally valued artifacts of masculinity and femininity are superficial and external to the self. Yet, they are the very precepts by which people and cultures define physical attractiveness and gender. Alcoholics are pathologically set up to attempt to assimilate these artifacts in order to feel more masculine or feminine. Alcoholics perceive themselves as inadequately male or female. This characterological reality is synergistically reinforced by culture and the mediums of culture.

The following case history demonstrates a number of the identity-oriented conflicts of the male alcoholic:

> NW was a forty-two-year-old retired army sergeant. He initially entered an army alcohol and drug rehabilitation program some three years prior to his retirement. At that time, the patient was diagnosed as a "chronic alcoholic."
>
> Following the completion of a one-month residential treatment program, NW attended a weekly outpatient therapy group and infrequently attended AA (Alcoholics Anonymous). His wife was referred to the post-Al-Anon group and very quickly became an active member in this group. While involved in this treatment program, NW was able to remain totally abstinent from alcohol for a period of some five months. However, the patient believed that he could "control his drinking" and began to drink again. The patient's initial few weeks of drinking were relatively uneventful. He was able to drink "a few beers each night" while avoiding the "hard stuff." Within a matter of weeks, this pattern began to deteriorate and the patient was soon back to his earlier pattern of drinking roughly a fifth of vodka each day. After a period of two months of drinking, the patient was again placed in residential treatment by his company commander. A few days after entry into the residential treatment center, NW began to evidence severe personality dis-

organization in combination with symptomatology associated with alcohol withdrawal. As a result of these symptoms, the patient was transferred to the base hospital and placed on the psychiatric ward. At this time, the patient was diagnosed as suffering from a "psychotic decompensation, paranoid type." It was additionally noted by the ward psychiatrist that NW was an "alcoholic." NW was a psychiatric inpatient for ninety days. Subsequently, he was referred to the author for outpatient care specific to his alcohol addiction.

NW was seen by the author in three individual-therapy sessions. He and his wife were then referred to a weekly open-ended marital couples therapy group that the author was conducting. The W's attended this group weekly for 18 months. They finally discontinued treatment as a result of N's retirement from the army and relocation in another state. It was within the context of some 130 hours of marital couples group psychotherapy with NW that the following "identity"-oriented clinical data were obtained. This group was made up of couples in which one spouse was alcoholic. Each session was held for two hours weekly. The group was "open-ended" and consisted of eight to twelve couples.

The patient expressed no warm feelings for either of his parents. He particularly disliked his mother. Time and again in therapy, he described his mother as "colder than a witch's tit in a brass bra." The patient had grown up within the confines of a lower-class, rural southern family of six children. NW's father was reportedly "bad to drink," and NW was able to vividly recall the many whippings he had received as a child and adolescent by his father. His mother did not drink. According to the patient, she spent a good deal of her life engaging in various church activities. NW verbalized that his older brother (the family consisted of one older brother, a younger brother, and three younger sisters) continually "beat the piss out of me." NW recalled having always been "nervous around people" and feeling like an "outsider." At the age of forty-one, the patient viewed himself as "not knowing who I am – I guess I've never known who I am." After having been in therapy for some eight months and following eight months of total sobriety, the patient began to view his military career choice as related to a "search for identity." During these months, the patient frequently referred to himself as being "crazier than hell." Having quit school in the ninth grade, NW decided to join the army two-and-one-half years later in order to "make something out of myself." In actuality, NW had been more than reasonably successful in his military career. He had reached the rank of sergeant first class. During the initial months of treatment, NW expressed a good deal of resentment toward the military for the role "it" had played in "causing" his alcoholism. This sentiment changed radically during the later stages of therapy.

As an adolescent and an adult, NW was extremely aggressive and violent. On occasion, NW had literally attacked people for staring at him while he was drinking in different barroom settings. After spending a number of months in treatment, NW began to look at this behavior and reached the point of concluding that "I guess I was trying to be a somebody, but I went about it all wrong." It became apparent that NW had been overly suspicious and perhaps frankly paranoid during much of his adult life. Within the process of group treatment, this patient was continually attempting to deal with and resolve the matter of being somebody. This issue of being somebody was associated with "being a man" and more fundamentally being a person. The fights and aggressive demeanor of this patient, his history of extramarital affairs, and even his military career choice can be viewed as defensive strategies that were aimed at maintaining the identity of the patient. NW drank alcoholically in order to feel powerful and masculine. He was combative for these same reasons, and the masculinity and aggressiveness associated with his military career choice fits this same psychodynamic rubric.

Following military retirement, NW described himself as being continually "all squirreled up," referring to his internal feelings of anxiety and emotional turmoil. Much of this conflict revolved around NW's inability to find any kind of job or voca-

> tion following military retirement. After four or five months of "job hunting," NW finally secured a position as a nightwatchman for a small corporation. NW had mixed feelings about this position and referred to himself as "back in uniform and totin' a gun again." While NW expressed a dislike for the uniform associated with the nightwatchman job, at the same time he felt very good about once again having a gun. Six months after NW began working as a nightwatchman, he became extremely dissatisfied with his job and various other facets of himself and his family, and in a matter of days, decided to move his family to a rural Alabama community. This was where his "kinfolk" resided.
>
> As one might have predicted, NW reinitiated his alcoholic career subsequent to this move. A letter from NW's wife to the author nearly one year after the move to Alabama indicated that NW was "drinking heavily, doin' a little construction work, and mostly raisin' chickens and hogs" on a three-acre farm.

This patient had experienced a long history of conflicts associated with the matter of identity. The identity conflicts of this patient are characteristic of most male alcoholics. The patient felt inadequate and inferior and manifested self-system fragmentation.

Alcoholics frequently attempt to overcompensate for their identity vulnerabilities by acting out in an overdetermined sexually role-appropriate fashion. The alcoholic acts out in accord with his or her perceptions and beliefs pertaining to sexually role-appropriate behavior. Male alcoholics are especially prone to sexual and aggressive acting out in defense of their identity conflicts. Chronic intoxication serves the purpose of binding intense anxiety specific to self-system fragmentation and ego splitting (Forrest, 1979a). The identity pathology of the alcoholic is associated with the gender confusion. Most alcoholics intensely fear being homosexual, yet this is but one aspect of the identity-oriented pathology of the addicted person. Many alcoholics know or believe that they are not homosexual in spite of their anxiety and trepidation over this issue.

The identity conflicts of the alcoholic are a function of regressive ego pathology. As noted earlier in the chapter, the identity conflicts of the alcoholic are a manifestation of ego deficit or a structural weakness of the ego. The alcoholic is chronically anxious. Chronic, intense anxiety impairs the reality-testing operations of the ego and creates a persistent degree of self-system fragmentation. Intense anxiety causes the alcoholic to feel chronically uneasy in his or her relations with significant others. The ego boundaries of the alcoholic have never been adequately defined or consolidated. Thus, the ego structure of the alcoholic is always weak or vulnerable in the realm of anxiety tolerance. Chronic and intense anxiety can precipitate identity defusion. In order to defend his or her precarious ego structure, the alcoholic acts out in a variety of essentially overdetermined and pathological ways: (1) the alcoholic attempts to orally integrate the ego or self-system; (2) the alcoholic becomes progressively more obsessive-compulsive in life-style; (3) the alcoholic acts out sexually in an attempt to consolidate a gender based self-system or ego structure; and (4) the alcoholic develops a paranoid frame of reference. Depression, phobias, hypochondriacal trends (Evans, 1980) and other psychoneurotic features may also be utilized by the alcoholic in order to compensate for gross ego deficit. Additionally, the alcoholic becomes ever-increasingly narcissistic in his or her interpersonal relations.

Intrapersonally, the alcoholic vacillates between viewing self in a narcissistic, omnipotent, grandiose, power-fantasy-oriented manner (Forrest, 1978) and evaluating self as worthless, inadequate, no good and "shit." These primitive methods of compensating for ego deficit are not ego dystonic. They are ego syntonic in that they constitute the alcoholic character structure. These factors explain the alcoholic's lack of rationally or cognitively mediated behavior, impulse-ridden behavior, primitive oral rage and aggression. The pathognomonic aspects of the alcoholic ego or self-system include pseudo-hypersexuality, the avoidance defense system, overdetermined dependency needs, sadomasochism, infantilism, depression, acting out, guilt and the entire gamut of other clinical issues dealt with in this text.

Bipolarity is another important clinical dimension of the alcoholic ego and self-system. The self-system of the alcoholic is constructed vis-à-vis consistent, ongoing, dichotomous experiences of the "good me-bad me" variety. Alcoholics feel and behave in a chameleon-like fashion. The intrapersonal and interpersonal worlds of the alcoholic are filled with consistent ups and downs, good and bad, superman and turd, and so forth. In sum, the alcoholic is a bipolar person. Most people are familiar with individuals who are friendly, warm and likable when sober. After consuming a number of alcoholic beverages, these seemingly friendly individuals become overly assertive, aggressive, and perhaps even dangerous. Some alcoholics are like this. However, the stereotype of the warm, loving alcoholic who becomes a veritable madman following the consumption of a number of alcoholic beverages may or may not be accurate. Not all alcoholics fit this *specific* type of Jekyll-Hyde personality paradigm. Yet, the alcoholic is divided within. The bipolarity of the alcoholic ego or self-system is indicative of adjustment pathology associated with ego deficit and a structural flaw within the self-system.

Kernberg (1975, 1976, & 1980) has delineated the borderline personality adjustment and the function of the "splitting" process. According to Kernberg (1975):

> Splitting refers only to the active process of keeping apart introjections and identifications of opposite quality. The integration, or synthesis, of introjections and identifications of opposite qualities possibly provides the most important source of neutralization of aggression (in that libidinal and aggressive drive derivatives are fused and organized as part of that integration), and, therefore, one consequence of pathological circumstances under which splitting is excessive is that this neutralization does not take place sufficiently and an essential energy source for ego growth fails. Splitting, then, is a fundamental cause of ego weakness, and as splitting also requires less counter-cathexis than aggression, a weak ego falls back easily on splitting and a vicious circle is created by which ego weakness and splitting reinforce each other.

Kernberg (1975 & 1980) indicates that one manifestation of splitting may be a selective "lack of impulse control" such as is prevalent in the addictions and alloplastic disorders. Perhaps the best-known manifestation of splitting is the division of external objects into "all good" ones and "all bad" ones, with the concomitant possibility of complete, abrupt shifts – that is, sudden and complete reversals of all feelings and conceptualizations about a particular person. Extreme and repetitive oscillation between contradictory self-concepts may also be the result of the mechanism of splitting." The process just described pertains to bipolarity within the self-system and is an index of ego deficit. Fragmentation is central to vacillation within the self-system and within one's world of interpersonal relations.

A final dimension of structural weakness of the alcoholic ego is the propensity toward massive regression (Forrest, 1978 & 1983). Alcoholics have a low frustration tolerance. The alcoholic responds to frustration and stress in any number of inordinately regressive ways. Rather than responding to stress in an appropriate, problem-solving manner, the alcoholic tends toward "all-or-none" regressive solutions. A common example of this tendency toward impulsive, regressive problem solving in the face of frustration and stress (Della-Giustina et al., 1978) is that of going on a drunken bender following an argument with the spouse or employer. The propensity for massive regression is directly related to the ego deficit of the alcoholic. In essence, the alcoholic reverts to the use of regressive defenses and behaviors when forced to cope with stressful stimuli. Even minimal or short-term stress and frustration (Mines and Yost, 1983) can precipitate very regressive behaviors upon the part of the alcoholic. The propensity toward massive regression is perhaps best demonstrated by the alcoholic who initiates drinking after fifteen to twenty-five years of sobriety and adaptive living. Within a matter of hours or days, these individuals are psychologically and physically dysfunctional. This phenomenon may be indicative of a physiological or disease process. At any rate, these regressions are a direct result of ego deficit. The alcoholic acts in order to alleviate stress. Furthermore, the alcoholic behaves impulsively, regressively, and in an all-or-none fashion.

There are other characteristics of the alcoholic ego that are central to the pathology of alcoholism. An overdetermined search for power and control is another indication of ego deficit.

Grandiosity, power-fantasy ideation and megalomania are also indicative of ego deficit and self-system fragmentation.

PSYCHOTHERAPEUTIC CONSIDERATIONS

Abstinence from alcohol is a basic goal of psychotherapy with alcoholics. The alcoholic is unable to resolve his or her basic identity conflicts prior to the establishment of sobriety. Heavy drinking and chronic intoxication reinforce and exacerbate the alcoholic's identity pathology. Most alcoholics are able to modify and resolve their basic identity conflicts vis-à-vis extended psychotherapeutic treatment and concomitant long-term sobriety.

The therapist needs to begin the process of genetic reconstruction after the alcoholic patient is committed to sobriety and the therapeutic alliance (Forrest, 1983). This treatment technique helps the patient and therapist understand the historic or genetic components of the patient's identity pathology. A consistent therapeutic focus upon the patient's fragmented "good" and "bad" identity and self-system components must be maintained throughout the psychotherapy process. It is therapeutically efficacious to begin this process by exploring the patient's self-perceptions and feelings of inadequacy, inferiority, grandiosity and hyper-narcissism. The therapist must interpret, explore and confront the alcoholic patient's characterological bipolarity and self-system fragmentation.

It is also important for the therapist to actively explore the patient's feelings, behaviors and self-dialogue pertaining to sexual identity. Some alcoholics floridly act out their identity conflicts vis-à-vis sexual promiscuity. The psychotherapist needs to openly discuss these issues and point out the destructive and self-defeating aspects of acting out. Most alcoholics are anxious and uncomfortable discussing sexual problems and particularly the matter of homosexuality. The therapist should consistently and actively focus upon the patient's sexual doubts and fears. However, these are very sensitive treatment issues and they are grist for the treatment process after a working and productive therapeutic alliance has been established. The therapists's premature interpretations, confrontations and content focus can result in the alcoholic patient's fleeing from treatment or destructive acting out (Forrest, 1982a).

Effective psychotherapy with alcoholics results in self-system and identity consolidation. The therapist teaches, models and globally facilitates the process of patient-identity consolidation. It is essential for the alcoholic patient to develop a sense of basic security and trust in the psychotherapist and therapeutic alliance. Effective and productive therapeutic relationships enable the patient to begin the process of self and identity exploration. Insight and growth are fostered by the therapeutic process. Eventually, a significant reconstruction of basic identity and the self-system occurs.

SUMMARY

The various identity conflicts of the alcoholic were discussed in this chapter. Identity was also defined in this chapter. Alcoholics manifest a plethora of identity conflicts. The identity pathology of the alcoholic is multifaceted. Alcohol addiction does create many different types of identity-based conflicts, yet the identity struggles of the alcoholic originate very early in life. The process of developing an adequately consolidated nuclear sense of self begins shortly after birth and continues throughout life. However, this process is most crucially accomplished, or not accomplished, during the developmental epochs of infancy and childhood. It cannot be overemphasized that the self, or ego, is interpersonally created and shaped. The ego or self-system is shaped by genetic makeup and interpersonal experiences. The parameters of identity begin with the task of self-other differentiation. This task has been pathologically accomplished in the case of the alcoholic. As a result, the alcoholic neurotically stumbles through life on an unending search for identity.

The identity conflicts of the alcoholic (Forrest, 1979a & 1983) are basically related to ego deficit or self-system fragmentation. Many alcoholics act out this struggle vis-à-vis an overdetermined sexual search for self. Male alcoholics drink in order to feel more powerful and more masculine. Women alcoholics drink in order to feel more feminine. The alcoholic's flight into heterosexual promiscuity can be viewed as a defense against gender pathology. Alcoholics are rarely homosexual or sexually deviate in an object sense. Our culture strongly reinforces macho (machismo) drinking for males (Knauert, 1979). Macho drinking kills many alcoholics each year. Cultural and societal cues reinforce drinking behaviors.

Alcoholics drink in order to construct or consolidate an identity. Paradoxically, drinking works in the sense that the alcoholic is able to avoid identity fragmentation by remaining intoxicated. However, this pathological process invariably fails. At some point, alcoholism creates further identity conflicts and self-system fragmentation. Alcoholism takes away identity! As the male alcoholic drinks to become more masculine, in reality he makes himself physically and psychologically less masculine. Women alcoholics become progressively less feminine as a result of chronic intoxication.

The alcoholic's ego deficit is manifest in a chronic sense of anxiousness, a bipolar adjustment style, a propensity toward massive regression, and other secondary clinical symptoms. Low frustration tolerance, an overdetermined flight into heterosexual roles and behaviors, and even chronic vocational changes can be associated with the structural makeup of the alcoholic ego or self-system. Intense anxiety creates self-system fragmentation. The identity conflicts of the alcoholic can often be significantly modified or resolved by intensive psychotherapy. In order to change and grow, the alcoholic must accept self as an alcoholic. The alcoholic chronically struggles against and denies this aspect of his or her identity. Within the confines of a successful psychotherapy relationship, the alcoholic synthesizes the fragmented components of the self-system. The curative therapeutic process includes a consolidation of identity. Developing a more reality-oriented and integrated understanding of "who I am" enables the alcoholic to make significant strides in the realm of identity consolidation. Abstinence (Forrest, 1980) is the first and most important step in this curative process.

Chapter Eight

ALCOHOLISM AND PARANOIA

INTRODUCTION

CLINICIANS have long recognized (Forrest, 1980 & 1982a) that paranoia is a significant feature of the alcoholic character structure and personality. However, little has been written on this subject. There is a dearth of research data pertaining to alcohol addiction and the various paranoid conditions. Freud (1953) briefly touched upon the psychodynamic issues of alcoholism, paranoia and homosexuality. Other clinicians (Fenichel, 1945; Meissner, 1978) have also briefly touched upon these clinical areas. This chapter encompasses an in-depth exploration of the relationships between pathological alcohol dependency and the paranoid states.

Paranoid reactions are attempts to escape from tension and anxiety through denial and projection defenses. This process results in the development of more or less systematized delusions. Delusions may be persecutory, jealous, grandiose, or erotic. Delusions are belief systems that are incongruous with social reality.

There are several paranoid states. Paranoia, paranoid schizophrenia, involutional paranoia and the paranoid personality constitute the major paranoid states (Meissner, 1978). The paranoid personality involves a basic characterological distortion. The paranoid personality is characteristically "hypersensitive, argumentative, suspicious, constantly maintaining a guarded and defensive attitude toward other people in his environment and the world around him. The rigidity and suspiciousness of these personalities make their personal relationships extremely difficult and trying, particularly on people around them. They avoid close involvement and are quite prone to jealousy and angry outbursts" (Meissner, 1978). In contrast to the other paranoid states, the paranoid personality is not psychotic.

The pathology of paranoia and related paranoid states is often associated with alcoholism (Knauert, 1980; Forrest, 1983) and chemical dependency. Paranoid trends are basic to the alcoholic character structure. Typically, the alcoholic's paranoia is well controlled during periods of sobriety. Many alcoholics become floridly paranoid during drinking bouts and periods of intoxication. Loss of control follows intoxication. Both of these processes foster the development of paranoid ideation.

The paranoid trends of the alcoholic are etiologically associated with infantile and childhood narcissistic need and entitlement deprivation. As discussed in Chapter Seven, infantile and childhood experiences involving rejection, unlove, and a lack of interpersonal warmth and concern upon the part of significant others initiate basic identity conflicts and pathology. The identity problems of the alcoholic are chronic. The paranoid dimension of the alcoholic character structure evolves from these early life narcissistic injuries. Narcissistic injury precipitates the development of a less than syntaxic self-system. Quite simply, early life experiences with significant others that convey a sense of rejection, neglect, hurt, and unlove contribute to the development of a less than adequately consolidated self-system. Alcoholics have never successfully resolved the basic issues pertaining to the question "Who am I?" Interpreting and relating to the world in a basically paranoid manner (Forrest, 1983) is clinically associated with identity confusion. Self-system fragmentation and identity pathology precipitate the paranoid dimensions of the alcoholic character structure.

ALCOHOLISM AND THE DEVELOPMENT OF PARANOID CONDITIONS

The alcoholic male tends to manifest overt identity problems and paranoia. Alcoholic women also have serious identity problems, but they tend to be less paranoid than male alcoholics. Cultural and social factors may be related to these dynamics. Several of these issues were discussed in Chapter Seven.

The paranoid dimensions of male and female alcoholics are related to basic identity pathology. A lack of consistent and ongoing gender-oriented consensual validation experiences creates the basis for the development of paranoid characterological features. The mother object is the primary source of narcissistic injury. She is sexually bipolar to the male infant. In the absence of a healthy relationship with the mother, the male infant develops an inadequate and distorted identity. The male infant's distorted identity does not include a nuclear sense of "maleness." A warm, nurturant, loving relationship with the mother object enables the male to establish close, meaningful interpersonal ties with her that are conducive to sexual differentiation. Being loved and essentially one with the mother object eventually facilitates the process of resolving the symbiotic ties of infancy and childhood. This process also helps the male accept and differentiate his physical and psychological being from the mother object. Obviously, healthy, early life mother-son relationships create the optimal pre-conditions for healthy father-son relationships. The male consolidates his masculine identity through his various transactions with the father object.

The identity process is different for the woman alcoholic. Having experienced an initial homosexual relationship with the mother object, women are less prone to the experience of potentially catastrophic feelings of anxiety relative to the matter of sexual identity. The paranoid process pertaining to sexual identity is of less clinical significance in the psychotherapy of women alcoholics. While the woman alcoholic's identity conflicts persist, they are less anxiety and fear producing than those of most male alcoholics. Identity confusion and homosexual conflicts are not as threatening to the woman alcoholic. Males have not experienced an early life homosexual relationship with the mother object. The male alcoholic fears the possibility of being homosexual. Unconsciously and pre-consciously, the male alcoholic perceives homosexuality as one of the most catastrophic of possible human transactions that might happen to him. This is a male dilemma.

The woman is "given" her psychological and physical identity vis-à-vis her relationship with the mother object. In this sense, women are not chronically involved in the process of working through or establishing their identities. The male sense of masculinity seems to be rather precarious. A multiplicity of culturally determined variables synergize these realities.

The paranoid dimensions of the alcoholic character structure are also associated with mother-son dependency, attachment and other forms of psychopathology. All alcoholics are pathologically dependent. The alcoholic needs to be "mothered." The roles and marital behaviors of the wife of the male alcoholic (Paolino and McCrady, 1977; Forrest, 1978) are often more akin to those of a mother than a spouse! Male alcoholics choose a spouse to meet their inordinate dependency needs and fill the roles of a surrogate mother. This neurotic pattern of spouse selection represents an attempt to magically undo the hurt, pain, rejection and deprivation experienced at the hands of the real mother object. This repetition compulsion may be acted out via several marriages. Ritual undoing is basic to this process. Attempting to establish a nuclear identity is also a basic ingredient in this process. Male and female alcoholics can never fully integrate the reality of having had a punitive, rejecting, inadequate, unloving mother. In spite of contrary appearances and verbalizations, the alcoholic unconsciously denies this reality.

Male alcoholics attempt to recreate vis-à-vis marriage a caricature of their mother-son relationship. This is an attempt to (1) love both self and the mother object, (2) sexually differentiate between self and the mother object, and, finally, (3) establish a loving relationship with the father, thereby consolidating an adequate sense of maleness. Alcoholics perceptually attempt to gain the missing love and affection of the original mother object. Unfortunately, this task can never be satisfactorily accomplished. In reality, the mother object was not capable of sustaining a loving, nurturant-type relationship with the alcoholic. The mother object was not and will never be capable of adequately meeting the alcoholic's narcissistic needs and entitlements. In a very real sense, the mother object's narcissistic injuries can never be undone. Unconsciously, many alcoholics are enraged at the mother object. In the event that the alcoholic was able to magically re-create the original mother-infant relationship, he or she would either murder the mother object or otherwise retaliate à la lex talionis. These factors explain the male alcoholic's perpetual difficulty in relating to women!

Many alcoholics verbalize that they dislike their mothers and never wish to see them or converse with them again. Nevertheless, these relationships are highly overdependent and pathologically symbiotic. Some alcoholics consciously reject and deny any form of loving or meaningful relationship with the mother object. A significant aspect of the experience of having been unloved and rejected by the mother object is that of chronically wondering "What was so catastrophically wrong with me that made my mother reject me to such an extent?" This form of ideation is paranoid.

Some male alcoholics have experienced an overdependent mother-son relationship. These overtly dependent and symbiotic mother-son relationships are also pathologically erotic in nature. Infrequently, the mother and son have engaged in incestuous sexual behaviors (Martin, 1980; Forrest, 1982b). The never-married male alcoholic of forty-five to fifty years of age who has remained with the mother object is overdependent and mother fixated. Symbolically, these alcoholic males have married the mother object. Unconsciously and pre-consciously, many of these alcoholics harbor a great deal of anger and rage for the mother object. These mothers chronically infantilize their alcoholic sons.

Overdetermined ego fusion with the mother object is an etiological factor in the development of paranoia. Ego fusion makes the alcoholic unable to break his infantile ties with the mother. Therefore, he is unable to consolidate a nuclear male identity. Self, in a gender sense, is never adequately differentiated from the mother object. Ego fusion also results in a simultaneous sexual fusion with the mother object. The alcoholic is chronically infantilized and feminized by this experience. This process fosters identity conflicts specific to the matter of masculinity and femininity. Family constellations that lack a father object for the son to identify with, emulate, and model appropriate male behaviors also foster identity problems. The mothers of some male alcoholics are aggressive, assertive and domineering, while their fathers tend to be weak, passive, withdrawn and inadequate (Wegscheider, 1981). Such a family system robs the son of an adequate male model. This process creates identity and role confusion and, hence, contributes to the development of a paranoid character structure.

Mothers of alcoholics also manifest significant identity confusion. Very few are overtly homosexual. However, a significant number of these mothers are markedly masculine in stature, appearance and general mannerisms. The mothers of many male alcoholics harbor a great deal of resentment, hate, and rage for males in general. Some have conveyed these messages to their sons throughout life. This process serves the pre-conscious and unconscious purpose of demasculinizing the son. The unconscious magical dynamic force that underlies this process involves turning the son into a female, a daughter.

This global process creates a paranoid characterological makeup. The predisposition to the development of a paranoid character structure evolves from a pre-conscious, if not conscious, awareness of (1) having been feminized by the mother object and/or being disallowed by her the opportunity to establish a nuclear male identity vis-à-vis a healthy father relationship, (2) realizing that as a male, one is somehow different from other males as a result of this experience, and (3) fearing that others know, or primitively understand, the sexual pathology basic to a disturbed form of mother-son relationship. All of these points have to do with understanding that one is somehow significantly different from other males. The alcoholic male always questions whether or not others comprehend his self-system fragmentation and identity pathology.

As mentioned earlier, women alcoholics also manifest basic identity pathology. However, this matter does not consistently relate to the development of a paranoid character structure in alcoholic women. The alcoholic woman does *not* consistently develop a paranoid character structure as a result of (1) the psychobiologic experience of enduring a prolonged homosexual relationship with the mother object and (2) sociocultural factors specific to womanhood and female identity. Many alcoholic women verbalize that they feel different and do not fit in. These self-perceptions can become reinforced by social reality. These factors actively and continuously synergize the paranoid struggles of some alcoholic women.

Various intrapersonal and interpersonal processes (Meissner, 1978) reinforce paranoia and the paranoid conditions. These processes are associated with the paranoid dimensions of the alcoholic character structure. The alcoholic life-style also creates paranoid ideation and a paranoid world view. Alcoholism can cause paranoid thinking. Most alcoholics (Forrest, 1978 & 1983) have engaged in various aberrant and socially deviant behaviors. Alcoholics assume deviant social roles. Indeed, most alcoholics become social deviates prior to acquiring the label "alcoholic." The alcoholic-labeling process is also tantamount to a scapegoat-role engagement. Familial and social consensual validation is essential to the labeling and scapegoating processes. The developmental and historic experiences of many alcoholics have included chronic role and behavioral deviance. Deviant roles can be devastating to the person's sense of self-esteem and self-worth. Early life deviant role entrapment reinforces deviant behaviors and roles during subsequent developmental stages. At some point, deviation and paranoia become ego-syntonic processes.

Any situation in which one deviates significantly from the accepted group standard or norm can create feelings of paranoia. In general, people are very conformity oriented. Most people experience a good deal of anxiety when they are perceived by others as deviating significantly from established and accepted normative standards. Infantile, childhood and adolescent sources of paranoia become the quid pro quo for the alcoholic. The alcoholic is an example par excellence of a social deviant. Alcoholics engage in various forms of socially unacceptable behavior. The social behaviors of the alcoholic can be bizarre. The paranoid dimensions of the alcoholic character structure are continually reinforced and exacerbated by alcohol-related and facilitated deviant social transactions. The alcoholic also becomes progressively more alienated from his or her primary reference groups. This process further reinforces deviant-role entrapment.

All alcoholics do not become involved in grossly inappropriate or deviant forms of social behavior. However, most alcoholics experience a great deal of guilt, anxiety and paranoia over intrapersonal conflicts and fantasies specifically associated with drinking. The alcoholic is paranoid and anxious as a result of the belief that significant others are aware of the inappropriate or bizarre interpersonal transactions and intrapersonal fantasies with which he or she has continually struggled. Alcoholics live a life of controlled paranoia. Social and cognitive deviance precipitates and reinforces paranoia. Arrests, debauchery, automobile accidents, job losses, marital discord and possibly multiple divorces, physical beatings and child abuse can be basic to the process of deviant socialization that accompanies alcoholism. The alcoholic experiences progressive feelings of alienation. In reality, the alcoholic should and does perceive the world from a progressively more paranoid perspective. The police, spouse, employer and significant others do begin to be on the lookout for the alcoholic once he or she has been labeled a social deviant!

Interpersonal transactions of this nature are infantile in nature. These transactions reinforce the paranoid ideation and perceptions of the alcoholic. Many alcoholics are perpetually caught up in the game of cops and robbers. Accordingly, the spouse, employer and police are in reality out to get the alcoholic. Within these contexts, the alcoholic has assumed the role of a victim or scapegoat. The spouse, employer and significant others become persecutors. These interpersonal transactions are parataxic. The socially deviant sexual behaviors of the alcoholic (Forrest, 1982b) also synergize paranoid ideation.

Many alcoholics engage in socially deviant behaviors while experiencing an alcohol-induced blackout. The alcoholic blackout is a poorly understood phenomenon. An alcoholic blackout (Forrest, 1978) is simply amnesia for a single event or extended episode during a drinking bout. The blackout typically occurs in the absence of extreme intoxication and does not involve loss of consciousness. The individual who experiences a blackout has no recall of a sequel of behaviors carried out while under the influence of alcohol. The blackout phenomenon is a controversial issue among experts in the field of alcoholism. Nonetheless, blackouts can also be a precursor to the development of paranoid ideation. Many alcoholics have had experiences of blacking out, then regaining full consciousness and hearing on the radio of a hit-and-run accident that took place during the drinking episode. These individuals are anxious, paranoid and wonder if they might not be the guilty party! Alcoholics sometimes act out violently, wreck cars, and beat up the spouse and children with no recall whatsoever of these activities after sobering up. Paranoia is often associated with these transactions. Fitting together the experiences of last night, or perhaps three or four days, reinforces paranoid ideation. The alcoholic may experience marked feelings of paranoia specific to a blackout, yet on literally hundreds of subsequent occasions he or she will repeat this experience! It is apparent that alcoholics make themselves paranoid.

The following case studies demonstrate the paranoid features and dimensions of the alcoholic character structure. In each of these cases, the psychotherapeutic management of the patient's paranoid ideation and behaviors assumed a major role in the treatment process.

Case 1. Earl M. was a forty-three-year-old Caucasian army sergeant. He was initially referred to the Fort Gordon Alcoholic and Drug Addict Rehabilitation Center as a result of intoxication while on duty. The patient had also been AWOL.

The patient had grown up in a New York City ghetto community. He was the oldest child in a family of six. Reportedly, one of his three sisters was a "drunk." The patient referred to his father as an "out-and-out alcoholic." The father was a lifelong construction worker and the mother had been intermittently employed as a domestic. The parents had experienced chronic marital difficulties relative to the father's alcoholism during Earl's childhood and adolescence. His father administered severe beatings to the mother and the four children.

Earl reported chronic feelings of isolation, fear, rejection and inadequacy during childhood and adolescence. In spite of average intelligence, Earl had managed to complete only the tenth grade prior to dropping out of school. After some eighteen months of living at home and working at various menial jobs, Earl enlisted in the United States Army. Prior to enlistment in the service, Earl had very few friends and viewed himself as a loner. However, he was emotionally attached to a younger sister. While Earl had come to disdain his father's drinking, he also harbored considerable resentment relative to his mother's constant "bitching" over the drinking issue. Earl related that he felt a deep distrust of people in general, to include both parents. Apparently, the only lasting and trusting relationship that Earl had been able to maintain was the one with his sister. The patient had infrequently consumed alcoholic beverages and gotten drunk prior to entry into the army, but he had experienced no social or interpersonal difficulties as a result of his drinking behavior before entering the army.

The patient's military career had been somewhat checkered. An older sergeant attempted to homosexually seduce the patient during his second year of enlistment. Apparently, both men had been drinking a good deal when this episode took place. Following this event, the patient reported that he terminated all social relations with the sergeant, feeling upset, guilty and disgusted over the entire matter. It was two years later when the patient began dating his present wife. He was twenty-two years of age at that time. Prior to this the patient reported having dated very little. The patient apparently met his wife at a nightclub in the same community in which he was stationed. She was a registered nurse. Following a relatively brief period of courtship (some four months), the couple decided to marry. Mrs. M became pregnant during the period of courtship. Mrs. M had grown up in a small rural community and had five brothers and sisters. Her father, a heavy drinker, had been a rather violent man and was prone to a great deal of acting out within the community and family constellation.

The initial ten to twelve years of the marriage encompassed having two more children, two military-precipitated separations of approximately eighteen months duration each, and a limited number of mutual extramarital affairs. These mutual marital affairs very quickly became a major source of marital dissonance. Earl manifested very little guilt or remorse about the women he became involved with, as everybody "did the same damn thing while they were in Korea." However, similar behaviors upon the part of Mrs. M were extremely threatening to the patient. He handled or managed these situations by administering violent beatings to his wife. In spite of having her upper right femur broken by the patient (he had broken her femur with a single blow of the butt of a twelve-gauge shotgun while in an alleged alcoholic blackout), Mrs. M continued to persist in the marriage. Meanwhile, she maintained an ongoing clandestine affair with a sergeant major. Earl progressively consumed more and more liquor and became increasingly dysfunctional in his marriage, family and job.

At the point of entry into treatment (the patient had been ordered into treatment by his commanding officer), the patient appeared to be self-assured, in control of his behavior, pleasant, and most enthusiastic about his involvement in the rehabilitation program. The patient and his wife were seen together in weekly conjoint therapy by the author. The patient was also involved in weekly group psychotherapy. Earl was encouraged to attend Alcoholics Anonymous and his wife was encouraged to become involved in the center's Al-Anon program. Psychological assessment of the patient with the Minnesota Multiphasic Personality Inventory (MMPI) indicated a 6-4-9 profile. The patient was diagnosed a sociopathic personality with concomitant paranoid personality features. An obvious factor in the patient's apparent complete acceptance of the treatment program was his scheduled retirement within approximately eight months. The patient attended all scheduled conjoint and group psychotherapy sessions and AA meetings for three weeks. He then began to miss treatment appointments. Shortly thereafter, Earl informed the treatment staff that he was quite capable of "controlling" his drinking, since he was now "limiting" his drinking to beer. The patient's wife had also intermittently attended Al-Anon during this time. She was also seen with her husband in three conjoint therapy sessions.

Mr. and Mrs. M were not seen in treatment for six weeks. Then the author received a distressed phone call from Mrs. M in which she related that Earl had been acutely intoxicated for ten days. It should be noted that Mrs. M was a rather sociopathic woman with significant acting out problems. She was also a problem drinker. The patient had severely beaten his youngest daughter (age 13) for her alleged marijuana smoking. He then sustained a superficial gunshot wound in the shoulder as a result of his attempts to subdue the "pusher" who had given his daughter the marijuana. Throughout the course of this drinking episode, Earl had also verbalized that he was going to kill the sergeant major who was involved with his wife.

During the few therapy sessions preceding this alcohol-facilitated regression, the patient was floridly paranoid. The patient's intrapersonal dialogue and fantasy ideation were highly paranoid in nature: "The Army is out to get me"; "My wife is a no-good whore" (with concomitant expressed fears of contacting venereal disease from her); "A lot of people want me locked up on the 'psycho' ward, particularly *the* sergeant major"; etc. Rather than confronting the patient with the basic craziness and paranoia inherent in these verbalizations, I had assumed a more supportive therapeutic role. This treatment technique facilitated both trust and an openness conducive to the patient's expression of highly guarded paranoid thought content.

Within one hour after the distressed call from Earl's wife, Earl appeared at the author's office. He requested an "emergency" session. During this session, the patient was acutely intoxicated, highly agitated, manic, fragmented and capable of acting out against his paranoically constructed persecutors. Moreover, the patient had a .45-caliber pistol with him. He informed the author that he was going to proceed immediately to the office of the sergeant major and kill him. Immediately following the patient's exit from the author's office, the chief of psychiatry was notified of the direness of the situation and the military police were called. Within minutes, the patient was apprehended. He was then interviewed by the chief of psychiatry and involuntarily hospitalized. The patient's wife was notified of this course of events.

After a period of seventy-two hours of sobering up, the patient continued to manifest poorly controlled feelings of anger, hostility and paranoid ideation. The patient harbored a good deal of hostility toward the author relative to his role in the hospitalization process. He verbalized that the author "betrayed him and sided with the enemy." On numerous occasions during the initial week of hospitalization, the patient threatened to kill the author. Rorschach and Thematic Apperception Testing at this time resulted in a diagnosis of paranoid schizophrenia and chronic alcoholism. During six weeks of hospitalization, the patient gradually experienced a general remission of symptoms. He became actively involved in group psychotherapy, ward government, individual psychotherapy, and began attending Alcoholics Anonymous on a regular basis. At the time of hospital discharge, the patient appeared to have resolved his rage and resentment toward the author for his role in the hospitalization process. However, he then blamed his wife for the hospitalization. Furthermore, he continued to manifest significant paranoid symptomatology.

Intermittent therapy and follow-up contacts and feedback from the AA community indicated that Earl again initiated drinking. The patient did retire from the U.S. Army. He subsequently separated from his wife and family and left the community. The patient was seen in four follow-up psychotherapy sessions conducted over an eight-month interval. Unfortunately, precise treatment outcome data on this patient are not available. However, in the absence of meaningful and ongoing treatment engagement, this patient could be expected to maintain a borderline adjustment.

Case 2. Tom C was a thirty-two-year-old army sergeant. He was treated on a self-referred basis at the Fort Carson Alcoholic and Drug Addict Rehabilitation Center. The patient was treated for chronic alcoholism and severe depression. At the point of contact with this agency, the patient was extremely despondent and considered a high-suicidal risk. The patient was immediately placed in a halfway house setting for a period of some six weeks and started on antidepressant medication. Tom had been stationed at an army base in Germany. While on a drunken binge, he had taken leave to return to the United States to visit his wife and children. He then planned to commit suicide.

The patient had grown up in a small rural community in Texas with his grandparents and other relatives. His mother had given him to her parents. She had been unmarried and in no position to emotionally or financially support the patient. The mother had been married numerous times, lived common law intermittently, and from time to time maintained herself by prostitution. The patient had one brother and two sisters. The second-oldest daughter was also left in the grandparents' keeping. She was emotionally close to Tom. This relationship had remained intact. Tom recalled his grandfather being a heavy drinker. He also noted that when he "visited" his mother and her various boyfriends, both were intoxicated or drinking heavily.

From the time Tom entered school until he quit in the tenth grade, he encountered a plethora of difficulties. For the most part, these problems were focused around his inability to get along with peers and significant others. Chronic difficulties with teachers, principals, and peers always seemed to relate to fights, aggressive acting out, and poorly controlled rage. Academically, the patient managed to pass from grade to grade. The patient enlisted in the United States Army at the age of eighteen.

The patient developed full-blown alcoholism at age twenty-nine. The military life-style had been a rewarding experience for the patient. Eventually, his ten-year history of controlled heavy drinking collapsed.

While stationed in Germany, the patient married a German woman. She was divorced and had a four-year-old son by a previous marriage. Marital difficulties began early in the marriage. Typically, drinking and mutual physical outbursts were basic to the couple's marital problems. The patient was involved in numerous transient affairs. His wife avoided such affairs until the latter years of the marriage when she became involved with a civilian physician. The patient was in Vietnam at this time, drinking heavily, debauching a great deal, and not providing monetary support. for his family. His wife alleged that she became physically involved with the physician out of physical necessity for herself and the children. This relationship was terminated after the patient returned from Vietnam. However, the psychological impact of this affair remained a chronic source of marital dissonance. The patient never tired of using this affair as a rationale for physically abusing his wife and children. Within two years of his return from Vietnam, the patient was reassigned to Germany. His wife refused to accompany him on this tour of duty. During this unaccompanied tour of duty, which ultimately resulted in the patient's engagement in treatment, the patient rapidly deteriorated. He was hospitalized for "drying out." The oldest son (age 11) had attempted suicide by hanging and was subsequently referred to a local community mental health center for psychotherapy.

Shortly after treatment engagement at the Fort Carson agency, the patient was reassigned to that installation. Once involved in the treatment program, the patient evidenced rapid and dramatic improvement. Within two months, the patient's depression was in remission. His wife frequently attended Al-Anon and both attended a weekly marital couples therapy group. The oldest son continued treatment at the community mental health center. Some four-and-one-half months later, Tom and his wife again began to experience marked marital discord. Resentments, primarily upon the part of his wife, proceeded from verbal abuse to outright physical assaults. The dyadic verbal and behavioral exchanges between this couple were steeped in aggression and hostility. Indeed, it seemed as though Tom and his wife were consciously determined to destroy one another.

Prior to this time, treatment had not encompassed the paranoid parameters of the patient's character structure. With the exacerbation of conflicts via the decompensation of the marital relationship, the patient began to evidence marked paranoid pathology. The initial clue to the patient's paranoid ideation was his sudden concern over his wife's marital fidelity. Tom began to "drop in" unexpectedly on his wife two or three times a day. Shortly thereafter, he began to call her at work ten or more times each day. The patient's regressive paranoid ideation reached the point of nightly inspections of his wife's undergarments. He would look for traces of semen that would indicate her unfaithfulness. Rather than reacting to the patient's increasing paranoid behaviors with withdrawal, a sense of personal threat and anxiety, the wife instead became increasingly combative and hostile toward the patient. Needless to say, the marital relationship quickly deteriorated.

Throughout this regression, the patient remained sober and regularly attended both Alcoholics Anonymous and group therapy. Feedback and support from these sources reinforced a marital separation. A marital separation did facilitate an apparent remission of the patient's paranoid psychopathology. Within the context of group therapy, the patient eventually began to explore his fear, hostility and distrust of females. He also began to view these components of his self-system within the context of viewing and interacting with others in a distorted, paranoid fashion. The patient remained totally abstinent. His depression remained in clinical remission. His paranoid ideation also remained controlled. The patient's wife discontinued all therapeutic contacts, to include Al-Anon. She took the children and moved in with another man. Eventually, she divorced the patient. The patient remained in psychotherapeutic treatment for over two years. He continues to attend AA and has been sober for over seven years.

Both of these case histories demonstrate the paranoid characterological features of the alcoholic. These patients did not trust their wives. They felt sexually inadequate and feared losing control of their wives. Both patients began to manifest florid paranoid symptomatology specific to the sexual acting out of their wives. Fears of being sexually inadequate, impotent and unable to keep the wife "sexually satisfied" were clinically associated with these patients' overt paranoid trends. Unconsciously, both patients feared homosexual contamination vis-à-vis the extramarital affairs of the spouse.

PSYCHOTHERAPEUTIC CONSIDERATIONS

It is difficult to ascertain the time at which the alcoholic begins to manifest paranoid symptomatology. The paranoid process usually becomes overtly malignant as the alcoholic progresses into the middle stages of the addiction process (Forrest, 1978). Within the context of the psychotherapeutic alliance, it can be established that many alcoholics have been consciously aware of their paranoid conflicts since the time of late adolescence. Alcoholics verbalize that they felt different, as though they did not fit in, during adolescence. Alcoholics struggle to control their paranoid conflicts. When the patient becomes floridly alcoholic, the paranoid process often breaks down or becomes pathologically uncontrollable. Acute or chronic situational stress can result in the outcropping of paranoid symptomatology. Paradoxically, it is after treatment or rehabilitation engagement that some alcoholics become paranoid and agitated. The ingestion of alcohol can serve a secondary purpose of masking or partially controlling paranoid ideation. Approximately 20 percent of alcoholics entering psychotherapy and rehabilitation display florid paranoid symptoms for the duration of even extended treatment.

Hostility, anger and rage (Meissner, 1978) are fused with paranoid psychopathology. Indeed, the paranoid personality is potentially volatile and explosive. The interaction of chronic alcoholism and a paranoid characterological makeup makes this an even more significant clinical consideration. The hurt, rejection and interpersonal pain experienced throughout life by the alcoholic enables him or her to "blame" others, project, and act out against these persecutors. Thus, it is ego syntonic for the alcoholic to retaliate against others in an overdetermined, paranoid manner.

The psychotherapist helps the alcoholic resolve and modify paranoid ideation by (1) facilitating a trusting, open therapeutic alliance, (2) helping the patient understand and terminate alcohol-determined inappropriate social behaviors and roles, and (3) resolving the patient's basic identity and sexual pathology. The patient must be committed to sobriety and the therapeutic process in order to therapeutically resolve identity and sexual conflicts.

After the alcoholic patient has been abstinent from alcohol for a few months and actively involved in the therapeutic process, the psychotherapist needs to begin an in-depth exploration of the patient's acting out behaviors, sexual adjustment style, self-concept and historic identity conflicts. The therapist needs to openly discuss with the patient all historic and present forms of paranoid thinking. It is therapeutically efficacious to actively point out how the patient has made himself or herself paranoid. The therapist must also help the patient explore and resolve chronic paranoid and disturbed self-perceptions and self-dialogue pertaining to being different, bizarre, or not fitting in.

It is very difficult for many alcoholics (Forrest, 1982b) to openly discuss their sexuality and sexual problems. Alcoholics tend to find it very difficult to discuss their bisexual and homosexual conflicts. The therapist needs to supportively help the alcoholic deal with these issues. A therapeutic exploration and resolution of paranoid ideation associated with sexual concerns and pathology is essential to the successful psychotherapy of alcoholism. The therapist's active interpretations and supportive confrontations are basic to the therapeutic process of resolving paranoid ideation.

SUMMARY

The paranoid dimensions of the alcoholic character structure were discussed in this chapter. Early life narcissistic injury results in self-system fragmentation and a paranoid character structure. Self-system fragmentation and identity deficit constitute the predisposition toward paranoid decompensation. Early life narcissistic need and entitlement deprivation results in a less than adequately consolidated self-system. The ego boundaries of the alcoholic (Forrest, 1979a & 1982b) are fragmented, poorly defined, and thus identity distorted. Alcoholics have never resolved their basic sexual-identity conflicts. They have failed to incorporate an adequate sense of masculinity or femininity, which precipitates a chronic fear of homosexuality and ego defusion. For most alcoholics, these are unconscious or pre-conscious processes. In theory, the homosexual relationship between the female alcoholic and her mother partially accounts for her relative lack of anxiety and fear relative to homosexuality and other sexual-identity issues.

The outcropping of florid paranoid symptoms is usually associated with the middle and later stages of alcoholism (Forrest, 1978). At this time, the alcoholic dynamism begins to globally collapse. A paranoid decompensation often appears to be precipitated by the termination of alcohol ingestion. Terminating alcohol addiction is difficult and anxiety producing.

The paranoid trends of the alcoholic are multifaceted and variably determined. It is essential for alcoholism counselors and psychotherapists to understand this particular dimension of the alcoholic personality and character structure. Once the alcoholic has reached the psychotherapist's office, it is imperative that the therapist (Forrest, 1979c) initiate therapeutic interventions that will help extinguish the patient's deviant role behaviors. This treatment technique is essential to the successful psychotherapy of alcoholics who are pathologically paranoid and actively reinforcing their paranoid trends. The alcoholic makes himself or herself paranoid via alcohol-facilitated, grossly inappropriate social behaviors. Each blackout reinforces the alcoholic's paranoia. Spouse beating, child neglect, job losses, and arrests also reinforce paranoid thinking. These sources of paranoid ideation are relatively accessible to the interventions of the psychotherapist. Therefore, they should be actively pursued during initial-treatment contacts.

Once engaged in the therapeutic process many alcoholics are able to understand these sources of paranoia. With adequate psychotherapeutic treatment, they are capable of modifying deviant or bizarre roles and behaviors. The patient becomes less paranoid by engaging in more healthy and appropriate social roles and behaviors. The patient then becomes more capable of exploring the psychogenic, identity-based roots of this characterological dynamism. Alcoholic patients need to deal with the sexual, identity-oriented conflicts that precipitate their paranoid ideation and behavior. In the absence of a therapeutic resolution of these issues, the sober alcoholic will continue to evidence paranoid symptomatology.

Chapter Nine

ALCOHOLISM AND SADOMASOCHISM

INTRODUCTION

ALCOHOLISM is not generally viewed as a variety of psychopathology encompassing sadism, masochism, or even secondary psychodynamic components of this typology. There are limited clinical and research data in the behavioral science literature (Schad-Somers, 1982; Forrest, 1983) dealing with alcoholism, sadism and masochism. Sadism, masochism and sadomasochism are clinical terms that are poorly understood, inadequately defined, and distorted by the nature of the affective connotations with which they are often associated.

Stekel (1929) is one of the few clinicians who investigated the issues of sadism and masochism. Unfortunately, Stekel failed to explore the clinical interrelationships between sadism, masochism, and alcoholism. Rather than merely focusing upon the pain-pleasure dimension of sadomasochism, Stekel (1929) emphasized that this type of behavior is psychosexually infantile and indicative of an obsessive character that manifests itself as a repetition compulsion. Sadomasochism is a disorder of the environment relating to specific experiences of childhood. According to Stekel, all sadomasochists are "affect hungry" individuals, who, in addition to their sexual pathologies, are essentially incapable of love. Stekel (1929) defined sadism as a "paraphilia in which the will to power is sexually accentuated" and masochism as "a paraphilia in which the will to submission is sexually accentuated." Stekel demonstrated in his case studies the persistence of the original sadistic disposition in those who are crippled or otherwise harshly treated by nature, fascists, and Ku Klux Klan members. He characterized the sadomasochist as "a dreamer who forces himself to the daily duties of life; one who lives in the past although apparently striving toward the future."

These general clinical descriptions of sadistic and masochistic behavior are readily applicable to many facets of the alcoholic character structure and the behavioral style of alcoholics. This chapter includes (a) a behavioral definition and description of the sadomasochistic adjustment style of the alcoholic, and (b) a discussion of the primary etiological components of this particular dimension of the alcoholic character structure.

ALCOHOLISM AND THE DYNAMICS OF SADOMASOCHISM

It is difficult to construct a precise behavioral definition of sadism, masochism or the sadomasochistic dynamism. Aberrant behavior or deviation is always relative. Sadistic and masochistic patterns of behavior are not bipolar characterological dimensions. Sadism and masochism coexist and are ego fused. Thus, the term *sadomasochistic* describes the ego syntonic nature, or ego fusion, of sadistic and masochistic characterological trends. Stekel (1929) indicates that the pain-pleasure and physical-abuse dimensions of sadomasochism are clearly of secondary or tertiary clinical importance. This position is incorrect. A basic hallmark of the alcoholic's sadomasochism is that of an overdetermined need to inflict physical and/or emotional hurt or pain upon the self and significant others. The number of suicides, homicides, automobile accidents, alcohol-induced physical symptoms, divorces, cases of child neglect and abuse, and nervous breakdowns specific to any random sample of alcoholic individuals clearly supports this position. Behaviorally, the alcoholic consistently inflicts a very pathological degree of pain upon self and significant others. The singular processes of being chronically intoxicated or acutely intoxicated are extremely sadomasochistic. Hangovers, being sick for days following a drinking spree, ending up in jail, and paying fines for driving while intoxicated are but a few of the many pain-oriented ingredients associated with alcoholism.

Most definitions and descriptions of sadomasochistic behavior (Fenichel, 1945; Schad & Somers, 1982) emphasize the sexual component of this pattern of behavior. Sexually sadomasochistic patterns of behavior are rarely a part of the behavioral repertoire of the alcoholic. This form of sexual aberration is no greater among alcoholics than among the general population (Forrest, 1982b). *Primary* sadomasochistic sexual deviation is an area of little clinical relevance to the psychotherapist involved in the treatment and rehabilitation of alcoholics. Symbolically, the sexual encounters of both male and female alcoholics are sadomasochistic. Extramarital affairs, divorce, numerous divorces, and the various behaviors of the alcoholic in the throes of an alcoholic-facilitated debauch involves sadomasochistic elements. A great deal of emotional pain, turmoil, and hurt accompanies these transactions. Sadomasochism includes various dimensions of emotional or affective pain.

The alcoholic family system is sadomasochistic. Indeed, the overt and covert *modus vivendi* of the alcoholic family system involves diffuse punitive interaction. Physical and emotional survival are paramount issues for the family members of the alcoholic family system (Forrest, 1978; Wegscheider, 1981). The alcoholic is often perceived as the family victim at the point of treatment engagement. However, the alcoholic family member is also a persecutor within the family system. Scapegoat, victim, rescuer and persecutor are the primary pathogenomonic roles within the alcoholic families (Forrest, 1978 & 1979b). The additional turmoil, pain and pathology created by perpetual role reversals and role slippage within these family systems reinforce sadomasochistic acting out. Pathologic familial roles and transactional games are exaggerated within the alcoholic family system. The non-addicted spouse is masochistic. The non-addicted spouse pathologically tolerates physical abuse, psychological hurt, and the sadistic and brutal confrontations of the alcoholic. The spouse of the alcoholic derives a good deal of secondary gain vis-à-vis masochistic roles and behaviors. The non-addicted spouse also engages in marital and familial roles that are sadistic.

The sadomasochistic dimensions of the alcoholic character structure are the product of arrested personality development. The behaviors, affects and cognitive style of the drinking alcoholic are much akin to those of the early adolescent. Poor impulse control, acting out, an inability to delay gratification, egocentricity, immaturity, irresponsibility, and problems with authority are but a few of the characterological features of the alcoholic that are regressive and infantile. It is during the stage of adolescence that the overt behavioral acting out of sadomasochism becomes floridly manifest. Temper tantrums, physical assaults against peers and significant others, and verbal aggression may be evident during the anal, oedipal, and latency eras. However, during adolescence, the alcoholic begins to actualize the physical and psychological behaviors that are fundamental to sadomasochistic patterns of interaction. At this time, the lust dynamism (Sullivan, 1953) becomes actively fused with the more primitive aggressive drives of the organism. The need to sadistically retaliate and punish others derives from being hurt or treated sadistically by significant others. Guilt, remorse and anger at the self serves to help create the masochistic component of the sadomasochistic dynamism. In addition, the experiences of having been unloved, unwanted, and rejected during infancy and childhood reinforce masochism. Unconsciously, the alcoholic masochistically internalizes these narcissistic injuries and behaves according to the self-dictate, "I deserve to be punished." Pathological drinking patterns (Forrest, 1983c) are often initiated during adolescence. The prodromal sadomasochistic trends of the alcoholic are synergized and reinforced by the initiation of the drinking process. The control of sadomasochistic behavior is diminished significantly once the addiction process is activated. Paradoxically, the ingestion of alcohol serves the purpose of neurotically controlling or binding the sadomasochistic trends of some alcoholics. Nonetheless, sadomasochistic behavior and sadomasochistically overdetermined interpersonal transactions are extremely infantile and indicative of regressive adjustment.

The infantile nature of sadomasochism is clearly related to psychosexual development. This is particularly true with regard to the alcoholic character structure. Most alcoholics do progress to the genital stage of psychosexual development. However, the psychosexual adjustment of the alcoholic remains a precarious matter. Alcoholics have an overdetermined oral and anal characterological makeup. These characterological factors are associated with sadomasochistic pathology. Unresolved oedipal conflicts can also reinforce sadomasochistic behaviors. Psychosexually oriented conflicts and identity pathology are primary psychogenic factors in sadomasochism.

Within the context of alcoholism, sadomasochism refers to those behavioral transactions in which the alcoholic overtly or covertly inflicts physical and/or emotional pain and/or injury upon self, significant others, and objects tangential to the self. Moreover, the sadomasochistic trends of the alcoholic encompass (a) the ego fusion of sadism and masochism, (b) behavioral, as well as intrapersonal, regression, and (c) psychosexual arrest and bisexuality.

Sadomasochism is basic to the alcoholic character structure. This premise is based primarily upon the alcoholic's manifest behavioral style, intrapersonal ideation and fantasy life. In the absence of adequately controlled longitudinal studies (Emrick, 1979), clinicians are limited to theory and inference as methods for explaining the behavior of the alcoholic. As indicated earlier, the sadistic and masochistic behaviors of the alcoholic are ego syntonic or fused. It is important to clinically explore (1) from which of these originally bipolar characterological functions the ego fusion emerges and (2) the intrapersonally and interpersonally oriented dimensions of this process of bipolar ego fusion.

The reality of infancy and childhood is such that human beings are totally dependent upon and controlled by parents, parental models, and significant others. Parents or parental introjects can be harsh, rejecting, physically abusive or punitive, and emotionally psychonoxious in their interpersonal transactions with infants and children. There is very little that the infant or child can do to counteract these painful and anxiety-producing sources of stimulation. The cognitive and affective characteristics of the infant preclude a conceptual awareness and understanding of narcissistic injury. However, these hurtful and painful experiences are neurologically and pre-conceptually recorded or programmed into the individual.

The sadomasochistic dimensions of the alcoholic character structure evolve in this general fashion and are initiated during these developmental epochs. As an infant, the alcoholic is first gravely hurt and injured by significant others, particularly the mother object. As the infant is subjected to a multiplicity of narcissistic injuries by parents and significant others, he or she experiences a primitive need to retaliate or strike back. The need to retaliate is primitive and almost reflexive in nature. The retaliatory hate, rage and aggression of the infant is first manifest vis-à-vis "nipple attack" and often becomes associated with excretory functions, temper tantrums, disturbed peer relations, and family pathology. As an infant and child, the alcoholic acts out against his or her parental persecutors. These transactions are more intense and affective than the typical responses of most infants and children to infrequent narcissistic injury, forced limits, and delayed gratification. The parents or parental models of the alcoholic have also experienced considerable narcissistic injury. Thus, sadomasochism and family pathology are basic to the addiction process.

The infantile need to retaliate and act out against significant others is an attempt to ritually, or magically, undo narcissistic injuries of the past. Getting even is another ingredient in this process. These processes are lifelong dilemmas for most alcoholics. Alcoholics attempt to escape the masochistic message of infancy and childhood, "I deserve to be punished." As a repetition compulsion, this process becomes one very significant ingredient in the neurotic, conflict-ridden interpersonal style of the alcoholic. Every alcoholic harbors a great deal of hatred, resentment and rage specific to the narcissistic injuries that he or she has experienced at the hands of parents and significant others during infancy and childhood. Sadistic behavior and ideation is later fused with masochistic pathology. The subdued sadistic attempts of the human infant or child to strike back at significant others, or to defend the self from the emotional or physical abuses and deprivations of parents and parental images, are very often life sustaining and survival oriented.

Characterological sadism is a precursor to the development of the sadomasochistic dynamism. The infant-child-mother-object relationship facilitates the development of characterological sadism. The mother or surrogate mother is the most significant source of narcissistic need and entitlement deprivation. The narcissistic injuries that are experienced by the male alcoholic vis-à-vis the mothering relationship are etiologically associated with the chronic and pervasive conflicts that male alcoholics experience in their subsequent relationships with women. Male alcoholics sadistically punish or abuse women (Forrest, 1978) as a result of their unresolved hatred and rage for the mother object. All women become extensions of the original mother object. These factors are related to the frequency of divorces, extramarital affairs, and wife beating characteristic of the male alcoholic (Ackerman, 1980; Wegscheider, 1981).

The infant and young child act out sadistically against parents or parental models for their narcissistic need and entitlement deprivations. These attempts at sadistic retaliation result in (1) sadistic impotence and (2) the internalization of sadistic rage and reinforcement of masochism. It is ultimately futile for the child or infant to sadistically attack or attempt to retaliate against parents and significant others. In fact, when the child does attempt to display anger and aggression against parental models, he or she very quickly becomes the recipient of further narcissistic injury, frequently including punitive physical abuse. Within this context, the infant or child learns to internalize sadistic behavior and fantasies. The infant and young child also unconsciously believes that he or she masochistically deserves to be punished. The unconscious masochistic process is thus reinforced through reality associated with the child's sadistic acting out. The child continually internalizes anger and rage that was originally directed at parents or parental models. Masochism is concomitantly reinforced and learned vis-à-vis this process. These processes in adjunct with the primitive belief that one deserves to be punished facilitate the ego fusion and ego syntonic nature of sadism and masochism. Thus, the sadomasochistic dynamism is formed.

The alcoholic systematically learns and is conditioned to punish self (behaviorally as well as unconsciously and ideationally) for attempting to act out anger and rage specific to parental narcissistic injuries. Eventually, self-punishment and masochism can be precipitated by the child's fantasy ideation. Even the fantasy of acting out a talion murder is an extremely threatening matter for the infant or young child. The child's primitive conceptual apparatus does not preclude the possibility of the parents' ability to read the child's mind. In the mind's eye of the child, the parents may decide to murder or annihilate the child (consciously, the child may believe that he or she deserves to be murdered for harboring murderous fantasies against the parental objects). These matters constitute catastrophic sources of anxiety for the child. This form of infantile ideation is primitively realistic. The parents have behaviorally validated the reality that they are capable of murdering the infant or child! It is sometimes necessary for the child to inflict physical hurt or pain upon self in response to fantasies involving the murder of their parents or the wish that they might somehow die. This is a process of ritual undoing. This emotional and behavioral rubric serves to teach, reinforce and synergize the sadomasochistic dynamism.

This process has a profound impact upon subsequent personality development and character structure. This form of early life experience creates the psychopathology of latency, the various stages of adolescence and adulthood. Sadomasochism is one by-product of this initial experience in living. Resentment, anger, rage and "getting even" with others stem from the sadomasochistic dimensions of the alcoholic character structure. Guilt, depression, "arranging" to be a chronic failure, anxiety and an utter sense of personal worthlessness are also associated with this dynamism. Being destroyed and destroying significant others are chronic intrapersonal and interpersonal realities for the alcoholic. This process is infantile and sadomasochistic.

The alcoholic manifests an overt sadomasochistic behavioral style. Inflicting physical and psychological pain upon self and significant others is a hallmark of alcoholism. The singular process of ingesting alcohol is sadomasochistic. All drinking that involves physical and/or emotional discomfort and pain to self and/or others is sadomasochistic. For many chronic alcoholics, the ingestion of alcohol precipitates (Forrest, 1978; Wooddell, 1982) gastrointestinal symptomatology, neurologic dysfunction, nutritional disorders, cardiac difficulties and blood-sugar problems. These are only a few of the major medical-biologic complications specific to alcoholism. A red thread in all of these alcohol-facilitated physical disorders is that of self-inflicted tissue destruction. This is the example par excellence of self-destruction. Alcoholism is a masochistic process. Frequently, tissue destruction involves the total human organism. Alcoholism also potentiates and actualizes suicide. Suicide is an ultimate form of masochistic behavior.

The alcoholic becomes increasingly involved in the process of self-destruction vis-à-vis self-induced tissue destruction. Those closest to the addicted individual (Forrest, 1980; Wegscheider, 1981) also experience concomitant emotional and physical pain. Significant others begin to experience psychological hurt and pain prior to the appearance of physical or psychiatric symptoms upon the part of the alcoholic. The processes of inflicting emotional and physical pain upon parents, spouse, children and friends reflect sadistic dimensions of the alcoholic character structure and the addiction process. Divorce, numerous divorces, child neglect and abuse, and the loss of friendships are sadomasochistic transactions. The guilt, anxiety, depression, rage and other negative affective states that accompany such sadomasochistically overdetermined transactions reinforce further sadism and masochism. These factors explain how the sadomasochistic dynamism is reinforced and maintained.

Significant others sadistically retaliate against the alcoholic. They inflict pain on the alcoholic. Sadomasochistic transactions and behaviors are highly reciprocal and mutually reinforcing. These behaviors can be cancerous. As noted earlier, the alcoholic punishes or acts out sadistically against significant others; experiences guilt, depression and anxiety as a result of these sadistic transactions; and then masochistically punishes self. Significant others inconsistently tolerate the sadistic attacks of the alcoholic and then retaliate à la lex talionis. Typically, the sadistic retaliations of significant others against the alcoholic precipitate similar feelings of guilt, anxiety and depression. This process also activates the masochistic needs of significant others. These patterns of interaction are extremely neurotic. Nonetheless, this is a transactional sine qua non of the alcoholic family constellation. Every member in an alcoholic family system (Forrest, 1978; Ackerman, 1978; Wegscheider, 1981) can readily identify with the process of personally hurting, hurting others, and being hurt by others. Such a paradigm of family interaction conditions, reinforces and teaches each family member to behave sadomasochistically. This process, in part, explains why so many daughters of alcoholics marry alcoholics and why the children of alcoholics tend to develop alcoholism. These processes are associated with the psychological and physical pain and hurt that occurs within the alcoholic family system. It must be emphasized that the alcoholic acts out sadistically as a result of being hurt and/or experiencing emotional and physical pain at the hands of significant others. The alcoholic masochistically internalizes experiences involving narcissistic injury and then sadistically retaliates.

Most clinicians involved in the treatment of alcoholics are aware of the sadomasochistic conflicts of these individuals. Yet, relatively few clinicians describe the behaviors of the alcoholic as sadistic, masochistic or sadomasochistic. There are many threatening connotative meanings associated with the words sadism, masochism and sadomasochism. Categorizing behaviors as sadomasochistic can inappropriately mean that the individual so labeled is somehow hopelessly bizarre or sexually perverse. As discussed earlier, very few alcoholics are sexual sadomasochists. Sadomasochistic behaviors and the addiction process *in toto* are the products of learning, conditioning, and social reinforcement. The sadomasochistic behaviors of the alcoholic are the result of a particular constellation of life experiences, as well as direct and incidental learning and reinforcement specific to these experiences. This type of behavior is basic to both the alcoholic character structure and the addiction process.

It is essential for the psychotherapist to deal directly (Forrest, 1979c) with the sadomasochistic conflicts of the alcoholic. This is an integral part of the recovery process. Learning more healthy, effective and rewarding patterns of behavior helps extinguish pathologically sadomasochistic adjustment patterns.

Four brief clinical case studies will be presented to illustrate the alcoholic's sadomasochistic character structure and behavioral style.

Case 1. Peggy J was a divorced, forty-three-year-old registered nurse. When initially interviewed by the author, the patient had a twenty-six-year history of alcoholism and poly-drug abuse and addiction. The patient had just completed a three-month inpatient psychiatrically oriented rehabilitation program specific to her addiction. She was seeking employment as an alcoholism counselor at the agency in which the author was then employed.

The patient had been parented by grandparents and had led a markedly sadomasochistic life-style. At the age of six, she had "fallen" out of a moving car, breaking her leg. Her adolescence was a time of conflict with grandparents and peers alike – she recalled "running away from home, physical and emotional confrontations with classmates, and one school suspension." Following high school graduation, the patient became pregnant. The father of the baby left the community, and the patient had an abortion.

Her addiction history per se was clearly sadomasochistic – numerous medical and psychiatric hospitalizations specific to alcoholism and other chemical dependencies, one divorce and multiple affairs, two children were placed in foster homes, the loss of license to work and practice as a registered nurse, and numerous job failures. Immediately prior to her last hospitalization, the patient had the experience of having been covered with lighter fluid and set on fire (while intoxicated to the point of stuporous) by a transient male whom she had "picked up" while on a drinking spree. She had taken this man to her apartment for sexual purposes. This episode resulted in 20-30 percent second- and third-degree burns to her entire body.

Peggy had, in effect, lived a life-style constructed around being hurt, hurting, and subsequently hurting others. Physical and emotional pain were central to her life-style, to include alcoholism and poly-drug abuse and addiction.

Case 2. Tommy H was a single, nineteen-year-old SP4 in the United States Army. He was first evaluated by the author while an inpatient. The patient was being treated for alcoholism, poly-drug abuse, and depression. The patient manifested chronic adjustment difficulties and marked depression.

A native of western Texas, this young man had experienced a plethora of difficulties prior to his military enlistment at age seventeen. Born out of wedlock, the patient was abandoned to the care of an aunt and uncle. They, in turn, placed the patient in a foster home. This was the beginning of a series of subsequent foster home placements. The longest of these foster home placements encompassed grades nine through eleven, at which time the patient "quit school." He joined the army shortly thereafter. This patient had been arrested and jailed five times prior to his military enlistment. Two of these arrests were a direct result of public intoxication and suspected drug involvement. The patient's history of assaultive acting out began at age five or six. The patient had numerous cigarette burns over his body. He related that he had simply "put my cigarettes out on my arm or stomach." Indeed, the patient's case history was none other than a documentary of being rejected and hurt by people and subsequently attempting to strike back and get even.

Following some four weeks of inpatient care, the patient was released to his unit and placed in an outpatient group psychotherapy program. Within one month following the patient's placement in the outpatient group therapy program, he successfully acted out the ultimate sadomasochistic act. The patient terminated his life via an overdose of alcohol.

Case 3. Earl M was a married forty-one-year-old retired army sergeant. He was seen in psychotherapy by the author for a number of months prior to his retirement. The patient entered treatment as a result of alcohol-facilitated behavior pathology. This individual had led a very sadomasochistic life-style.

The patient had grown up within a functionally intact family system. His father was an alcoholic. The father had been extremely volatile and physically abusive in his marital and family relationships. The patient had experienced a good deal of reinforcement to act out violently. The patient had been removed from elementary school (6th grade) as a direct result of a physical assault against a fellow student. Earl persisted within the school system through grade eleven. He then "dropped out." Police arrests, drinking and getting into trouble were basic to his daily routine prior to enlisting in the military. The patient's military career included a good deal of drinking, fighting and debauching.

The patient was referred for alcoholism treatment as a result of numerous AWOLs, behavior difficulties within his unit, and marital difficulties. The entire family system became involved in the treatment process. In the course of family therapy, it became apparent that Earl was extremely sadomasochistic. The patient physically assaulted his wife and children on a daily basis. The patient had lacerated his eight-year-old son's skull while enraged at his wife (he had thrown the telephone at her, after ripping it from the wall and missed, hitting the son). He had broken his wife's right femur with a single blow of a twelve-gauge shotgun butt. Earl had been shot with a .22-calliber pistol while attempting to accost an alleged "drug pusher" who had given or sold his daughter a few marijuana cigarettes. Moreover, the patient acknowledged having wrecked five cars while being intoxicated. He had been incarcerated for short periods of time on numerous occasions as a result of a variety of alcohol-facilitated acting out behaviors. He had also been psychiatrically hospitalized as a result of threatening to kill a fellow enlisted man who had become sexually involved with his wife. The psychological and physical damage that this patient had inflicted upon his entire family was catastrophic.

Case 4. Howard S was a thirty-two-year-old married patient who was seen by the author in psychotherapy. The patient's wife also initiated treatment for herself, as she felt she could no longer "take it" and wanted a divorce. Howard became involved in treatment as a result of his wife's concerns about his drinking and violent behaviors.

Howard was a construction worker. He had grown up in eastern Kansas and then moved to Colorado three years after high school graduation. He reported having never really gotten along well with his parents. While in school, the patient frequently experienced physical confrontations with classmates. On one occasion, he had been suspended from class attendance for a period of three days following one of these altercations. As an adolescent, Howard recalled having enjoyed shooting cats and "torturing" other animals.

After moving West and finding a construction job, Howard began dating his wife. She had grown up in an alcoholic family (her father was an alcoholic). The patient had been physically and emotionally abusive toward his wife during courtship. During one of her initial therapy sessions, Mrs. S stated that prior to marriage she felt as if Howard "controlled" her. Mrs. S was also physically afraid of Howard, but she felt that things would get better, or "work out," once they were married. Shortly after marriage, it became apparent to Mrs. S that things were not going to get better. Howard began to drink more. He became more abusive and their relationship began to steadily deteriorate.

After nearly two years of marriage, Mrs. S initiated treatment. The final precipitating event that led to her seeking treatment was an extended "drunk" on the part of Howard. This binge terminated in a rather bizarre sexual episode. Howard severely beat Mrs. S and then forced her to submit to anal intercourse while hanging out of their second floor bedroom window. During a course of extended psychotherapy, it was found that Howard manifested primary sexual psychopathology and alcoholism. The patient's sexual pathology was also highly sadomasochistic.

Chronic alcoholism is central to each of these case studies. Clearly, these case studies also demonstrate borderline psychopathology, depression and sexual aberration. Each of these patients had experienced marked long-term sadomasochistic interpersonal and intrapersonal conflicts.

PSYCHOTHERAPEUTIC CONSIDERATIONS

The psychotherapist must help the alcoholic resolve and extinguish his or her sadomasochistic behaviors. Indeed, recovery from alcoholism may be impossible if the alcoholic is unable to modify the sadomasochistic conflicts that facilitate and maintain the addiction process.

By focusing upon the pain-pleasure dimensions of the drinking process, the therapist enables the alcoholic to consciously understand self-inflicted pain and punishment. The therapist actively and consistently points out how the alcoholic makes self psychologically and physically sick vis-à-vis drinking. Termination of drinking is a primary goal in the psychotherapy of alcoholism. The alcoholic stops punishing self when the addiction process is terminated.

The therapist needs to explore the historic dynamics associated with the alcoholic's self-destructive behaviors and lifestyle. It is important to point out to the patient that he or she does not "deserve" to be punished. Alcohol-facilitated hangovers, physical illness associated with intoxication, arrests, marital and family discord, depression and other psychological problems and vocational difficulties are therapeutically viewed as forms of self-punishment.

A consistent therapeutic exploration (Schad-Somers, 1982) of the alcoholic's feelings of hurt, anger and rage often leads to a resolution of the patient's need to sadistically punish significant others. The psychotherapist needs to explore patterns of family and marital interaction and point out to the patient the sadomasochism inherent in these relationships. This treatment technique is often fostered by an extended therapeutic focus upon the various dynamics associated with the patient's family of origin.

It is very important for the therapist to avoid becoming involved in therapeutic roles and interactions with the patient that are sadomasochistically flavored. Counter-transference distortions (Forrest, 1982a) do not contribute to the effective and successful psychotherapy of alcoholism. It is psychonoxious for the therapist to become angry and enraged at the patient when he or she drinks or experiences a slip while in treatment.

Many alcoholics find it difficult to cope with consistent success and prosperity. Alcoholics are self-defeatists. The therapist must point out, interpret and confront these sadomasochistic patterns of behavior. Effective psychotherapy helps the alcoholic modify and overcome the various destructive aspects of his or her sadomasochistic character structure and life-style.

SUMMARY

The sadomasochistic dimensions of the alcoholic character structure were discussed in this chapter. Sadistic and masochistic characterological features appear to be bipolar. However, sadism and masochism are always ego syntonic and fused. The sadomasochistic dynamism represents an ego fusion of sadism and masochism. Alcoholic individuals manifest a pathological sadomasochistic character structure. As an infant and child, the alcoholic attempts to act out sadistically against parents (especially the mother object) and significant others in retaliation for the narcissistic need and entitlement deprivations they have inflicted upon the individual. Pervasive early life narcissistic injury programs the alcoholic to feel worthless, inadequate and inferior. Later in life, this experiential process becomes the masochistic equivalent of the verbal message "I deserve to be punished." When the young child attempts to act out or retaliate against parents and significant others, he or she learns that retaliations do not work. Furthermore, the child discovers that these futile attempts at sadistic retaliation may result in a physical or psychological annihilation of self. At this point, a process of masochistic internalization is effected. Anger, rage and diffuse hostility are internalized and channeled back into the self-system. This process explains the ego-syntonic nature of sadistic and masochistic characterological components.

Sadomasochistic struggles are a lifelong dilemma for the alcoholic. Acting out, "getting even" and retaliating followed by guilt, depression, and self-hatred is the alcoholic sadomasochistic dilemma. The attempts of the alcoholic to sadistically get even with significant others usually fail. The sadistic retaliations of the alcoholic are impotent measures geared to convince self and others that the self is powerful and significant. These attempted sadistic reprisals frequently become very masochistic experiences and transactions. Those closest to the alcoholic (Forrest, 1980) become entrapped in an interpersonal milieu that is psychonoxious and congruously sadomasochistic. Every member of the alcoholic family system continuously experiences pain or hurt, hurts or inflicts pain upon other family members, and is then hurt in retaliation by family members. This process always ends masochistically for the alcoholic. The pleasure and sadistic triumphs of today become the pain and masochism of tomorrow.

The sadomasochistic dimensions of the alcoholic adjustment style do not usually include the bizarre, deviant, sexual pathology historically associated with sadism, masochism and sadomasochism. In this chapter, the process of chronically and pathologically inflicting emotional and physical pain upon self and significant others is defined as "sadomasochism." The sadomasochistic behaviors of the alcoholic are caused by faulty learning, conditioning and reinforcement experiences. Sadomasochism is an essential component of the alcoholic adjustment style. Sadomasochism is a clinically significant factor in the development and maintenance of the addiction process.

The sadomasochistic trends of the alcoholic are extremely infantile in origin and nature. A pathological fusion with the lust dynamism also occurs in every case of sadomasochism. The sadomasochistic conflicts of the alcoholic are obsessive-compulsive. They originate during the initial developmental eras of life and persist throughout life in the absence of psychotherapeutic treatment and recovery. Even with successful psychotherapeutic intervention, the alcoholic character structure remains refractory to radical modification (Forrest, 1979b). However, the sadomasochistic trends of the alcoholic can be significantly modified by psychotherapeutic intervention.

Hopefully, the brief clinical case studies presented in this chapter will help the reader better understand the sadomasochistic dimensions of the alcoholic character structure and adjustment style. Sadomasochism is universally basic to the alcoholic character structure. Alcoholics who are involved in effective psychotherapy begin to evidence significant behavioral change and characterological growth. These recovering persons are no longer the endless victims of their own sadomasochistic and self-defeating behaviors.

Chapter Ten

ALCOHOLISM AND ACTING OUT

INTRODUCTION

THE alcoholic tends to be viewed by the clinician as a character behavior disorder. Hill, Haertzen and Davis (1962) suggest that social deviance is the only personality characteristic associated specifically with alcoholism, narcotic addiction or criminality. Research evidence consistently indicates that alcoholics and addicts are sociopathic (Sutker, 1971; Hoffman, Jackson and Skinner, 1975; Emrick, 1979). The clinical and research data dealing with alcohol addiction and sociopathy (Matuschka, 1978) tends to be limited to behavioral descriptions of the alcoholic. The behavioral style of the alcoholic (Forrest, 1980 & 1983) is similar to the sociopath and character behavior disorder. The differential diagnosis of alcoholism (Forrest, 1978; Knauert, 1982) can be difficult and confusing.

Gilberstadt and Duker (1965) delineate four primary clinical MMPI profiles that are indicative of heavy drinking. Their approach to the clinical diagnosis of alcoholism is based upon behavioral descriptions that fit each of these four particular profiles. A behavioral description of the alcoholic, based upon the psychological (MMPI) assessment studies of Gilberstadt and Duker (1965), includes the following symptoms: "heavy drinking, chronic alcoholism which may lead to delirium tremens, anxious, inferiority feelings, guilt, dependent upon wives and others, under-achieved in academic performance, in vocational performance they were usually described as good workers on a particular job, but because of alcoholism, job histories reflected much instability, highly immature, depressed, egocentric, father alcoholic, alcoholism most frequent single symptom, acting out, a history of broken families or poor family conditions were noted in about half of the cases, severe marital conflict, and psychopathic occupations."

This descriptive model of the alcoholic includes a rather specific characterization of drinking behavior, vocational adjustment, affective style, and even academic performance. Gilberstadt and Duker (1965) state "the 4-9 patient is described as having been a child of athletic build who was generally precocious in early development." It should be noted that Gilberstadt and Duker do not include the diagnosis of chronic alcoholism as one of their 19 primary diagnostic categories.

Historically, the behavioral science professions have viewed chronic alcoholism as a symptom (Forrest, 1978) that is indicative of more severe underlying psychopathology. Chronic alcohol addiction (Forrest, 1978) can also be viewed as a relatively unitary psychopathological disorder. The alcoholic may have experienced various emotional difficulties prior to initiating the addiction process. However, the alcoholic eventually solidifies a primary adjustment choice (alcoholism) that is addiction based. According to this model, marital discord, vocational difficulties, depression, guilt and other indicators of maladjustment are the symptoms of alcohol addiction. The addiction per se is the most important psychopathological process to be dealt with in the treatment of alcoholics. Successful therapeutic resolution of the patient's alcoholism (Knauert, 1982) results in the remission of such secondary symptoms as depression, marital failure, anxiety and acting out.

Frequently, clinicians have diagnosed or labeled the alcoholic a "psychopath." The terms psychopath, sociopath, character behavior disorder, and passive-aggressive personality described similar behaviors and adjustment styles. The alcoholic has often been included within these diagnostic subgroups. Pre-alcoholic and alcoholic adjustment styles do appear to be generally sociopathic. However, the acting out symptoms of the alcoholic are resolved or go into significant remission in at least 70 percent of cases that are successfully treated in psychotherapy (Forrest, 1983). In a corollary fashion, alcoholics who reject treatment frequently become progressively more symptomatic. The drinking alcoholic experiences a global deterioration. The deterioration process includes a predominance of psychopathic or acting out behaviors. Alcoholics manifest pathological anxiety, depression, and guilt. They also become more asocial as the addiction process unfolds. The addiction process always results in a loss of control over behavior and intrapersonal ideation. These realities reinforce the development of multifaceted socially deviant roles. Deviant social-role engagement often results in the alcoholic's seeking treatment or being forced into a rehabilitation program.

The matter of clinically evaluating the alcoholic as a character behavior disorder, sociopath, or passive-aggressive personality is a problem of differential diagnosis (Knauert, 1982). The clinical associations between alcohol addiction, sociopathy and the impulse disorders stem from the acting out dimensions of the alcoholic. These issues can be clinically confusing. Acting out is a salient behavioral dimension of alcoholism and the impulse disorders. However, the acting out symptomatology of the alcoholic differs significantly from that of the individual manifesting a bonafide sociopathic or impulse disorder adjustment.

A number of the clinical aspects of the acting out symptomatology of the alcoholic are discussed in this chapter. The origins of the acting out dimensions of the alcoholic character structure are also considered. The alcoholic adjustment style is alloplastic. However, few alcoholics are sociopaths. Alcoholics have tended to be evaluated by clinicians as manifesting a character behavior disorder or impulse disorder. This has occurred as a result of the common denominator of acting out symptomatology associated with alcoholism and the impulse disorders. Strategies of psychotherapeutic intervention and even proper legal management of the alcoholic are closely related to an accurate differential diagnosis.

ALCOHOLISM, ACTING OUT AND THE IMPULSE DISORDERS

The pathological acting out behaviors of the alcoholic do not originate during the developmental eras of adolescence or adulthood. Many alcoholics have been hyperactive or highly anxious during early childhood. Alcoholics consistently describe themselves as having always been "nervous," "uptight," or hyperactive. Furthermore, parents and significant others consistently report that the alcoholic was motorically hyperactive during childhood and infancy. Hyperactivity is a characteristic of many individuals who eventually become addicted to alcohol. Hyperactivity, anxiety and nervousness describe similar behaviors. Chronic uneasyness, restlessness, exaggerated motor activity, distractability, poor "stick-to-itive-ness," and always being "on the go" are behavioral characteristics (Forrest, 1978 & 1980) of the alcoholic.

The endogenously depressed (Della-Giustina and Forrest, 1979) alcoholic is anxious and behaviorally hyperactive. Alcoholics who remain chronically intoxicated in order to manage depression often manifest an underlying agitation. It is difficult to explain why the alcoholic is chronically anxious or hyperactive. Constitutional and genetic factors may operate to determine this particular aspect of the alcoholic adjustment style. Blood-sugar problems or metabolic dysfunction can be variables that determine the hyperactivity of some alcoholics. Minimal brain dysfunction and various neurological factors (Castor, 1982) may be related to the chronic hyperactivity of some alcoholics.

The diffuse acting out behavioral style of the alcoholic is precipitated by intense and chronic anxiety. More specifically, acting out is behaviorally associated with (Ellis, 1979) a generalized low frustration tolerance, poor impulse control, action rather than cognition, iconoclastic attitudes, and socially inappropriate or abrasive patterns of interpersonal relating. Thus, the alcoholic responds to minimal or moderate stress inappropriately. The problem-solving style of the alcoholic is generally one of acting *without* adequate rational assessment of alternative solutions or courses of action. The alcoholic tells others to "go to hell" rather than internally and intrapersonally dealing with these sentiments and feelings. The alcoholic may engage in grossly inappropriate acting out transactions, such as assaulting the spouse or children, drinking on the job, and driving under the influence.

The rather broad parameters of the alcoholic's pathological style of acting out are determined during the epochs of infancy and childhood. Pervasive early life narcissistic need and entitlement deprivation results in diffuse acting out symptomatology. The acting out behaviors of many alcoholics are overtly manifest during early childhood.

The overdetermined acting out behaviors of the alcoholic are life sustaining and survival oriented. The alcoholic acts out in order to physically and psychologically survive early life narcissistic injuries. The mother or surrogate mother and significant others comprising the interpersonal world of the alcoholic reinforce acting out and poor impulse control. Eliciting attention pertaining to the needs to be held, cuddled, fed, loved and even having one's diapers changed can be difficult for the infant. The mother object and significant others of the alcoholic have been insensitive to these very powerful needs. In response to the stress and anxiety created by factors such as these, the alcoholic must scream and evoke a near total organismic response in order to elicit life-sustaining behaviors from the mother object and significant others. The prototaxic intrapersonal and interpersonal experiences of the alcoholic are consistently anxiety ridden (Forrest, 1978).

The various members of the alcoholic family system (Ackerman, 1978; Wegscheider, 1981) are pathologically encapsulated in their own neurotic conflicts and struggles. It is very difficult for them to respond appropriately to the needs of their children. In general: (1) overdetermined acting out behaviors are basic to the experience of infancy and childhood in the case of the alcoholic; (2) in many respects, this particular adjustment style is adaptive in nature; and (3) the acting out behavioral style of the alcoholic persists throughout subsequent developmental stages. It is possible that chronic organismic overstimulation in early life may precipitate central nervous system, neurological, or other body-system changes that facilitate the acting out behavioral style on a lifelong basis. Interpersonal learning plays a major role in the persistence of acting out symptomatology.

The psychopathic or sociopathic personality is the product of extreme and prolonged early life psychological and physical abuse (McCord and McCord, 1964). The sociopath has experienced narcissistic injury and physical abuse, beatings, neglect and severe punishment during infancy and childhood. These experiences are interpersonally more physical and violent than those experienced by the alcoholic. The early life interpersonal experiences of the sociopath are consistently violent. This same form of emotional climate persists within the family constellation or surrogate family constellation of the sociopath during latency and the various stages of adolescence. The sociopath is a product of a family system that consistently reinforces the belief that "others are to blame." Correspondingly, the sociopath feels that he or she has been victimized and thus has the right to retaliate or "get even." A sociopathic parental model and possible neurological impairment (hypothalamus) may also be significant factors in the causation of psychopathic or sociopathic adjustment styles (McCord and McCord, 1964; Knauert, 1982).

Acting out is a methodology employed by the alcoholic to bind or control anxiety. Early life hyperactivity or borderline hyperactivity is a reality with which many alcoholics have been forced to live. During adolescence, many alcoholics become aware of their internal feelings of anxiety and agitation. The epoch of adolescence is also characterized by a more integrated awareness of oneself and problems with impulse control and acting out. Adolescence is a developmental era that is characterized by an increase in acting out conflicts and struggles for people in general. These acting out conflicts are often accompanied by psychological growth, an increased ability to differentiate between self and others, the development of a value system, and numerous other psychological essentials prerequisite to effective human living. Most people proceed through this era without experiencing serious acting out problems. Such is not the case for many alcoholics. Adolescence exaggerates the alcoholic's conflicts that are associated with impulse control.

Adolescence is a developmental era that involves many new stresses as well as an exacerbation of chronically unresolved historic conflicts. Many alcoholics begin to drink pathologically during the teen years (Forrest, 1983). Frequently, clinicians encounter a great deal of difficulty in their attempts to ferret out the role of pathological drinking or alcoholism in maladaptive adolescent adjustments. These issues are even more perplexing and confusing for parents, peers, and school authorities (Sena, 1979). The interpersonal and intrapersonal conflicts of the alcoholic adolescent can be overwhelming or catastrophic. Rather than merely rebelling at parental dictates and other authority figures, the adolescent alcoholic learns that he or she can be overtly angry, resentful, and violent in relationships with parents and others. Moreover, the alcoholic finds out that he or she can act out these strong affects in a number of rather rewarding ways. The alcoholic eventually discovers that his or her acting out behaviors are unproductive and ineffective. Confrontations with parents, police, peers and school personnel over matters pertaining to overdetermined acting out synergize the anxieties of the alcoholic.

In short, most alcoholics make very little progress in the resolution of their adolescent conflicts. The emergence of active sexuality, changes in family psychodynamics and peer relations, the impending reality of vocational choice, future educational questions, and the matters of courtship and marriage present new obstacles of major threat for the alcoholic as he or she enters adolescence. These new demands upon the adolescent precipitate further anxiety experiences.

It is during late adolescence and early adulthood (Forrest, 1978) that many alcoholics begin to detach themselves from significant others. This process of social withdrawal and isolation is closely associated with the development of alcohol addiction. Eventually, the alcoholic severs virtually all of his or her interpersonal attachments. Alcoholics do remain superficially attached to drinking cohorts and "friends" who are also heavy drinkers or alcoholic. The marital relationship also suffers and deteriorates in numerous respects as the addiction process unfolds. Frequently, separation and divorce (Paolino and McCrady, 1977; Wegscheider, 1981) is the result of the grossly inappropriate and intolerable behaviors of the addicted spouse. Marital difficulties accompany the alcoholic marriage from its inception. Verbal confrontations, constant arguing and bickering, and perhaps "controlled" physical violence frequently become marital realities during the initial weeks and months of marriage. The process of moving away from significant others and encountering progressive interpersonal difficulties occurs when many alcoholics are between the ages of fifteen and twenty. Alcoholics often state that they have always been outsiders or loners and that they have always had people problems. Marriage can represent a neurotic solution for these dilemmas.

As the alcoholic continues to act out during late adolescence and adulthood, he or she accordingly moves into a plethora of socially deviant roles within the family constellation and the larger social community. The processes of progressive interpersonal detachment and concomitant social deviant role entrapment results in the alcoholic's becoming more anxious. The alcoholic could extinguish anxiety feelings by simply terminating socially deviant role behaviors. However, the drinking and intoxicated alcoholic is incapable of terminating deviant familial and community role behaviors. In addition to the anxiety created by the processes of moving away from significant others and assuming a social role of deviant, the alcoholic experiences a good deal of anger, rage and resentment over these matters. This particular combination of processes and the affective responses that accompany them synergize the alcoholic's acting out pathology. Anger, rage and resentment are always apparent in the acting out demeanor of the alcoholic. However, the aggressive or violent acting out behaviors of the alcoholic are usually secondary to the experience of anxiety.

Alcoholics are most prone to pathological acting out when they are acutely anxious. The alcoholic acts out as a result of acute or chronic anxiety that can be associated with various sources. Many alcoholics are relatively unaware of feeling anxious, and some are not even aware of what particular events or situations cause them to become anxious. Many alcoholics consistently deny the experience of acute or chronic anxiety. The alcoholic learns to live neurotically with his or her anxiety. Alcoholics fail to learn how to extinguish feelings of anxiety or change behavioral patterns that precipitate anxiety. However, the alcoholic responds to the experience of acute and potentially ego-disorganizing anxiety by acting out. The acting out pathology of the alcoholic can be viewed as a regressive defense maneuver in the service of the ego. Acting out is a primitive and yet functional defense mechanism employed in the service of the ego to control or bind anxiety. Indeed, the alcoholic responds to acute anxiety in a reflexive manner. Acting out in response to interpersonal and internal anxiety constitutes the *modus vivendi* of the alcoholic (Forrest, 1982a). Acting out and impulsive behaviors are also generally quite repetitive.

The acting out behaviors of the alcoholic that eventually prove most destructive of the alcoholic involve intoxication, sexuality and aggression. Alcoholics experience various difficulties as a result of alcohol-facilitated sexual and aggressive acting out. Acting out encompasses drinking behavior and alcoholism per se. In the therapeutic management of the alcoholic patient (Forrest, 1979a, 1979c, & 1982a), it is imperative that the therapist first focus upon the patient's alcohol-facilitated acting out behaviors. Alcoholism and intoxication potentiate acting out behaviors. Alcoholism is acting out. Unfortunately, psychotherapists and other behavioral scientists (Bratter, 1982) often fail to appreciate the clinical significance of acting out and impulse deficit associated with alcoholism and acute intoxication.

Acute anxiety can result in the psychological incapacitation of the alcoholic. Remaining chronically or periodically intoxicated offers the alcoholic a viable and pragmatic means for coping with the experience of being acutely anxious. Acting out sexually or aggressively also reduces and blocks the alcoholic's awareness of being catastrophically anxious.

The alcoholic manifests a morbid fear of going crazy or becoming insane. Even more prototaxically, the alcoholic experiences profound anxiety over the matter of death (Scott, 1979). It is during adolescence and adulthood that the alcoholic becomes overwhelmingly aware of the personal experiences of anxiety and intrapersonal trepidation and correspondingly fears going crazy and dying.

Being markedly anxious, becoming aware of this unpleasant and threatening experience and in a resultant fashion becoming even more anxious and agitated amounts to a neurotic entrapment from within. In order to control struggles from within, the alcoholic acts out in any number of pathologically overdetermined ways. The acting out behaviors of the alcoholic always involve motor activity. Acting out enables the alcoholic to better control fantasy ideation, self-dialogue, and other intrapersonal processes that mean to the individual that he or she is extremely anxious and possibly going crazy. A crucial source of gain afforded the alcoholic vis-à-vis acting out symptomatology is that of focusing or directing behavior and intrapersonal awareness at targets external to the self. The alcoholic derives neurotic gain from various facets of the addiction process.

The alcoholic's fear of insanity is closely associated with a morbid fear of death and dying. Death is the ultimate uncontrollable transaction. Alcoholics (Scott, 1979) experience considerable difficulty accepting their own mortality. They are extremely anxious about the matter of dying. Alcoholics are also obsessed with being in control of self. Alcoholics are obsessed about controlling self, significant others and the phenomenal world. Yet, the drinking alcoholic is a person without inner control. Many alcoholics become totally out of control. It is paradoxically logical that the alcoholic is so chronically ridden with anxiety and fears pertaining to the issues of madness and death!

Initially in this chapter it was emphasized that alcoholics differ significantly from individuals manifesting primary sociopathic and impulse disorder pathology. In addition, these differences are consistent and multiple. The point has been made that alcoholic patients act out in a pathologically overdetermined fashion as a defense against the experience of anxiety. A hallmark of the sociopath or psychopath is the lack of capacity for internally experiencing anxiety (McCord and McCord, 1964; Cleckley, 1964; Matuschka, 1978). The psychopath is a rather affectless individual who is essentially refractory to the experience of being chronically anxious. This situation is the antithesis of the chronically anxious alcoholic. The psychopathic, sociopathic, character behavior disorder and impulse disorder diagnostic categories include individuals who lack the capacity to be anxious. The issue of whether or not the sociopathic individual experiences internal anxiety can be recondite. The quantitative assessment of anxiety can be difficult. Sociopathic individuals do experience some degree of internal anxiety, but significantly less so than the chronic alcoholic. Sociopaths and people with impulse disorders are not chronically anxious and agitated. The sociopath cathects or externalizes anxiety more effectively and pathologically than the alcoholic. The alcoholic is anxious from within. The sociopath does not consistently internalize the experience of anxiety. The anxiety that is experienced by the sociopath is minimal, transient and does not precipitate gross personality disorganization. In addition, the sociopath is not trapped from within. Sociopaths and impulse disorders are not *chronically* the victims of their internal experience of being anxious and affectively disturbed (i.e. depressed or guilty).

The behavioral transactions that the alcoholic engages in to externally victimize himself or herself are also alcohol-facilitated. Typically, the alcoholic is not asocial. The sociopath is asocial and without values. Violent asocial behaviors may be actualized by the alcoholic when he or she is acutely intoxicated. The alcoholic's angry, asocial acting out episodes are followed by feelings of depression, remorse and guilt. After attaining sobriety, the alcoholic frequently experiences pervasive guilt and depression as a result of the behaviors he or she has engaged in while intoxicated. Alcoholics often employ these uncomfortable and threatening feelings as an excuse for further drinking. Violence, rage and aggression are often expressed by the alcoholic via automobile accidents, self-destruction, and psychophysiological symptomatology. The alcoholic acts out against himself or herself. Sociopaths and impulse disorders channel violence and acting out directly against all others. The alcoholic tends to direct violence at the self and limited significant others. The alcoholic often attacks, destroys and acts out against family members (Forrest, 1980). Alcoholics experience depression and intense guilt feelings as a result of familial conflict. The sociopath lacks the ability to internalize conflict and respond appropriately in an affective sense. Sociopaths and impulse disorders lack the capacity to experience genuine affect. They also lack the capacity for experiencing significant and meaningful interpersonal attachments. The alcoholic is a very poor manager of his or her affective life. Nonetheless, the alcoholic is an affective person. The affective dimensions of the alcoholic form the basis for effective psychotherapeutic intervention (Forrest, 1979a & 1983).

Sociopaths and alcoholics are manipulators par excellence. However, these types of people manifest different manipulative styles. Sociopaths are far more narcissistic and vicious in their manipulative transactions than the alcoholic. They encounter marked difficulty functioning on any interpersonal level, even among fellow "cons" and with other sociopathic persons. The psychopath trusts no one. Survival is a matter of ruthlessly manipulating and using others. The sociopath (Cleckley, 1964) experiences no empathy or affective attachment for those who fall victim to his or her vicious and mercenary manipulations. The sociopath also experiences no guilt, depression or remorse over his or her damaging use and abuse of others.

Alcoholics are also skilled manipulators (Shostrom, 1967; Forrest, 1982a). However, alcoholics tend to be quite capable of establishing significant object attachments with those whom they manipulate. The manipulations of the alcoholic are far less ruthless and vicious than those of the sociopath or impulse disorder. The alcoholic usually has some degree of concern and affective involvement with the target of his or her manipulations. For example, the alcoholic is usually a master in the art of manipulating the non-addicted spouse. In spite of the alcoholic's irresponsibility associated with paying bills, work, marital fidelity and legal matters, the non-addicted spouse persists in the role of familial manager. Manipulation (Forrest, 1980a) is also basic to the drinking *modus vivendi* of the alcoholic. It can be astonishing to find out just how much the alcoholic can procure to drink in the complete absense of having any money or credit! This feat is often accomplished through the financial assistance of drinking cohorts and alcoholic colleagues. The majority of alcoholics are not withdrawn, isolated, seclusive drinkers. Bartenders and liquor store owners also tend to be manipulated into a free drink or a free bottle from time to time by the alcoholic. Alcoholics are very adept at maintaining the manipulative ability to continue supporting their addiction.

The alcoholic develops an interpersonal support system. Many alcoholics drink with the same people over an extended period of time. These relationships are alcoholically determined and maintained. However, these relationships are very different from those established by the sociopath or impulse disorder. The sociopath (Cleckley, 1964; Matuschka, 1978) is not capable of maintaining meaningful and in-depth relationships over an extended period of time. Indeed, the sociopath is an individual who may make reasonably good first impressions. These individuals appear to be pleasingly sociable and glib on a short-term basis, but invariably they are "moving on" interpersonally and geographically. In contrast, the alcoholic is capable of maintaining a functional interpersonal network for years or perhaps a lifetime.

The manipulative style of the alcoholic changes rather drastically following the achievement of sobriety. However, even with extended periods of sobriety, most recovering or recovered alcoholics continue to be somewhat manipulative.

The manipulative style of the sociopath is a movement against others. The manipulative style of the recovering alcoholic vacillates between an attempted (often neurotic) movement toward others and a movement with others. Drinking alcoholics are more like the sociopath and impulse disorder in manipulative style.

The acting out pathology of the alcoholic is most apparent during the later stages (Forrest, 1978) of the addiction process. This is particularly true with regard to the acting out of bizarre, socially deviant behaviors. Bizarre, grossly inappropriate acting out behaviors often result in the alcoholic being forced into treatment. Most, if not all, alcoholics become socially deviant during the later phases of their addiction careers. With the advent of physiological addiction and the later stages of the addiction process, the alcoholic begins to act out in a grossly socially inappropriate and uncontrollable fashion. At this time, the alcoholic behaviorally acts out what were earlier fantasies having to do with seducing a neighbor, telling the boss to "kiss my ass," "knocking some damn sense into my wife's head," and perhaps even incest (Martin, 1980; Forrest, 1982b). The social deviance and acting out of the alcoholic progressively encompasses such behaviors as public intoxication, job absenteeism, driving while intoxicated, and inappropriate verbal and physical confrontations.

Unfortunately, many alcoholics are never identified as social deviants. These alcoholics are unfortunate in that they are never identified as being alcoholic and subsequently "pushed" into treatment or rehabilitation. Collectively, people view the skid-row alcoholic as a bona fide social deviant. In general, people are less tolerant of the alcoholism and acting out behaviors of the lower-class alcoholic than they are of the middle- or upper-class alcoholic. Collectively, people share the tacit assumption that one must act out in an alcohol-facilitated "crazy" fashion in order to really be an alcoholic. Within industry, families and communities, alcoholics are permitted to drink alcoholically as long as they do not act out in ways that are deemed to be deviant, socially inappropriate, or bizarre. Alcoholic housewives have long been "permitted" to drink alcoholically as long as they remained within the confines of their homes! Alcoholic women who remain at home, drink at home, and refrain from grossly deviant acting out within the community at large tend to rarely be labeled "alcoholic." Priests, high-ranking military officers, and members of the more prestigious professions (medicine, law and dentistry) likewise tend to be hidden and permitted to be alcoholic by their families, significant others, and the community. It is ego alien and threatening for most people to accept the fact that housewives, priests and other members of the clergy, high-ranking government officials, and family physicians are addicted to alcohol. Some alcoholics are not prone to deviant acting out during the course of their addiction. It is simply easier for significant others to covertly reinforce, rationalize and thus permit these individuals to remain alcoholic.

Acting out and subsequently being identified as an alcoholic and social deviant can result in treatment engagement. Acting in, or being alcoholic and not prone to acting out, can result in various unfortunate consequences. Alcoholics that act in are often not pushed in the direction of seeking some form of help or rehabilitation.

The following clinical case study illustrates the process of social reluctance to identify select individuals as being alcoholic in the absense of gross acting out psychopathology. This alcoholic patient manifested a long-term history of covert acting out.

Mrs. S was a thirty-one-year-old attractive mother of two children. She was involved in a divorce proceeding which focused upon the matter of child custody. Her husband was a thirty-seven-year-old airline pilot employed by a major airline company. He had legally contested the mother's assuming child custody upon the ground that she was either presently alcoholic or incipiently alcoholic. The husband was a non-drinker. During the course of the child-custody hearing, it was disclosed that Mrs. S was the daughter of an air force general. During adolescence she had experienced rather marked and chronic difficulties in the realm of family interaction and family living. It was apparent that Mrs. S got along quite poorly with both parents. Matters pertaining to staying out late, choice of male companions and peer relationships, and attitudinal and value system differences were basic to many of the conflicts between Mrs. S and her parents.

Following the completion of one year of college, Mrs. S became pregnant and subsequently gave birth to an illegitimate child. The child was given up shortly after birth and placed in a foster home. Approximately two years later, Mrs. S became an airline stewardess employed by the same airline as her husband. Shortly after gaining employment with the airline company, Mrs. S began dating her husband who was frequently assigned to the same flight crew with her. A good deal of their courtship centered around parties, social events, and other activities that included heavy drinking. Both Mr. and Mrs. S were socially active and moderate to heavy drinkers at this time. After some four months of dating, Mrs. S again became pregnant. Both parties decided upon an abortion for Mrs. S rather than marriage or another illegitimate birth. Within the following eight months, the couple married. Approximately two years later a daughter was born, to be followed by a son two-and-one-half years after the birth of the daughter.

The initial four years of marriage involved a good deal of socializing with friends and other couples. Typically, the social activities and events Mr. and Mrs. S participated in revolved around drinking or at least consistently involved significant drinking. Both Mr. and Mrs. S described their first four years of marriage as essentially "happy." Mr. S became increasingly concerned about the drinking behavior of both himself and his wife and the impact of this behavior upon their children. As a result of these concerns, Mr. S completely terminated his drinking behavior. Moreover, Mr. S initiated an active church and religious life immediately following his decision to quit drinking. It soon became evident that the marital relationship changed and, in many respects, suffered as a direct consequence of Mr. S's decision to quit drinking and his religious involvement. It was the sentiment of Mrs. S that somehow Mr. and Mrs. S, as a couple, no longer "fit in" among the other couples with whom they had socialized. Mrs. S also noted that she "resented" this social change as well as her husband's abstinence and religious interests. By the fifth year of marriage, both Mr. and Mrs. S began to be mutually aware of the deteriorating nature of their marital relationship. Furthermore, Mrs. S indicated that she continued to drink even more following her husband's termination of drinking. It was pointed out by Mr. S that his own mother was an alcoholic and that he began to fear that perhaps his wife was becoming an alcoholic.

For the duration of the final two-and-one-half years of their marital relationship, Mrs. S stated that she consumed approximately one quart of wine every night. In addition, she infrequently drank a "light CC and water or two" per evening following her nightly wine consumption. Her daily drinking pattern never began prior to five o'clock in the afternoon and ended with the television late show. She was also quick to point out that she had only been sick or "passed out" as a result of intoxication on four or five occasions during the final two-and-one-half years of the marriage. No extramarital affairs had been initiated by either spouse. Mrs. S had no history of job loss or legal difficulty as a result of her drinking behavior. She was perceived as a "good mother" according to the testimony of friends, neighbors and the teacher of their daughter. The social case worker who was involved in the evaluation of parental fitness for child custody in this case reported that she did feel Mrs. S had a "problem" with drinking, but that this problem in no way was detrimental to the children.

In the course of the legal hearing, it was brought out that Mrs. S had consulted a psychologist a few weeks earlier with regard to her "problem" with drinking. Based upon two 1-hour clinical interviews and psychological testing, Mrs. S's psychologist testified that she was not an alcoholic and that she did not have a significant drinking problem. Psychological assessment, according to the psychologist's expert testimony, indicated that Mrs. S "felt good about herself," – "was confident," "and generally well-adjusted" – "certainly not the type of person who in my experience is or becomes addicted to alcohol." However, it was the stated recommendation of her psychologist that she continue in psychotherapy in order to assure that she did not develop an alcoholism problem in the future.

My own expert testimony as a psychologist for the defendant in this case, Mr. S, very directly suggested that the pattern of consumption that Mrs. S had maintained for two-and-one-half years was indicative of a very significant drinking problem, if not alcoholism. Additionally, I pointed out the more covert acting out pathology of Mrs. S that is central to the alcoholic adjustment style. Following my testimony, I was cross-examined at length about the near total lack of alcoholic or alcohol-related acting out upon the part of Mrs. S. Her lawyer emphasized over and again to the court that Mrs. S did not frequent bars, nightclubs and lounges, that her "social drinking" in no way interfered with parenting abilities, and that in no way was it possible for the defense to show the court that Mrs. S was an alcoholic or problem drinker. The lawyer also pointed out that Mrs. S was able to stop drinking, with the exception of two social get-togethers with friends, for three weeks prior to the hearing. He also stressed the point that Mrs. S had only imbibed a few times in the past "few years" to the extent of regurgitation or "passing out," this certainly being no indication of her being an "alcoholic!"

After a night's deliberation, the judge ruled that Mrs. S should have child custody. It was his judgment that "there is no indication of Mrs. S's being a chronic alcoholic, or for that matter, there is no indication that she has a problem with her personal drinking behavior." An interesting and perhaps clinically significant anecdote related to Mr. S by a next-door neighbor of Mrs. S (Mr. S had, a number of months earlier, moved into an apartment a few miles from their home) was that on the night following the decision of the judge, Mrs. S had a party and "pitched a good one." On this occasion, she drank to the point of passing out. It is obvious that the professional legal denizens involved in this case were poorly versed in the areas of alcohol addiction and alcohol abuse.

This brief case study quite lucidly demonstrates several irrational cultural beliefs that are associated with alcoholism and deviant acting out. In order to be perceived as a "real" alcoholic, one must act out in a bizarre, grossly, socially inappropriate fashion. The general public is beginning to realize the fallacy and inaccuracy of such stereotypic thinking. The alcoholic can be identified and treated prior to entry into the stage of extreme pathological acting out. This case study demonstrates the more covert dimensions of the acting out pathology of the alcoholic and incipient alcoholic. The covert acting out of the alcoholic is viewed according to such sociologically related factors as education, power and status within a community, race and socioeconomic class. Generally speaking, the more perceived power, status and prestige an alcoholic manifests within a given community, the more he or she is permitted to act out. Overt acting out is also evaluated as a function of these variables.

The alcoholic experiences chronic emotional disturbance as a result of acting in. Sociopaths do not experience emotional conflicts as a result of acting in. Alcoholics manifest chronic pathology in the intrapersonal or acting in realms. In the case of the alcoholic, acting out pathology is always juxtaposed to acting in pathology (Ellis, 1979). Intrapersonal conflicts play a crucial role in the actualization and maintenance of the addiction symptomatology choice. The sociopath is generally refractory to the experience of disturbing intrapersonal ideation and acting in.

The sociopath rarely, if ever, becomes physiologically addicted to ethyl alcohol. This has been my consistent clinical observation over the past twelve years. In the event that this clinical position is correct, it follows that drinking behavior per se will diagnostically differentiate the alcoholic and the sociopath or psychopath. Hopefully, this position will eventually prove heuristic. The sociopath is invariably a heavy drinker. Typically, the sociopathic individual will consume more than four drinks on at least three or four occasions per week. Intoxication or partial intoxication prior to and during criminal activities is standard behavior (Yochelson and Samenow, 1977) in the case of the psychopath. The incarcerated sociopath frequently claims that he or she is an alcoholic and is going to join Alcoholics Anonymous. Joining AA is often interpreted to mean that the sociopath is changing for the better, or being successfully rehabilitated in the eyes of the correctional facility staff. By purporting to be an alcoholic, the psychopath avoids accepting personal responsibility for his or her criminal activities. In a multiplicity of ways, the sociopath simply uses the idea or concept of being an alcoholic. Less than 10 percent of the incarcerated criminals engaging themselves in Alcoholics Anonymous or other alcoholism-rehabilitation modalities while incarcerated continue these treatment contacts once they are released from confinement. While on parole status, the sociopath may continue to see a therapist or attend a group such as Alcoholics Anonymous. These are "conning" transactions. Once the psychopath escapes external pressure to modify drinking behavior and other behaviors, he or she again begins to act out.

In contrast to the alcoholic, the sociopath has no controls from within. However, the sociopath does have a significantly greater ability to control his or her drinking behavior than does the alcoholic. The sociopath does not end up in a medical detoxification ward over and over again. Indeed, the psychopath does not lose control of his or her drinking. Sociopaths and impulse disorders do not consume a fifth or quart of vodka per day for month after month or year after year. The sociopath is almost invariably a heavy drinker and psychologically dependent upon alcohol. Yet, these individuals do not decompensate into florid alcohol addiction. Medical and social histories of forty- to fifty-year-old alcoholics and sociopaths reveal consistent and rather dramatic differences between these populations with regard to (1) drinking behavior per se, (2) the outcomes and effects of drinking, and (3) acting out symptomatology in general. Sociopaths drink for many of the same reasons that alcoholics drink, yet they do not become chronically addicted. Some alcoholics appear to manifest a predisposition to tissue addiction (Knauert, 1982). Sociopaths do not seem to be physically predisposed to develop alcoholism.

A valuable clinical means for differentially assessing the alcoholic and sociopath is that of behavioral follow-up. This diagnostic barometer can be extremely useful even within the confines of a one-month residential treatment program. The sociopathic behaviors of the alcoholic very often undergo a rapid and drastic remisssion following the initiation of sobriety. This is particularly evident in the case of alcoholic persons who maintain their sobriety and continue in psychotherapy or some other form of rehabilitation. The sociopath who is an alcohol abuser persists in a floridly sociopathic life-style following the initiation of sobriety. Sociopaths also tend not to establish long-term abstinence.

The passive-aggressive personality is relatively less symptomatic than the sociopath or impulse disorder. The behavioral patterns associated with the passive-aggressive personality diagnosis are much more akin to those of the alcoholic than those associated with the diagnosis of sociopath or impulse disorder. The passive-aggressive personality is immature, irresponsible, prone to acting out, frequently a heavy drinker, manipulative and self-centered.

PSYCHOTHERAPEUTIC CONSIDERATIONS

The successful psychotherapy of alcoholism encompasses an ever-present therapist focus upon the patient's acting out behaviors. Most alcoholics terminate their deviant and grossly inappriate patterns of acting out subsequent to establishing sobriety and entering psychotherapy. The therapist must point out to the patient early in the treatment process that (1) drinking facilitates acting out, (2) drinking and acting out are self-defeating patterns of behavior, (3) drinking and acting out while in therapy are unacceptable forms of behavior, and (4) recovery and growth occur as a function of the patient's increased capacity to internalize and resolve conflicts rather than impulsively and narcissistically act out.

A rather extended therapeutic exploration of the alcoholic's acting out characterological style is essential to the successful treatment process. The psychotherapist needs to explore the patient's impulsive and acting out behaviors associated with the developmental epochs of adolescence and childhood. The role of anxiety in acting out must be elucidated and worked through. Affects such as rage, anger, depression, low self-esteem and guilt are associated with the alcoholic's acting out pathology. These various issues need to be therapeutically managed and resolved.

The alcoholic must learn to openly discuss and talk about his or her feelings and emotions rather than denying, repressing, projecting and neurotically acting them out. Alcoholics have not learned how to internalize and work through conflicts and threatening affects. It usually takes a great deal of therapeutic work and time for the alcoholic patient to learn how to internally work through painful feelings and conflicts.

A long-term goal of psychotherapy with alcoholics involves the modification of the avoidance defense system and repression. The patient is less prone to impulsive acting out and binge drinking following a therapeutic modification of the avoidance defense system. The patient's style of repressing all threatening feelings and conflicts is very destructive. Effective psychotherapy helps the alcoholic patient internally resolve acting out problems rather than to defensively repress and deny these sources of conflict.

SUMMARY

Pathological acting out is central to alcoholism and the impulse disorders. Etiologically, alcoholism, sociopathy and the impulse disorders evolve as a result of similar interpersonal factors. However, the sociopath is the product of significantly more physical abuse and interpersonal violence during the early epochs of life. The sociopath moves against others. Alcoholics move away from others. The alcoholic's movement away from others also encompasses a driving need to move towards others. These interpersonal movements are neurotically actualized via the ingestion of alcohol.

The alcoholic is chronically anxious. Bio-physiological variables can play a significant role in the long-term anxiety experiences of the alcoholic. The sociopath is pathologically non-anxious. The sociopath is pathologically affectless. The symptomatic acting out behavior of the alcoholic can be viewed as a defense against anxiety or a pathological methodology for binding or controlling interpersonal and intrapersonally determined anxiety. In contrast, the sociopath acts out not as a result of the experience of intense internal or interpersonal anxiety but more as an attempt to retaliate or get even with others.

Rage is a primary affect that the sociopath experiences. The alcoholic is the affective victim of his or her interpersonal and intrapersonal anxiety. Acting out does afford the alcoholic several paradoxical sources of internal strength. In this respect, acting out is neurotically adaptive.

Alcoholism per se can be viewed as a process of pathological acting out against self, significant others, and the phenomenal world. As the alcoholic becomes increasingly chemically dependent, the frequency of acting out in grossly bizarre or socially deviant ways also increases. Alcoholics become social deviants. The sociopath acts out against others. Guilt, anxiety, depression, and remorse are not experienced by the sociopath as a result of the acting out process. Alcoholics are more capable of forming interpersonal attachments than are sociopaths.

Most alcoholics terminate a good deal of their acting out pathology following the establishment of sobriety. The sociopath who *appears* to be alcoholic persists in his or her style of pathological acting out after achieving abstinence from alcohol and mood-altering chemicals. The differential diagnosis of alcoholism-sociopathy-impulse disorder can be difficult. Narcissistic self-attachments and locus-of-control factors also clinically differentiate alcoholics and sociopaths.

The sociopath rarely becomes tissue addicted to alcohol. The sociopath is almost always a heavy drinker or alcohol abuser. However, sociopaths do not lose complete control over their drinking. The sociopath is an individual without effective internal controls. Yet, the sociopath is more in control of his or her drinking than the alcoholic. Sociopaths often purport to be alcoholic as a means of conning judges, correctional facility staff, and self. In comparing the social histories and medical records of alcoholics and sociopaths, it becomes apparent that these clinical populations drink, behave and emote quite differently. Research efforts need to be directed at these areas.

Most alcoholics are capable of rather marked positive behavioral growth and change as a result of psychotherapeutic treatment. Approximately 70 percent of alcoholics (Armor, Polich and Stambul, 1978; Forrest, 1978; Emrick, 1980) becoming engaged in comprehensive alcoholism-treatment programs evidence significant positive change. Cleckley (1964) sums up the antithetical treatment response of the psychopath:

> Having regularly failed in my own efforts to help such patients alter their fundamental pattern of inadequacy and antisocial activity, I hoped for a while that treatment by others would be more successful. . . . I have now, after more than two decades, had the opportunity to observe a considerable number of patients who. . . were kept under treatment not only for months but for years. The therapeutic failure in all such patients observed leads me to feel that we do not at present have any kind of psychotherapy that can be relied upon to change the psychopath fundamentally.

More recently, Yochelson and Samenow (1976 & 1977) likewise reported an unfavorable prognosis for the psychotherapeutic treatment of the sociopath.

This chapter poses a number of clinically controversial issues for the psychotherapist and clinician. Acting out pathology is central to the impulse disorders and the addictions. Hopefully, the material discussed in the chapter will prove heuristic.

Chapter Eleven

ALCOHOLISM AND GUILT

INTRODUCTION

GUILT is basic to the psychopathology of alcoholism. The role of guilt in the development and maintenance of alcohol addiction is poorly understood. Historically, the alcoholic has been viewed as "morally depraved." Alcoholic persons have also been viewed as "evil" in various cultures. Alcoholism has been perceived as a moral issue. Some people believe that intoxication or the ingestion of an alcoholic beverage is a sin. The morality of drinking and alcoholism was a matter of such social significance in twentieth century American culture that prohibition was instituted. Throughout the world, alcoholism has been associated with morality, sin or evil, and guilt.

It is important to clinically define and describe guilt. Guilt has received sporadic attention in the behavioral science literature. Nosologically, guilt has frequently been associated with depression and depressive reactions. Psychoanalytic theory (Fenichel, 1945; Freud, 1953; Gaylin, 1968) emphasizes that neurotic guilt arises as a result of an overly strict and punitive superego. Other schools of counseling and psychotherapy identify guilt as an affective force that affects behavior in a rather wide variety of ways. Reality operations, self-concept, self-dialogue and various affects are associated with guilt.

Mowrer (1961 & 1964) has written extensively about the role of guilt in the etiology of various emotional disturbances. According to Mowrer (1964), guilt is "the fear a person feels *after* having committed an act which is disapproved by the significant others in his life, before the act is detected or confessed. Guilt, in short, is the fear of being found out and punished." Furthermore, Mowrer notes that guilt persists "for precisely the reason that in human society the mere passage of time does not reduce culpability. The original act (which causes guilt) is, moreover, compounded by deception which becomes an ongoing 'sin' which was not merely committed *then*, but is still being practiced and perpetuated, here and now." It is noteworthy that Mowrer (1964) states that a neurosis "it seems, is nothing but a state of guilt that has been neither admitted nor atoned for, and the notion that a person needs some special kind of professional treatment to deliver him from such a condition is surely one of the great illusions of modern times." In this same vein, Mowrer goes on to say that "neurosis is, therefore, the 'trouble' which conscience causes when a person of basically good character in some way compromises himself and persistently refuses to do anything about it." Guilt, and thus neurosis, is experienced as a result of a mistake which is then protected and protracted by means of a lie. Mowrer (1964) also explores how Protestantism has had the tragic consequence of leaving people without defined and effective methods for dealing with *personal guilt*.

Other definitions and clinical descriptions of guilt (Cameron, 1963) also emphasize the fact of committing a breach of conduct and the feeling of culpability related to such behaviors. Mowrer's (1964) definition of guilt emphasizes fear, behavior, feelings and the role of significant others in the process of experiencing this very powerful affect. Early in life and rather consistently throughout life, all people are taught many "thou shall nots." The Ten Commandments and other biblical sources prescribe social norms and regulate social behaviors. A breach of conduct is any act that is disapproved of by significant others and/or society. Fear is closely associated with committing a breach of conduct. Most people experience marked guilt feelings if they steal a friend's car or money. People are taught and conditioned to behave according to such dictates as "thou shall not steal," "thou shall not commit adultery," "thou shall not kill," and so forth. The process of socialization effectively teaches most people to actually fear these select transactions. People do not engage in these behaviors and transactions because they fear the consequences of so doing.

Mowrer indicates that fear is experienced after committing an act that is unacceptable in the eyes of significant others and society. He also implies that confession can result in an exoneration of guilt associated with unacceptable or misbehavior. Affects other than fear often accompany misbehavior under the guise of guilt. In other words, a breach of conduct or misbehavior may be followed (or preceded) by feelings of depression, despondency, rage and anxiety. Other psychotherapists and clinicians (Glasser, 1965; Bratter, 1982) have noted this point. Some depressive reactions are precipitated via the misbehavior, guilt, self-punishment and depression paradigm.

It is important to recognize that people vary considerably with regard to what they perceive as a "breach of conduct." The criminal experiences virtually no guilt as a result of his or her criminal activities (Yochelson and Samenow, 1976 & 1977). Criminals live in a collective that actively disapproves of criminal behavior. However, the interpersonal world of the criminal is often made up of individuals who reinforce criminal behaviors. In effect, criminals teach each other not to experience guilt as a result of their asocial behaviors! At the other end of the continuum, we find individuals who feel extremely guilty about receiving a speeding ticket. Receiving a B instead of an A for a college course may result in marked guilt feelings for select students. Perfectionistic strivings can precipitate chronic struggles with guilt. Behavior usually causes guilt feelings. This can be a confusing issue. The mere thought of committing a breach of conduct or misbehaving can result in the experience of guilt for some persons. Generally speaking, the graduate student feels guilty about receiving a C because he or she did not study and prepare adequately for a course. A married man may feel guilty because he seduces his neighbor's wife. In these situations, it is the behavior or act that determines the experience of guilt. Guilt typically occurs after the behavior or act. In many instances, the person is discovered or found out as a result of his or her behavior. Reik (1961) considered this possibility in his book, *The Compulsion to Confess.* Guilt feelings can result in one's being found out. According to Reik (1961), this process demonstrates the compulsion to confess.

The compulsion to confess operates as a superego function alleviating guilt specific to an unacceptable act.

This chapter is devoted to an exploration of the various forms of guilt that facilitate and reinforce the alcoholic symptom choice. Early life narcissistic injury is associated with the alcoholic's irrational guilt. Alcoholics make themselves guilty vis-à-vis the addiction process. A good deal of the alcoholic's guilt is rational.

ALCOHOLISM AND THE VICISSITUDES OF GUILT

While drinking and between alcoholic episodes, the alcoholic is consistently preoccupied with thoughts and feelings of guilt. Drinking alcoholics neurotically manage their feelings of guilt. It is only after the alcoholic has been actively committed to psychotherapy and sobriety for a number of months that he or she is capable of effectively resolving guilt conflicts.

A majority of alcoholics report having been aware of guilt conflicts prior to early adolescence. Typically, the alcoholic verbalizes these early feelings of guilt as "I can remember as a child feeling like something was always wrong, and somehow it was always my fault; I constantly felt bad about something. I guess I must have done something, but I don't think I know what it was that I had done wrong most of the time." The alcoholic is the recipient of early life messages vis-à-vis significant others that convey a sense of personal guilt.

During infancy and childhood, the alcoholic is told that he or she is inadequate, worthless and unloved. As a child, the alcoholic experiences guilt as a result of interpersonal messages that communicate a basic sense of non-well-being. As a child, the alcoholic feels guilty because he or she is *ipso facto* a failure within the family constellation. Alcoholics feel that there is something pervasively wrong with them. Furthermore, alcoholics blame themselves for these various inadequacies and flaws. In essence, the alcoholic feels guilty as a result of his or her inability to be loved, adequately cared for, and treated with dignity and respect by significant others. Guilt is one affect that can be associated with infantile and childhood rejection by significant others. Unfortunately, it is extremely difficult for the young child to comprehend that he or she is, in fact, not flawed and thus should not feel guilty.

In his work with skid-row alcoholics in New York City, Doctor Arthur P. Knauert observed this same pattern of intense guilt associated with select familial experiences. More specifically, Doctor Knauert has found that many successful physicians and lawyers who end up being skid-row alcoholics very often have struggled with extreme feelings of guilt associated with the death or lifelong crippling illness of another family member. The alcoholic primitively believes that he is responsible for the sibling's or parent's death. This irrational belief fosters lifelong guilt conflicts. The young child can also blame himself or herself for an object loss resulting from parental divorce.

Intense guilt is an affective vector that facilitates and maintains the alcoholic's self-destructive behaviors. The alcoholic believes and *knows* (consciously as well as preconsciously and unconsciously) that he or she deserves to be punished. The pervasive self-destructive trends of the alcoholic are associated with guilt conflicts. The addiction process creates and reinforces guilt feelings. The alcoholic engages in an ever-increasingly self-destructive repertoire of behaviors.

Guilt feelings can be extinguished by atonement, restitution, ritual undoing, or confession. Obviously, confession is atonement, restitution, and a form of ritual undoing. Confessing one's guilt can also reinforce maladaptive behaviors and establish a warped self-concept. This is exactly what happens in the case of many alcoholics. Many alcoholics accept their guilt and continually and neurotically confess their guilt for a lifetime.

The alcoholic is always angry about his or her chronic interpersonal conflicts. Guilt associated with the issue of interpersonal failure becomes fused with a morass of angry, hostile feelings. As the alcoholic enters the adolescent years, he or she frequently begins to act out these feelings of anger and rage against significant others. The alcoholic feels even more guilty as a result of acting out against others and subsequently punishes self. The alcoholic concretely demonstrates to self that he or she is, in fact, no good and, therefore, deserves to be punished. As an adolescent and an adult, the alcoholic behaves according to the guilt precipitated dictate "I deserve to be punished."

In an overdetermined fashion, the alcoholic acts out against self for two reasons. Acting out against the self is congruous with the lifelong interpersonal and intrapersonal messages that the alcoholic has internalized. Guilt is basic to these processes. Secondly, the alcoholic behaves in a self-destructive manner as a means of ritual undoing or confession. The alcoholic primitively attempts to exonerate guilt through the process of punishing the self. The ingestion of alcohol represents a primitive magical process that partially extinguishes guilt. Sobering up is also an atonement or undoing mechanism. When the chronic alcoholic begins to get sober, he or she experiences considerable physical and psychological pain. This pain *is* self-destruction. The alcoholic achieves atonement and confession by becoming abstinent. Drying out or detoxification is a "purge." The alcoholic primitively purges self when he or she achieves sobriety. The alcoholic begins again or is "reborn" via sobriety following weeks, months or perhaps years of chronic intoxication (Forrest, 1978).

The guilt feelings of the alcoholic are fused with anger and oral rage. Each year thousands of alcoholic persons destroy themselves alcoholically via the oral ingestion of alcoholic beverages. The destructive guilt of the alcoholic is associated with ego pathology. Splitting (Kernberg, 1976) is basic to the ego structure and adjustment style of the chronic alcoholic. Alcoholics have sustained such a degree of early life narcissistic injury that in order to survive they have learned to dichotomize their experiential world of object relations. Guilt is associated with the "bad me" or "not me" components of the ego apparatus. The alcoholic chronically attempts to deny, repress or dissociate "bad me" or "not me" experiences. Furthermore, the alcoholic always has a vacillating superego structure. Whenever the alcoholic begins to feel happy, comfortable with self and significant others, and when things begin looking up, the alcoholic responds by punishing self. This behavioral pattern (Forrest, 1979a & 1979c) is baffling to the neophyte clinician working with alcoholic patients. The "bad me" component of the alcoholic ego structure demands punishment from the superego. It is almost as if the alcoholic says to himself or herself, "I should not feel good; I should feel guilty about feeling good!" At this point, the alcoholic punishes self in order to avoid guilt feelings associated with pleasure. The alcoholic compartmentalizes life. Everything is all or none. The alcoholic is a superman or a shit. This life-style generates guilt conflicts.

Initially in life, the irrational guilt conflicts of the alcoholic are imposed upon the addicted person vis-à-vis interpersonal relations. During the stages of childhood, adolescence and adulthood, the guilt conflicts of the alcoholic become increasingly self-imposed. As the alcoholic experiences peer difficulties, academic difficulties, vocational problems, and marital discord, he or she feels progressively more guilty. Many alcoholic persons find the challenge of education difficult. In fact, it is common to find that the alcoholic has given up and failed academically by the time he or she was in the sixth or seventh grade. These individuals feel guilty about their academic failures. However, many alcoholics are bright and perform extremely well in an academic sense. Interpersonal failure is often a significant hallmark of even the bright, professionally successful alcoholic. It is the behaviors of the alcoholic that cause guilt. Most alcoholics are ill prepared for the increasing complexities and responsibilities that accompany adult living. As such, alcoholics become increasingly guilty as a result of their marginal ability to manage new and more difficult life tasks. Some alcoholics feel extremely guilty as children *because* their parents are divorced. These persons experience even more profound guilt over the failure of their own marriages. Many alcoholic persons are determined to make their marriage work.

It is axiomatic that the older the drinking alcoholic becomes, the more dysfunctional he or she becomes. Behaviorally, the drinking alcoholic is out of control. The alcoholic's *modus vivendi* can only create guilt. It is basically irrational to feel, perhaps for life, guilty because one's mother and significant others were unable to provide adequate love and parenting. It is more irrational to chronically make oneself guilty as a result of explicit here-and-now behaviors and transactions. The drinking alcoholic continually compounds his or her childhood and adolescent guilt conflicts vis-à-vis the addiction process. The guilt which the drinking adult alcoholic experiences as a result of concrete here-and-now behavioral transactions is paradoxically rational. It is logical and rational for the alcoholic to feel guilty over such matters as not providing adequate food and clothing for the family. The alcoholic who abuses and beats his or her children while intoxicated certainly has a reality-oriented basis for feeling guilty. A woman alcoholic that I treated a few years ago actually ran over her four-year-old daughter as she was playing in the family driveway. The woman was inebriated at the time of this grave mishap. This alcohol-facilitated accident resulted in a broken leg for her daughter. The guilt that this mother experienced as a result of this incident was rational.

It is important for the psychotherapist to focus upon the very rational and understandable basis for the guilt that the alcoholic feels (Forrest, 1979c). Guilt is very often associated with the inappropriate or crazy behaviors of the drinking alcoholic. It is therapeutically efficacious for the therapist to point out to the alcoholic that he or she makes self guilty as a result of inappropriate, alcohol-determined behaviors. Irresponsible behavior upon the part of the alcoholic creates rational and irrational guilt conflicts. Many of the irrational dimensions of the alcoholic's guilt conflicts have to do with infantile and childhood experiences. However, the drinking alcoholic almost always manages guilt feelings irrationally. This is an important point. In response to guilt feelings (rational guilt) having to do with being fired from his fourth job in two months, one alcoholic patient went on a two-month "bender." This is a typical response set upon the part of the alcoholic. In order to avoid or deny guilt associated with irresponsible behaviors, the alcoholic often drinks more. Many alcoholics drink alcoholically, in part, as a defense against guilt feelings. Alcoholism creates a reality-oriented basis for guilt. Every person who drinks alcoholically engages in behavior that results in guilt. It is important for the counselor or psychotherapist to be able to recognize when the alcoholic is drinking in order to cope with guilt. Yochelson and Samenow's (1977) view that there is a "goodness of guilt" is correct. The alcoholic must learn how to rationally come to grips with guilt while sober. Guilt operates to maintain and even synergize the addiction process.

Paradoxically, guilt can also play a crucial role in the termination of the alcoholic's dependency (Ellis, 1979; Forrest, 1983).

Many alcoholics consciously choose to drink in order to escape profound guilt feelings. These individuals are often capable of terminating their addiction. However, after achieving abstinence, they experience a guilt-facilitated depression. Some of these alcoholics are able to quit drinking without intervention. They are motivated to give up their addiction. Intense guilt evolves as a result of a conscious awareness of personal irresponsibility in these cases. The patient may "fall off the wagon" several times. The therapist needs to actively deal with the patient's guilt as soon as he or she sobers up. Many alcoholics neurotically *use* guilt in the service of their addiction. As one patient explained this process, "I feel so damn guilty when I get sober that I've just got to get drunk again." Therapists (Bratter, 1983; Forrest, 1983) must let their alcoholic patients know that sobriety will not be easily accomplished, and that a good deal of emotional pain and turmoil will accompany the initial weeks and months of recovery. The psychotherapist must also point out to the alcoholic (Forrest, 1979c) that pathological guilt can only be resolved through sobriety and work.

It is imperative that the alcoholic stop making himself or herself guilty in the here-and-now. An important first step in this process involves terminating all drinking. Every alcoholic is guilty about his or her addiction. The alcoholic is guilty about making self sick vis-à-vis the addiction process. Alcoholics are guilty about their self-destructive addiction symptom choice. Many alcoholic persons are emotionally elated after achieving sobriety. In addition to the many overt and objective sources of gain derived from sobriety, the alcoholic experiences a catharsis associated with the more primitive levels of change and growth associated with the achievement of long-term sobriety. The sober alcoholic can begin to experience life for the various purposes of living rather than experiencing life in a destructive, guilty, death-oriented fashion (Scott, 1979).

Guilt can be a driving force that underlies the alcoholic's depression and depressive conflicts. As discussed in Chapter Six, many alcoholics are chronically depressed. The alcoholic has experienced numerous reality-oriented failures, which can be interpreted to mean that he or she does deserve to be depressed and, therefore, punished. Frequently, it is guilt that actually causes the depressed alcoholic to commit suicide. It is beneficial to point out to the alcoholic that he or she cannot go back and live life differently in order to cope with current guilt conflicts. However, the alcoholic can diminish feelings of guilt that are related to the past by living responsibly today. The therapist must be able to differentiate (Knauert, 1980) between the patient's depression and guilt and then help the patient recognize how guilt contributes to depressive conflicts.

Alcoholics are depressed and guilty about family matters (Wegscheider, 1981; Forrest, 1982b) and sexuality. Drinking alcoholics put their families through hell. Angry outbursts involving spouse and children, gross neglect of parenting responsibilities and refusing to pay bills are but a few of the areas in which the alcoholic creates family conflict. In short, the alcoholic consistently creates emotional turmoil and chaos within the family system. The drinking alcoholic consciously realizes what he or she is doing *to* the family, yet alcoholism acts as a buffer or a defense against the guilt related to his or her pathological family transactions. When sober, the alcoholic is confronted by the family system relative to his or her various unacceptable and crazy behaviors. Most recovering alcoholics experience a good deal of guilt about their aberrant family interactions. To make things worse, the non-addicted spouse frequently attacks the alcoholic (Forrest, 1978) during the initial months of recovery. The children and spouse of the alcoholic may actively persecute the addicted family member subsequent to sobriety, thus compounding guilt conflicts. In effect, the sober alcoholic must live with the emotional pathology that he or she helped facilitate in each and every family member.

The alcoholic often feels directly responsible for the behavioral difficulties of the children. In order to remain abstinent and grow psychologically, the alcoholic must learn how to cope with family conflict (Forrest, 1980a). Alcoholic family systems sometimes include an emotionally disturbed son or daughter. The alcoholic must personally come to grips with these family situations. In so doing, the alcoholic family member overcomes guilt conflicts related to family living.

Many alcoholic marriages fail *after* the addicted spouse has terminated the addiction process. Divorce or separation is accompanied by a sense of loss, depression and guilt. Psychotherapists who are working with a recovering alcoholic in the process of divorce should explore the rational and irrational dimensions of the patient's guilt associated with the divorce. The florid psychopathology basic to some alcoholic marriages can only be terminated by divorce. Rebirth (Forrest, 1978) may begin for both marital partners following a separation or divorce. The spouse of the alcoholic sometimes finds that she or he cannot tolerate living with the non-drinking partner. In order to deny profound guilt feelings associated with such a marital situation, the alcoholic sometimes intransigently and parasitically clings to the non-addicted spouse.

The alcoholic consistently feels extremely guilty with regard to his or her relationships with the children. Alcoholic husbands feel just as guilty as alcoholic wives over the issues of child neglect and abuse. Invariably, the alcoholic parent does neglect and psychologically abuse the children. It is common (Ackerman, 1980) for the alcoholic parent to physically abuse the children while intoxicated. Violence is basic to the alcoholic family system. Recovering alcoholics can and do recognize the impact they have had upon their children. When the alcoholic realizes just how deeply the children have been hurt, guilt and depression follow. Guilt associated with inadequate parenting is frequently rational. The psychotherapist can help the alcoholic deal more rationally with guilt stemming from poor parenting by encouraging the alcoholic to seek professional help for the child. Children growing up in alcoholic families have drug and alcoholism problems, they often fail in school, they encounter difficulties with the police, and quite often they choose to leave home prematurely (Wegscheider, 1981). The alcoholic learns that he or she cannot magically undo the various conflicts of the children. Yet, the alcoholic can relieve his or her guilt by encouraging the children to seek professional and/or self-help treatment.

Family therapy (Forrest, 1978; Wegscheider, 1981) can be a very effective treatment strategy for helping the alcoholic parent deal with guilt related to maladaptive parenting. The alcoholic family system very often suffers with a form of collective guilt. In such instances, family therapy is essential to the resolution of the collective guilt experienced by the alcoholic family system. As the alcoholic family member becomes progressively more deviant in an interpersonal sense, the other non-addicted family members tend to assimilate and internalize the alcoholic's guilt. The spouse of the alcoholic begins to feel intensely guilty about the bizarre interpersonal behaviors manifest by the alcoholic. In order to make the alcoholic happy, many non-addicted spouses decide to drink with the alcoholic. This solution never works. The family that drinks together is not the family that stays together! Non-addicted spouses soon find that they cannot psychologically participate in the surfeited drinking activities of their alcoholic. Heavy drinking upon the part of the alcoholic's non-addicted spouse frequently results in sexual acting out (Forrest, 1981). The alcoholic uses such transactions against the non-addicted spouse. The non-addicted spouse can only feel angry, depressed and extremely guilty over transactions such as these.

When the alcoholic refuses to pay bills and fails to behave responsibly in other areas of living, the entire family feels guilty. As the alcoholic deteriorates, the family typically severs many community and interpersonal ties. The alcoholic family is isolated (Forrest, 1980) and alone. Guilt accompanies the process of family isolation and alienation from the community. Children living in an alcoholic family system feel embarrassed and guilty about the behaviors of their alcoholic father or mother. Children are afraid to bring friends home when one or both of their parents are alcoholic. In short, the children of the alcoholic share the experience of guilt. Furthermore, the non-addicted spouse and children of the alcoholic resent feeling guilty as a result of the behavioral demeanor of the addicted family member. Guilt thus becomes fused with anger, hostility and resentment within the alcoholic family system. Non-addicted family members sometimes attempt to retaliate against the alcoholic for the guilt feelings that he or she has created and perpetuated within the alcoholic family system. For these reasons, it is imperative for the therapist to help the alcoholic family system come to grips with the issue of family guilt.

The realm of sexuality and human sexual behavior (Forrest, 1982b) contributes to the guilt of many alcoholic persons. Alcoholics often can recall guilt feelings related to sexual behaviors dating back to childhood. Many alcoholics struggle with masturbation guilt. Alcoholics manifest various sexual dysfunctions, deviations and sexual problems.

Guilt feelings can stem from a multiplicity of sexuality behaviors and conflicts. Sexual acting out and promiscuity create profound guilt conflicts for many alcoholics. The sexually oriented conflicts of the alcoholic constitute one red thread of this book. Some alcoholic males have either approached another male sexually or even homosexually assaulted a drinking cohort. These transactions often involve married alcoholics who have children. Guilt can accompany any deviant or socially disapproved sexual act that the alcoholic carries out. Family guilt is often associated with interfamilial sexual pathology. While intoxicated, the alcoholic family member may behave and interact with other family members in a seductive or frankly sexual manner. Depending upon the specifics of such a family transaction, predictably a number of negative feelings may be acted out within the family system. It is a family tragedy when the alcoholic seduces a daughter or son (Martin, 1979). Sexual transactions of this variety take place within alcoholic family systems far more often than is recognized by even alcoholism experts. The most common form of incest within alcoholic family systems involves an alcoholic father and his early adolescent stepdaughter or daughter (Forrest, 1982b). Frequently, the alcoholic father has been sexually involved with his daughter or stepdaughter for an extended period of time. In many of these cases, the wife of the alcoholic is aware of the sexual relationship between her daughter and husband.

The sexual liaison between father and daughter becomes a family secret. Needless to say, every family member involved in the family secret is extremely guilty about this matter. Most alcoholics who are sexually involved with their children attempt to keep this issue known only within the family system. These pathologic familial transactions reinforce drinking and other forms of family conflict. When the incestuous daughter reaches the age of fifteen or sixteen, she may be the family member who initiates outside intervention. When this happens, the alcoholic is enraged and the mother is both depressed and profusely guilty. The daughter is confused and doubly guilty. She experiences intense guilt related to (1) her sexual relationship with her father or stepfather and (2) initiating outside intervention, which frequently results in forced treatment or incarceration of the stepfather. Daughters who are sexually victimized by an alcoholic father are realistically afraid. The alcoholic family system enduring such an experience lives with guilt. Furthermore, this guilt lives on in each family member. The alcoholic who facilitates such a family relationship requires extended psychotherapy and rehabilitation. Indeed, the incestuous daughter, mother and every family member in an incestuous alcoholic family system is in need of treatment.

Many alcoholics experience guilt conflicts as a result of their religious beliefs. Religion has been an influential vector in the lives of many alcoholic persons. The religion of the alcoholic is often steeped in fundamentalism. In describing his religious experiences, one of my patients emphasized that he had always been in trouble with God. As the patient elaborated upon this point, it became clear that he could long remember disobeying the many "thou shall nots" of his religion. This patient felt chronically guilty as a result of his many religious transgressions.

The religiously oriented guilt conflicts of the alcoholic are germinated in the interpersonal and ecclesiastical realms. The religious conflicts of the alcoholic are basically conflicts with authority. In a strictly religious context, the alcoholic is in conflict with God! Many alcoholics fight a battle with God and the church for most of their lives. The alcoholic constantly attempts to reject religion, God and all the "thou shall nots" that go with any religious doctrine. Why should this make the alcoholic feel guilty? In the first place, most people who behaviorally reject the basic "thou shall nots" of our society experience interpersonal conflict and intrapersonal dissonance. The alcoholic, then, manifests interpersonal and social conflicts following gross rejection of societal norms ("thou shall nots"). Secondly, the bipolar character structure of the alcoholic is interpersonally determined. Thus, guilt not only results from a violation of religious doctrine ("thou shall nots") but from a rejection by significant others and the ensuing rejection of authority figures and societal norms upon the part of the alcoholic. The alcoholic resents and attempts to reject every authority figure, not just God! However, the bipolar characterological makeup of the alcoholic is such that sobriety and serenity are possible only when he or she begins to deal with the reality of authority conflicts.

The first authority figures that all people must deal with in life are parents or surrogate parents. Usually, alcoholics have had a great deal of difficulty managing matters of control, power and authority as they relate to parents. The authority-oriented conflicts of the alcoholic involve anyone who is potentially somehow perceived as being superior or more powerful than the addicted person. Police, priests and ministers, the first sergeant or the general, the boss or job supervisor, doctors, and ultimately God are but a few of the people with whom the alcoholic has authority conflicts. Since the alcoholic feels that he or she is *the* ultimate authority, it is only logical to predict authority problems in many areas of living! In reality, the alcoholic very often experiences chronic authority conflicts. Guilt feelings arise as the alcoholic fails in such authority or power struggles. Guilt is, therefore, a part of the ongoing interpersonal struggle of the alcoholic. As the alcoholic rejects religion, God and his worldly superiors, he or she fails over and over again in an interpersonal sense and thus experiences guilt.

The religion and religious background of many alcoholic persons is of the "hell fire and brimstone" variety. A God or religion that emphasizes punishment and sin can reinforce guilt. The drinking alcoholic frequently places self in a double bind. These individuals feel guilty if they fail to go to church and eventually divorce themselves from their religion. Participation in the religious activities of the church can likewise create guilt. Most drinking alcoholics respond to a double-bind situation of this type by choosing to serve their addiction rather than their God and religion! They terminate religious activities, feel guilty, drink even more, and secretly pray to God for forgiveness.

Alcoholics Anonymous can help the alcoholic bridge the gap between a meaningful spiritual life and a life-style steeped in guilt (Emrick, 1979). Psychotherapy can also accomplish this same task. A healthy love relationship can do the same. However, sobriety must come first. Although Alcoholics Anonymous is not a religion per se, it is an organization constructed upon sound religious principles. The AA program of recovery (the 12 steps) includes "came to believe in a Power greater than ourselves that could restore us to sanity and made a decision to turn our will and our lives over to the care of God *as we understood Him*." The religious flavor of AA is such that many alcoholics can accept and live with its doctrine (the 12 steps). The fifth step of Alcoholics Anonymous requires the alcoholic to "admit to God, to ourselves and to another human being the exact nature of our wrongs." This step is very important. If the alcoholic works this step, he or she accepts God (or a variety of religion) and, more importantly, confesses in order to live rationally *without* guilt. In order to recover, the alcoholic must confess over and over again the pathology of his or her drinking career. Self-disclosure (Hountras and Forrest, 1970; Forrest, 1978) is a confession. In the process of confessing to God, self and another human being, the alcoholic additionally modifies his or her system of denial (avoidance defense system).

The capacity to experience guilt is a favorable prognostic variable in the psychotherapy of alcoholism (Forrest, 1982d). The therapist's goal is not to extinguish the alcoholic's ability and capacity to experience guilt. Rather, the psychotherapist needs to help the alcoholic learn to live in a manner that does not facilitate guilt resulting from misbehavior. Alcoholics also need to resolve their irrationally determined infantile sources of guilt. As the alcoholic makes himself or herself known within the context of the psychotherapeutic relationship, he or she can begin to know this self and become a real self. Confession and guilt work are central ingredients in the healing process.

At the onset of this chapter, it was suggested that guilt can constitute neurosis. Guilt feelings can precipitate maladaptive behaviors. Guilt feelings feed into and reinforce neurotic patterns of adjustment. Mowrer (1964) points out that "guilt persists for precisely the reason that in human society, the mere passage of time does not reduce culpability." Behavior that facilitates guilt tends to be repeated, compounded by self and other deceptions (denial), and thus problematic in the ongoing here-and-now experience of the alcoholic. In order to stop feeling guilty, the alcoholic must stop behaving in a manner that causes guilt. The alcoholic needs to terminate neurotic behaviors that create guilt feelings. Sordid, alcohol-facilitated maladaptive behaviors need to be openly explored within the therapeutic alliance. In so doing, the alcoholic makes a full confession to the psychotherapist. First and foremost, it is important for the alcoholic patient to be able to confess the reality of his or her addiction. The therapeutic process of working through involves integrating this confession ("I am an alcoholic") into the pre-conscious and unconscious levels of awareness. Alcoholics teach themselves to be honest by confessing the reality of their addiction. This is a very important educational process about the self. It is not atypical for the chronic alcoholic to be the last person to discover that he or she is an alcoholic! In spite of numerous hospitalizations specific to alcohol addiction, alcohol-facilitated divorces, job losses, and so forth, the alcoholic very often continues to perceive himself or herself as "not really an alcoholic."

PSYCHOTHERAPEUTIC CONSIDERATIONS

Psychotherapy is always constructed around the process of self-disclosure (Jourard, 1964; Forrest, 1970 & 1978; Hountras and Forrest, 1970). Self-disclosure can be viewed as a confession. Confession results in atonement, which can help the alcoholic recover. It is extremely difficult for the alcoholic to (1) diffusely confess within the confines of the psychotherapy relationship, (2) integrate the reality of these confessions within the self-system (to include an integration and acceptance of the reality of being addicted at the more primitive levels of consciousness), and (3) continue drinking and behaving irrationally. Chronic alcoholics who persist in an extended psychotherapy relationship cannot return to their alcoholic life-style without becoming more guilty and emotionally disturbed. The same can be said of the alcoholic who spends a good deal of time within the Alcoholics Anonymous community. The patient experiences the reality of his or her being in a psychotherapy relationship or by attending AA. Returning to an alcoholic life-style is tantamount to a sadomasochistic choice to feel more guilty. In contrast to a number of the other dynamisms discussed in this text, guilt is not a basic characterological feature that persists and determines behavior following several years of sobriety. The sober alcoholic who is committed to responsible living through a psychotherapy relationship, a rehabilitation program, or a self-help group such as Alcoholics Anonymous can overcome and resolve guilt.

The psychotherapist needs to consistently point out to the alcoholic patient how he or she makes self guilty vis-à-vis intoxication and inappropriate behaviors. After the patient has achieved abstinence and is committed to the therapy process, the therapist needs to actively explore the childhood origins of the patient's irrational guilt. Alcoholics need to learn how to accept themselves as they are.

It is very important to begin the process of therapeutic guilt resolution early in the treatment process. Therapist support, encouragement and interpretations facilitate this process. In some cases, it is therapeutically efficacious for the psychotherapist to point out to the patient that he or she has historically used guilt in the service of the addiction process. The therapist also needs to focus upon the patient's religious and sexual experiences, beliefs and values.

SUMMARY

The guilt conflicts of the alcoholic were discussed in this chapter. Guilt can be thought of as negative feelings associated with committing an act that is disapproved of by significant others. In order to experience guilt, an individual must behave in a manner that is socially unacceptable or socially disapproved. Behaving in a socially unacceptable fashion frequently results in a fear of being found out and perhaps even being punished for such misbehavior. The alcoholic chronically feels guilty. Much of the guilt of the alcoholic is irrational (Ellis, 1979) and etiologically determined during the early developmental stages of life. Commonly, alcoholics feel guilty about being unwanted and unloved as young children. The alcoholic accepts personal responsibility for a plethora of incomprehensible inadequacies and shortcomings. One result of this process is the internalization of tremendously powerful irrational guilt conflicts. Many alcoholic persons rebel as adolescents and adults and attempt to *give* their guilt to significant others. The alcoholic tries to escape guilt feelings by projecting and blaming significant others and the "world." Rational guilt (Ellis, 1979) is associated with the alcoholic's many alcohol-facilitated, crazy transactions and behaviors. A rational consequence of being a chronic alcoholic is feeling guilty. Invariably, the drinking alcoholic progressively behaves in more guilt-producing ways. As the alcoholic deteriorates, he or she acts out in a multiplicity of socially inappropriate ways that result in guilt feelings and conflicts.

Vocational failures, marital failures, poor parenting skills, sexual promiscuity or poor sexual performance, and religious beliefs are but a few of the areas in which the alcoholic experiences guilt. Guilt reinforces the addiction process. When the alcoholic does sober up, he or she is confronted with the reality of guilt associated with any or all of these matters. Paradoxically, alcoholics drink alcoholically in order to deal with guilt. Guilt synergizes depression (Della-Giustina and Forrest, 1979) and self-destruction. The alcoholic family system is collectively guilty. Sexual acting out within the alcoholic family system (Forrest, 1982b) creates the most pathological form of collective family guilt. Dogmatic religious beliefs can add to the guilt of the alcoholic.

In order to stop feeling guilty, the alcoholic must quit drinking. The capacity of the alcoholic to experience guilt can be a favorable prognostic treatment sign. Guilt becomes such a painful vector in the lives of many alcoholics that it pushes them into a psychotherapy relationship, Alcoholics Anonymous or a comprehensive rehabilitation program. The alcoholic is rarely a sociopath or character behavior disorder. Sociopaths lack the capacity to experience intense and prolonged guilt (Cleckly, 1964). Frequently, alcoholics have been inappropriately categorized or labeled as sociopaths and impulse disorders. Euphemistically, clinicians have pointed out that alcoholic persons struggle with guilt conflicts!

Recovery dictates confession. Psychotherapy, Alcoholics Anonymous, and rehabilitation programs provide the alcoholic with an opportunity to confess. As the alcoholic remains sober, changes behavior, discovers his or her being, and discloses to other human beings, he or she is no longer crippled and overwhelmed by feelings of guilt. Guilt can constitute a neurosis. Mowrer (1964) incorrectly asserted, "The notion that a person needs some kind of professional treatment to deliver him from such a condition (guilt-induced neurosis) is surely one of the great illusions of modern times." Although alcohol can do more good than harm for many people (Chafetz, 1977), drinking can create guilt feelings that often require professional intervention in the case of many alcoholics!

Chapter Twelve

ALCOHOLISM AS AN OBSESSIVE-COMPULSIVE DISORDER

INTRODUCTION

SIGNIFICANT scientific research studies (Forrest, 1978) have been made within the explicit realm of understanding the origins of alcoholism during the past fifty years. Nonetheless, there exists very little consensus of opinion in the alcoholism field about the causes of alcohol addiction. Within the various professions engaged in the treatment, rehabilitation, research, and understanding of alcoholism, there are a diversity of opinions relative to the etiology of alcoholism.

The American collective is confused and bewildered in its attempt to understand what alcoholism is and what causes alcoholism. Most people do agree that (1) there are literally millions of alcoholics in the United States, and (2) the alcoholic needs some form of treatment. There is also an emergent collective realization that alcoholics are capable of terminating their profound and pathological dependence upon alcohol.

Personnel involved in the actual delivery of alcoholic rehabilitation services are well aware of the position of the American Medical Association that recognizes and identifies alcoholism as a disease. However, physicians and medical experts (Knauert, 1982) also seem to question the categorization of alcoholism as a disease process. Many physicians reject the position that alcoholism is a disease. One very positive outcome of the AMA position defining alcoholism as a disease has been the increased medical and treatment benefits available for the alcoholic. This position has also facilitated less stigmatizing of the alcoholic, thus permitting more alcoholics to seek out treatment and rehabilitation.

Psychological theories of alcoholism generally emphasize the role of learning theory (Bandura, 1969; Wellman, 1979; Forrest, 1983) in the causation and maintenance of this disorder. Affective disturbance has been associated with the etiology of alcoholism. Most typically, the behavioral science professions have viewed the alcoholic behavior of an individual as being symptomatic of other more pathological underlying conflicts. This position suggests that certain people ingest alcohol and become chemically dependent in order to neurotically cope with more profound interpersonal and intrapersonal problems. Behavior therapists have recently achieved considerable recognition as a result of their controversial belief that many alcoholics can be successfully treated in the sense of being returned to the ranks of normal or social drinkers (Armor, Polich and Stambul, 1978).

Early infantile and childhood experiences have also been hypothesized by many clinicians to play an important role in the causation of alcohol addiction. More recent psychological models of alcoholism have focused upon family psychodynamics (Wegscheider, 1981) and transactional styles. Personality theorists have tended to view chronic alcoholism as evolving from a particular personality type or makeup. Personality theorists involved in alcoholism research and treatment have consistently viewed the alcoholic as an obsessive-compulsive personality type.

Sociological theories have also been applied to the problem of alcoholism. The incidence of alcohol addiction and problem drinking is on the upswing (Forrest, 1980 & 1982c) in most Western cultures. Sociologists have postulated that industrialization, technology, the communication media, and even schools have facilitated an increase in alcohol abuse and addiction. Behavioral scientists have referred to our culture as a sick society. A disturbed society breeds alcoholism, mental illness and criminality. The very real possibilities of nuclear attack and nuclear holocaust have been associated with the "collective neurosis" of the twentieth century.

It is apparent (Bratter and Forrest, 1983) that behavioral scientists do not know the precise causes of alcoholism. Within the explicit confines of the alcoholism rehabilitation field, everyone *seems* to know the relative causes of alcoholism!

Alcoholism is an obsessive-compulsive disorder (Blane, 1968; Forrest, 1978 & 1982a). The obsessive-compulsive pathology of alcoholism (Wegscheider, 1981) has been discussed in the alcoholism treatment and rehabilitation literature. Most clinicians recognize the compulsive nature of the alcoholic. However, the obsessive-compulsive dimensions of the alcoholic character structure have received only fragmented and superficial attention in the literature dealing with the psychopathology of alcoholism.

This chapter elucidates the role of obsessive-compulsive symptomatology in the creation and maintenance of alcoholism. The etiological basis of the obsessive-compulsive dynamism is discussed. Alcoholism is not simply an obsessive-compulsive disorder. However, the obsessive-compulsive dynamism constitutes a cardinal feature of the alcoholic adjustment style. Every alcoholic can be viewed as an obsessive-compulsive!

OBSESSIONS, COMPULSIONS AND ALCOHOLISM

The obsessive-compulsive disorders have been explored extensively in the clinical literature (Saltzman, 1968; Rachman and Hodgson, 1980). According to Saltzman (1968), the term "obsessive-compulsive neurosis" refers to "thoughts, feelings, ideas and impulses which an individual cannot dispel in spite of an inner desire to do so. The compelling nature of the activity – despite the fact that it may be illogical, undesirable and unnecessary – is the central issue." In spite of a wish for free will, or freedom of choice, the obsessive-compulsive individual is forced by internal pressures to engage in a variety of behaviors that are maladaptive and, frequently, even distasteful or frightening. Saltzman (1968) indicates that three basic elements constitute the obsessive-compulsive dynamism: "(1) behavior or thought which persists beyond the need for and/or in spite of voluntary action, (2) the presence of anxiety and somatic distress because of the ego-alien nature of such thoughts, and (3) insight into the illogical and unreasonable nature of the thought or action, which does not alter the behavior." The obsession is thus a persistent, ritualized, cognitive-behavioral pattern.

Prior to the development of grossly inappropriate or bizarre ritualized behavior, the obsessive-compulsive dynamism is typically manifest in personality and character structure. The obsessive-compulsive character structure manifests itself vis-à-vis a behavioral style that is characterized by orderliness, stubbornness, being perfectionistic and punctual, meticulousness, frugality and preciseness. Inflexibility, rigidity, overconscientiousness, a lack of adaptability, needs for order and discipline, and personal reliability are often associated with the obsessive-compulsive adjustment style. A major function of the obsessive-compulsive dynamism is that of maintaining control over both oneself and one's environment. Other features of the obsessive-compulsive adjustment style include philosophizing, rationalization and double-talk, intrusive homosexual thoughts, an avoidance of feelings and affective life in general, doubting and procrastination, ambivalence, ritualistic living, and grandiosity. Cameron (1963) defines obsessive-compulsive reactions as "apparently useless but irresistible repetitious acts, words or thoughts, whose aim is to reduce tension and anxiety by (a) indulging in something forbidden, (b) denying such indulgence or guarding against it, or (c) by punishing oneself for having had the impulse to indulge."

Obsessive-compulsive symptoms vary in complexity (Rachman and Hodgson, 1980). Obsessive-compulsive patients vary greatly with regard to their overt symptomatology. Chronic alcohol addiction can be viewed as essentially an obsessive-compulsive disorder. The drinking behavior, general life-style characteristics, and fantasy ideation of the alcoholic are obsessive-compulsive.

The obsessive-compulsive disorder(s) is an adjustment symptomatology that involves binding or controlling anxiety (Saltzman, 1968; Rachman and Hodgson, 1980; Forrest, 1983). Psychotherapists and psychopathologists (Fenichel, 1945) have viewed obsessive-compulsive adjustments as maladaptive methodologies that are utilized to control intense anxiety. Sullivan (1953) considered the obsessive-compulsive reaction to be one of the most primitive psychological means for defending the self-system against florid schizophrenic decompensation. The outcropping of acute obsessive-compulsive symptoms (Sullivan, 1953) is frequently associated with an impending or incipient schizophrenic episode. Obsessive-compulsive characterological and behavioral features have been associated with either bizarre adjustment styles or relatively unobtrusive characterological traits. The obsessive-compulsive dynamism has been associated with alcoholism and the addiction disorders (Forrest, 1978). Clinicians have referred to the alcoholic as an obsessive-compulsive personality.

An overdetermined process of binding anxiety is central to all obsessive-compulsive adjustments. This process is orally manifested in alcoholism. The process of orally binding anxiety is also a central ingredient in smoking, marijuana dependence, "pill-popping" dependencies and addictions, and obesity. Needle dependencies and addictions differ psychodynamically from the orally oriented addictions. Classically, the obsessive-compulsive disorders have been associated with handwashing rituals and compulsive "counters" and "doubters" (Rachman and Hodgson, 1980). Orality is not usually a fundamental psychodynamic issue in obsessive-compulsive reactions of these types. The obsessive-compulsive handwasher engages in this specific form of maladaptive behavior in order to control internal anxiety. Alcoholics drink alcoholically and obsessively-compulsively in order to defend the self-system from the primitive experience of being overwhelmingly anxious. Genetic, bio-physiological and related non-psychologically based variables may facilitate or even determine obsessive-compulsive behaviors.

A maladaptive motoric set is also basic to the obsessive-compulsive disorders. Alcoholics respond to their chronic anxiety by orally ingesting alcoholic beverages. This process partially extinguishes anxiety and other noxious affective states. The addiction process per se (purchasing alcohol, ingesting alcohol, and behaving alcoholically) is a relatively unique maladaptive motoric behavioral set or behavioral repertoire. This response set is unquestionably obsessive-compulsive. Other obsessive-compulsive disorders involve unique and ritualistic maladaptive behavioral motoric response sets. For example, obsessive-compulsive handwashers chronically and repetitiously engage in essentially the same anxiety-binding ritual. In the event that the handwasher is forced to change or modify his or her particular maladaptive response set, the experience of anxiety is exacerbated. A primitive exacerbation of anxiety-related conflicts occurs when the alcoholic is forced to temporarily terminate his or her drinking behavior. Obsessive-compulsive disorders originate as a maladaptive means for binding anxiety and eventually result in anxiety in the event that the obsessive-compulsive individual cannot act out his or her ritualistic pathology. Attempting to terminate an obsessive-compulsive disorder results in feelings of vulnerability, anxiety and threat.

For the alcoholic, compulsion refers most specifically to the compulsion to drink. Chronic intoxication, in part, extinguishes feelings of anxiety and other threatening affective states. The orality of the alcoholic (obsessive-compulsive) disorder evolves as a result of feeding disturbances during infancy, narcissistic injury, dependency conflicts that become manifest orally, parental modeling, the relative effectiveness of this symptom choice, and social reinforcement contingencies. Alcoholics drink compulsively to the point of intoxication. After the initiation of drinking, the alcoholic *must* compulsively continue to imbibe. The alcoholic has no control over his or her drinking behavior once alcohol has been ingested. The matters of control and compulsion operate paradoxically in the case of the alcoholic. Alcoholics drink in order to gain control over their interpersonal and intrapersonal worlds. Alcoholics also lose control over both of these domains after drinking. Logically and rationally, the alcoholic would seem to be able to choose whether or not to imbibe. Rationally, the alcoholic would likewise seem to be able to choose how much or how little to drink. In fact, the alcoholic is not able to control these very processes! The drinking alcoholic is controlled by his or her uncontrollable compulsion to drink. The compulsive character structure of the alcoholic is such that therapeutic and rehabilitation measures aimed at teaching the addicted individual to drink socially, drink with control, or drink in moderation generally fail. Controlled-drinking treatment approaches (Armor, Polich and Stambul, 1978) can be extremely psychonoxious because the alcoholic drinks from compulsion. The alcoholic has been involved in such an all-encompassing and extended learning paradigm, with regard to the drinking compulsion, that attempts to return to social drinking are futile and uneconomical. Future advances in the field of alcoholism treatment and rehabilitation may possibly render this position incorrect or invalid.

Saltzman (1968) accurately describes the compulsive dimensions of the alcoholic. He points out that obsessive-compulsive behavior persists in spite of voluntary action and that insight into the illogical and unreasonable nature of the action does not alter behavior. Most alcoholics attempt to quit drinking. They may attend Alcoholics Anonymous sporadically, attempt to become involved with the church, change jobs, divorce, and move in their attempts to quit or control drinking. The compulsion to drink controls the alcoholic. Paradoxically, the alcoholic comprehends his or her addiction dilemma. Insight, self-awareness, and rational thinking seem to have very little bearing upon the ability of the alcoholic to choose not to drink or to control drinking. This is but another paradoxical dimension of the alcoholic process. The alcoholic appears to rationally comprehend the scope and nature of his or her addiction symptomatology and yet he or she (1) paradoxically understands very little with regard to the alcoholic compulsion, (2) pre-consciously and unconsciously rejects his or her alcoholism, and (3) believes that he or she can control future drinking episodes. The alcoholic verbalizes logical reasons for not drinking or controlling drinking in the future. However, the alcoholic is behaviorally unable to follow through on these rational beliefs and decisions.

The alcoholic compulsion is always a highly ritualized affair. Adolescent alcoholics engage in rather stereotypic drinking behaviors. Middle-age alcoholics tend to consistently drink the same alcoholic beverage, frequent the same bars or consistently drink at home, and in numerous other behavioral ways evidence a ritualistic style of drinking. Indeed, each alcoholic eventually manifests a very individualistic pattern of consumption and alcoholism. An alcoholic pattern may include only weekend consumption and intoxication, a yearly "drunk," job termination prior to the initiation of drinking, and obvious depression prior to a drinking episode. The drinking pattern of some alcoholics revolves around drinking "when things are too good." As Goeth stated, "nothing is harder to bear than a series of good days!" The drinking ritual is one very important aspect of the alcoholic compulsion. A patient that I successfully treated had been on an alcoholic binge lasting only two or three weeks, five times in three years. On each of these occasions, the patient's wife had been hospitalized. As soon as the patient's wife had entered the hospital, he initiated drinking, consciously wished and fantasized her death, and "felt free." Psychotherapeutic exploration and resolution of this patient's pattern of alcoholism resulted in long-term total sobriety that included two subsequent hospitalizations of his wife. A key to successful therapeutic work with alcoholics is that of changing, modifying, or extinguishing the patient's drinking ritual.

Rituals and magical thinking are central to the alcoholic adjustment style. A major function of the alcoholic ritual is that of maintaining, or attempting to maintain, complete control over self and the environment. The ritualistic behaviors of the alcoholic originate during early childhood. Fantasies and wishes for the death, destruction and annihilation of parents and parental imagoes are controlled or magically undone vis-à-vis the child's development of a magical, ritualistic procedure for curtailing these forbidden thoughts and impulses. Rituals, ritualistic thought processes, magic, and undoing are all intimately associated with alcoholism and the obsessive-compulsive disorders. These same interpersonal and intrapersonal processes are clearly manifest within the context of religious practices and primitive societies. The alcoholic knows from experience that he or she is powerless over alcohol. Therefore, the alcoholic feels compelled to call upon superhuman powers to overcome his or her weakness or compulsion to drink. The drinking ritual with its magical properties serves this exact purpose. Ritualistic behavior also serves the purpose of binding anxiety.

After having succumbed to his or her compulsion, the alcoholic engages in some form of ritual undoing. The actual pattern of ritual undoing varies considerably from patient to patient and may not fully develop until the alcoholic has progressed into the later stages (Forrest, 1978) of the addiction process. Promising the spouse that he or she will "never touch the stuff again," going to church, "paying penance" through compulsive work, hangovers, and the "after-drunk depression" can all be viewed as undoing rituals. Prototaxically, the alcoholic believes that these undoing activities will magically exonerate the self from the responsibilities associated with various alcohol-facilitated crazy behaviors. The alcoholic is perceived as a truly tolerable member of the human race by his or her family following an alcoholic drinking spree! At this time, the alcoholic is tolerable as a result of his or her ritual undoing activities within the family system. The compulsion to drink, ritualistic behavior specific to the alcoholic compulsion, and the undoing ritual all consist of a series of maladaptive motoric behaviors. All of these transactions serve the purpose of binding anxiety, which serves the ultimate purpose of maintaining control over oneself and the environment. The drinking compulsion and ritual also diverts the attention of the alcoholic and significant others away from the addicted process. These processes facilitate a sense of personal control.

Rage, violence and hostility are associated with chronic alcoholism. The compulsive and ritualistic behaviors of the alcoholic are often a defense against violent acting out. Alcoholics are prone to violent acting out. The alcoholic's most aggressive and destructive acting out is directed against the self. Alcoholics also tend to act out violently against those with whom they are closest. The alcoholic's spouse, children, parents and significant others absorb the brunt of the alcoholic's verbal and physical confrontations (Wegscheider, 1981). Drinking to the point of gross intoxication can serve the purpose of controlling the alcoholic's acting out of violence against others. Alcohol-facilitated passing out, physical immobilization, and impaired rational faculties can bind or defuse the aggression of the alcoholic. However, intoxication can also result in the outcropping of hostile and violent behavior. Some alcoholics appear to be capable of violent acting out against others only following the ingestion of alcohol. Again, the alcoholic drinks compulsively in order to establish control. However, the alcoholic invariably experiences a global loss of control once entrapped in the addiction process.

Characterologically (Reich, 1942 & 1961), the alcoholic is pervasively compulsive. The pathologically compulsive adjustment style of the alcoholic involves an infinite number of more specific or compartmentalized behavioral dynamisms. The sexual life and adjustment of the alcoholic (Forrest, 1982b) is compulsive. Compulsive sexual acting out is central to the overall adjustment style of many male and female alcoholics. Multiple marriages, numerous affairs, and a rather polymorphously perverse sexual life-style characterizes the compulsive sexual adjustment of some alcoholics. By the same token, many alcoholics are pathologically compulsive and rigid in their adherence to fidelity, socially acceptable standards of sexual behaviors or total avoidance of all forms of sexual intimacy. These sexual adjustment styles reflect control and compulsion.

The sexual compulsions of the alcoholic are also utilized to bind or control anxiety. More specifically, the compulsive sexual acting out of the alcoholic can be viewed as a defense against self-system fragmentation and identity defusion. Compulsive sexual acting out is a distorted method for validating gender identity. Power is another clinical issue that is closely linked to the sexual compulsions of the alcoholic. Each sexual escapade or encounter is viewed by the alcoholic as a triumph or victory. Seduction involves the physical domination of another human being. Thus, the seducer controls and exhibits power over the person he or she seduces. For many male and female alcoholics, identity and peer status evolve from the ability to sexually seduce members of the opposite sex. Western culture reinforces these irrational beliefs. Males and females who fail in their social and interpersonal sexual "conquests" are sometimes labeled "faggots" or "bulldykes." Many alcoholics are acutely anxious over these identity-based matters. These processes foster compulsive sexual acting out.

The generalized compulsiveness of the alcoholic is evidenced within the realm of work. Many alcoholics are only satisfied with doing a "perfect" job. This perfectionism, or striving for perfectionism, permeates the self-work needs of the alcoholic regardless of actual position or vocational specialty. Striving for perfection very often provides the alcoholic with ample excuse for further intoxication. In reality, no one is capable of perfection for the duration of a career, let alone on a daily basis! Behaviorally, the alcoholic can be the antithesis of a perfectionist. While striving for perfection and viewing self as a perfectionist, the alcoholic usually fails to approach perfection. Many alcoholics work exceptionally hard and do a truly outstanding job for a few days or weeks. Then, suddenly and for no obvious reason, they quit or develop a "to hell with it all" attitude. The alcoholic invests a great deal of physical and psychological energy in the process of being compulsively perfectionistic. The alcoholic works so hard at this process that he or she invariably sets self up to fail. It is simply impossible for the alcoholic to consistently perform at his or her set standard of performance. This process involves another form of neurotic self-entrapment. The alcoholic tries over and over, in one realm of living after another, to be perfect and yet he or she perpetually programs self for failure vis-à-vis all of these endeavors.

Alcoholics who terminate their alcoholism often become excellent workers and employees. Many recovering alcoholics continue to be compulsive. Sober alcoholics have a tendency to become "workaholics." A successful psychotherapy experience can modify the perfectionistic strivings of the alcoholic and thus enable the individual to persist in a vocation without reengaging in the self-defeating process of being alcoholically perfectionistic.

Time structuring is an issue of the utmost important in the clinical management of alcoholic patients. Compulsively structuring six to twelve hours per day around drinking and drinking transactions is the *modus operandi* of many alcoholics. When the drinking compulsion is extinguished, the alcoholic must learn how to restructure this significant time segment of his or her life. Many alcoholics progress from the drinking compulsion to the work compulsion in order to structure time more effectively. Recovering or recovered alcoholics often make excellent employees, as they need to work extra long hours and they also strive to do a perfect job. Workaholism is also neurotic time structuring.

Disturbing and maladaptive intrapersonal processes are also clearly associated with the alcoholic symptom choice. Issues of power, control and grandiosity are associated with addiction symptomatology. Saltzman (1968) stresses the role of grandiosity in the addictive disorders. Power-fantasy ideation (Forrest, 1978), narcissism, omnipotence, and borderline megalomania are all closely associated with alcoholism. Obsessive intrapersonal ideation is intimately associated with the overdetermined power needs of the alcoholic. The prolonged experience of narcissistic injury dictates the creation of profound internal feelings of inadequacy, inferiority, worthlessness and interpersonal impotence. The self-concept of the alcoholic is made up of these long-term negative interpersonally determined affective experiences. The alcoholic's radical self-concept vacillation into personal grandiosity, narcissism and borderline megalomania serves to defend the self-system from overwhelming feelings of inadequacy, incompetence and inferiority. The ingestion of alcoholic beverages allows the alcoholic to become a superperson in his or her own eyes. Controlling interpersonal and intrapersonal sources of anxiety via the ingestion of alcohol enables the alcoholic to (1) feel that he or she is in control of self, (2) believe that he or she controls significant others, and (3) thereby omnipotently control his or her phenomenal world. Obviously, these processes are neurotic and tenuous. These processes facilitate unrealistic and distorted feelings of grandiosity and omnipotence.

Chronic intoxication and the unreality related to being intoxicated maintains and supports the alcoholic's system of ideational grandiosity. Grandiosity also supports the alcoholic compulsion. Terminating one's addiction and remaining sober for months or years eventually means dealing with reality. Indeed, the experience of long-term sobriety is invariably accompanied by an exacerbation of feelings of inadequacy, helplessness and impotence. However, recovery and getting better involves the growing capacity to accept personal limitations, integrate these limitations, and eventually gain a realistic and rational degree of control over self, others and the phenomenal world. Unconsciously and pre-consciously, the alcoholic has no desire to give up his or her addiction and primitively fears doing so. Early in the recovery process, sobriety is associated with loss of control. Alcoholics also deny the ultimate reality of their being – death. Every alcoholic has symbolically experienced death vis-à-vis intoxication and blackouts on hundreds of occasions.

In short, the compulsive need to be *in control* is central to both the drinking compulsion and the pathologically omnipotent strivings of the alcoholic. By simply ingesting alcohol, the alcoholic feels that he or she can become the controlling center of the universe. The grandiose and omnipotent strivings of the alcoholic include the irrational belief that self is in complete control of all drinking behaviors. As such, the alcoholic always irrationally believes that he or she can quit or control the drinking process. This belief system is non-reality oriented. Perhaps the ultimate paradox of alcoholism is that the drinking alcoholic individual is for all practical purposes completely out of control! The alcoholic always insists that he or she can drink and, likewise, that he or she can stop drinking at any time. In reality, the alcoholic is powerless over alcohol. The alcoholic (Forrest, 1980) is always going to quit drinking tomorrow but tomorrow somehow never seems to come! Every alcoholic drinks in order to control his or her life, yet becoming and being an alcoholic means progressively losing control over oneself and one's life. Sooner or later, the alcoholic compulsion crumbles and the addicted individual is confronted with the reality of just how out of control he or she is. Every alcoholic has a morbid fear of going crazy or becoming insane. Chronic alcoholism is functional insanity!

Matters of power and control are of pathological importance to all of the members of the alcoholic family system. However, it is the alcoholic who compulsively controls the family system. Although the alcoholic family member tends to be perceived as the family victim or scapegoat, he or she tends to rule the family system in an almost iron-fisted fashion. The alcoholic can be a familial dictator. Furthermore, the alcoholic obsessively and compulsively controls the family system. It is of the utmost importance for the alcoholic to be powerful and in control within the context of his or her family system. To be a "zero," impotent and powerless within the confines of the family system, is an extreme threat to the alcoholic. In defense of self, the alcoholic thus compulsively and pathologically seeks to control the family system. Alcoholics compulsively strive to be the "top dog" within the family system (Forrest, 1978; Wegscheider, 1981) and, yet, he or she often controls and dictates from the familial stance of "loser" or victim.

Obsessive ideation (Rachman and Hodgson, 1980) usually accompanies compulsive behavior. Compulsion describes behavior. Obsession refers to ideation. Obsessive thought processes (Cameron, 1963) include rather specific and repetitious ideas, feelings and impulses. Obsessive thoughts or feelings are very often alien to the conscious awareness of the individual. When experientially comprehended, obsessive thoughts are often threatening, strange and anxiety producing. The obsessive thought process is consistent with regard to content and is highly ritualistic in scope. The alcoholic is an obsessive personality type. The obsessive thought process of the alcoholic reinforces and maintains the addiction compulsion.

Obsessive thought processes become manifest during childhood. Most typically, the pathologically obsessive trends of the alcoholic emerge into conscious awareness during early adolescence. The rituals, magic and obsessive-compulsive ideation associated with childhood and adolescence are associated with the mastery of self, significant others, and the world. Obsessive-compulsive patterns of thought and behavior are utilized in order to defensively control interpersonal and intrapersonal processes. Fear that stepping "on a crack will break my mother's back" is one common example of obsessive-compulsive behavior and ideation operational during childhood and latency. This obsessive-compulsive pattern is a ritualistic procedure that serves the purpose of controlling or binding anxiety and guilt associated with the child's actual obsessive thoughts (wishes) regarding the death, injury or murder of a parent or parental imagoes. Furthermore, this procedure is an "undoing" ritual that exonerates the child from negative affects and ideational content relative to ego-alien and threatening thoughts (against) associated with parents or surrogate parents.

It is extremely difficult to ascertain precisely when the alcoholic has become pathologically obsessive. The alcoholic is floridly obsessive. The obsessive pathology of the alcoholic is overt and experienced consciously by the individual prior to becoming addicted and frequently during early adolescence. The obsessive ideation of the alcoholic often follows the development of functionally compulsive behavior patterns. Obsession tends to follow compulsion in the development of alcoholism. Perhaps compulsive symptomatology always accompanies obsessive thought patterns (Rachman and Hodgson, 1980).

Obsessive thought patterns involve matters of personal inadequacy and inferiority. Adolescent alcoholics and adult alcoholics obsessively struggle with feelings of worthlessness (Glasser, 1965 & 1976) and inferiority. Juxtaposed to these negative self-feelings and perceptions are exaggerated feelings of personal narcissism, grandiosity and megalomaniac trends. The alcoholic vacillates between feeling totally inadequate and feeling omnipotent. The fantasy life of the alcoholic is obsessive and bipolar in terms of self-oriented content. At times, the obsessive ruminations of the alcoholic are comprised mainly of narcissistic and omnipotent feelings about self. The alcoholic also obsessively contemplates his or her worthlessness, failures in life, and various other themes having to do with very negative self-perceptions and feelings. Obsessive trends create and maintain the addiction process.

The drinking alcoholic can be described as an obsessive personality. Alcoholics are obsessed with alcohol and drinking. Quite frequently, alcohol per se assumes the focal point of the alcoholic's obsessive style. The following case study demonstrates the obsessive-compulsive character style of the alcoholic:

> CW was a forty-one-year-old retired army master sergeant. He described himself as having been "born an alcoholic." The patient grew up in a rural West Virginia community and enlisted in the United States Army at the age of seventeen. CW reported that his initial experiences with alcohol took place at the age of fourteen, prior to his military enlistment. Even on these occasions, CW drank to the point of intoxication. An important aspect of his eventual decision to make a career of the army was

the fact that he "liked" the drinking associated with military life. He recalled having been preoccupied with liquor bottles during his first years of military enlistment. He enjoyed "browsing around the whiskey stores." During his incipient stage of alcoholism, CW spent considerable time on the weekends "just looking at all those pretty bottles in the Class-Six store."

Following a career of chronic alcoholism that lasted some fifteen years, CW finally achieved sobriety via Alcoholics Anonymous. He has been totally abstinent for thirteen years. The last five years of CW's alcoholic career involved the daily consumption of no less than a fifth of vodka. His obsession with alcohol still involved spending considerable time in military and civilian liquor stores "looking at all those bottles and thinking about how great it would be if I could drink the contents of all of them!" CW verbalized, "I guess all I really lived for during those years was alcohol – to drink and get drunk; all I thought about was alcohol – I even used to sleep with a fifth of vodka in my undershorts – every minute of my life revolved around alcohol in some way; I dreamed about alcohol, I talked about alcohol, and I continuously thought about alcohol."

This brief case study illustrates the degree to which the alcoholic becomes obsessed with alcohol. The obsession with alcohol, drinking, and all other alcohol-related transactions progressively generalizes and eventually encapsulates the alcoholic. Obsessive alcoholic thought content involves matters pertaining to (1) what to drink, (2) how to procure another drink, (3) where to drink, and (4) virtually all other issues related to maintaining an intoxicated state. Obsessive thought processes thus support and actively maintain the addiction process.

A primary concern of the alcoholic is simply that of remaining intoxicated or partially intoxicated. The alcoholic's obsessive thought content and obsessive style serves this purpose. The obsession serves the compulsion. In a reciprocal fashion, the drinking compulsion per se reinforces the alcoholic's obsessive ideation. Specific obsessive ideational thought content evolves with and following compulsive behavior or the development of a specific compulsive ritual. Subsequent to the development of the obsessive-compulsive dynamism, these separate processes (obsession and compulsion) always fuse and tend to generalize.

The alcoholic's obsessive cognitive style is also infused with sexual feelings, impulses and fantasies. The alcoholic obsessively ruminates about two primary sexual issues: (1) heterosexual seduction and (2) homosexuality. Few alcoholics are primarily homosexual (Forrest, 1982b) or overtly bisexual in the sense of sexual object choice. Yet, all alcoholics have chronic questions and doubts about their gender identities. The compulsive sexual acting out and obsessive sexual ruminations of the alcoholic are defensive strategies aimed at protecting gender identity. Some alcoholics do not experience intrusive homosexual thoughts or fantasies. However, many alcoholics experience considerable anxiety over the matter of intrusive homosexual fantasies. Many alcoholics fear possible primary sexual object deviation. Alcoholics are consistently able to deal with and modify intrusive, obsessive sexual ideation within the confines of the therapeutic alliance. Obsessive sexually oriented thought processes evolve as a result of (a) the reality or unreality of these sexual behaviors having been acted out in the past and (b) the internal need to deny or otherwise cope with sexual object deviation conflicts.

The sexually oriented obsessive trends of the alcoholic are primitive and often pre-genital in orientation. Orally and anally oriented themes are very much a part of the obsessive sexual ideation of the alcoholic. Consistently, orally oriented sexual themes are most obvious and accessible to the conscious awareness of the alcoholic. Anal thought process (Forrest, 1982b) tends to be more repressed by the alcoholic. However, some alcoholics are very much aware of their obsessive preoccupation with anality. The obsessive sexual ideation of the alcoholic is not limited to oral and anal content. Many alcoholics are obsessively sexual in a more polymorphous sense.

Paradoxically, the obsessive sexual thought processes of the alcoholic operate to control behavior, ideation and feelings. Obsessive ideation serves to actively reinforce overt behavioral acting out. Obsessive ideation can be utilized to control or eliminate intrusive homosexual obsessive material, obsessive homosexual thoughts and obsessive oral or anal cognitions. In sum, an obsession can be a defense against other obsessions! An obsession is a neurotic style of conflict resolution. These methods of self-regulation are extremely inefficient. Thus, the obsessive-compulsive dynamism frequently breaks down.

It has been indicated that the obsessive-compulsive is characterized by (1) "insight into the illogical and unreasonable nature of the thought or action which does not alter the behavior" (Saltzman, 1968) and (2) "indulging in something forbidden, denying such indulgence or guarding against it, and punishing oneself for having had the impulse to indulge" (Cameron, 1963). This is a description par excellence of the alcoholic. Every alcoholic has some degree of insight into the crazy or irrational nature of his or her drinking compulsion. Yet, this understanding does little, if anything, to alter alcoholic behavior! Every alcoholic indulges in the "forbidden." The alcoholic engages in forbidden behaviors, fantasies and drinking. Alcohol and sexuality are forbidden matters in the case of the alcoholic. All alcoholics are continuously guarding against their compulsion to drink. Sober alcoholics are obsessed with guarding against drinking. Alcoholics also continuously and viciously punish themselves for drinking and having the impulse to drink. The obsessive punishes self.

The alcoholic power fantasy (Forrest, 1978) is an obsession that is closely associated with control, power and anxiety-binding processes. Obsessive power-fantasy ideation is a defense against potentially overwhelming feelings of inadequacy, inferiority and worthlessness. Power-fantasy ideation defends the alcoholic from feeling like a zero. The obsessive style of the actively alcoholic person functions to deny or distort reality. Many alcoholic persons manifest rather specific power-fantasy obsessions. Typically, these individuals have experienced the same obsession for years. Diffuse grandiosity and overtly pathological narcissistic trends are the behavioral correlates of the alcoholic's obsession with power. Every alcoholic wants to be a big shot.

PSYCHOTHERAPEUTIC CONSIDERATIONS

Successful psychotherapy of the alcoholic requires a therapeutic modification of obsessive and compulsive pathology. The therapist needs to initially help the alcoholic terminate his or her drinking compulsion. In the event that the obsessive ideation of the alcoholic is not therapeutically resolved, the alcoholic will continue to drink compulsively. Likewise, the alcoholic compulsion synergizes obsessive ideation, which maintains and reinforces the addiction process.

Effective therapy and rehabilitation efforts (Forrest, 1979a & 1979c) always encompass concrete behavioral change as well as self-dialogue and ideational change. The alcoholic grows and changes vis-à-vis behavioral and cognitive strategies of treatment.

It is most efficacious for the psychotherapist to focus upon the patient's drinking compulsion early in treatment. As the patient establishes sobriety, the therapist begins to explore obsessive thought processes that actively support the drinking compulsion. Alcoholics obsessively and compulsively attend to liquor stores, nightclubs, television beer commercials and other alcohol-related stimuli. The therapist can utilize interpretation, support, thought-stopping and desensitization techniques in order to extinguish alcohol-oriented obsessive ideation and the compulsion to drink. It is also helpful for the counselor to have the alcoholic patient openly discuss the historic and logical consequences that are associated with his or her drinking.

Some alcoholics find it relatively easy to develop a positive addiction (Glasser, 1976; Forrest, 1979b) as an alternative to drinking. Therapists can actively support and reinforce the alcoholic's decision to develop a positive addiction. Positive addictions are obsessive-compulsive in nature. I have found that most alcoholics are in need of psychotherapy, an involvement in Alcoholics Anonymous, or some other form of ongoing intimate human relationship in addition to developing a positive addiction.

After several months of abstinence and work in psychotherapy and Alcoholics Anonymous, most alcoholics find that their compulsion to drink is less intense. These individuals are also less obsessed and less preoccupied with drinking and alcohol. Successful psychotherapeutic treatment results in the fading of obsessive-compulsive mechanisms that have created and maintained the addiction process.

It is also very important for the therapist to help the recovering alcoholic grow and change beyond an obsession and compulsion with sobriety. Sobriety alone is never enough (Forrest, 1978)! Far too many alcoholics simply achieve abstinence and remain rigidly obsessed with staying sober. These persons never grow beyond their compulsion to remain sober. Effective psychotherapeutic interventions foster global flexibility, growth and change.

SUMMARY

This chapter explored the obsessive-compulsive dimensions of the alcoholic adjustment style. Alcoholism is not simply an obsessive-compulsive disorder. However, alcoholism can be viewed as an obsessive-compulsive disorder. The obsessive-compulsive components of chronic alcoholism have only briefly been mentioned in much of the clinical and research literature (Blane, 1968).

The role of infantile and childhood narcissistic need and entitlement deprivation was discussed as a precursor to the development of alcoholism. The obsessive-compulsive dynamism functions to bind anxiety. The alcoholic's compulsion to drink was explored. Control and anxiety-binding processes are central to alcoholism and the obsessive-compulsive disorders.

The alcoholic drinks in a ritualistic fashion. Alcoholism is a ritualistic process that involves magical and primitive patterns of thought. Obsessive ideation can be viewed as a methodology for maintaining control over self, significant others and the phenomenal world. Obsessive ideation and compulsive behavior serve the purpose of maintaining the narcissism, grandiosity, and power needs of the alcoholic. Every alcoholic is literally obsessed with alcohol. Drinking alcoholics continually ruminate about drinking. The alcoholic life-style is constructed around the addiction process.

A brief case study was included to illustrate the obsessive style of the alcoholic. Intrusive homosexual thoughts, pre-genitally oriented sexual ideation, and a generalized preoccupation with sexuality characterize the obsessive thought process of many alcoholics. The alcoholic fits most clinical descriptions of the obsessive-compulsive personality (Rachman and Hodgson, 1980). Characterological compulsivity reinforces and supports the alcoholic's drinking obsession and generalized obsessive style. Obsessive ideation also maintains and reinforces compulsive behavior.

Recovering alcoholics (Forrest, 1983) continue to be pervasively obsessive-compulsive. Following successful psychotherapeutic treatment, the alcoholic continues to be obsessive-compulsive. Many successfully treated alcoholics switch or change addictions and become workaholics. Workaholism is also grist for the psychotherapeutic process. Many alcoholics find and maintain their sobriety via the Alcoholics Anonymous community. The movement into AA can be viewed as a relative change in obsession and compulsion. The recovering alcoholic continues to be compulsively and obsessively concerned about alcohol and alcoholism.

Punctuality, neatness, obsessive rumination, problems with money management, frugality, and even difficulties with constipation and defecation are but a few of the areas that reveal the obsessive-compulsive character structure of the alcoholic. Chain-smoking and the continual ingestion of coffee are rather well-known orally oriented compulsions associated with the behavioral style of the recovering alcoholic. The obsessive-compulsive dynamism involves a fundamental characterological armoring (Reich, 1961) that is relatively refractory to psychotherapeutic amelioration.

Chapter Thirteen

ALCOHOLISM AND FAMILY PSYCHODYNAMICS

INTRODUCTION

LITTLE has been written (Forrest, 1978) about the basic psychodynamics of the alcoholic family system. The literature specific to the alcoholic family system (Ackerman, 1978; Wegscheider, 1981) stresses the point that it is not only the alcoholic within these families that is emotionally disturbed. It has been emphasized that the spouse and children of the alcoholic are also emotionally disturbed. Indeed, the alcoholic family system is disturbed.

The extended experience of growing up within an alcoholic family system may program children to become addicted (Forrest, 1978). Research (Roe, 1945; Wilsnack, 1982) indicates that approximately 50 percent of children growing up within an alcoholic family system eventually develop alcoholism or chemical dependency. There are many theoretical explanations for this reality. The experience of living in an alcoholic family system involves continual reinforcement, learning and overlearning, which fosters the eventual development of alcoholism.

This chapter includes a discussion of the primary psychodynamics of the alcoholic family system and the alcoholic marriage. Many alcoholics have been parented by grandparents, relatives and foster parents. The experience of being parented by alcoholic relatives, grandparents, or foster parents presents a number of relatively unique and significantly different psychodynamic considerations. However, family conflict vis-à-vis narcissistic injury is basic to the etiology of alcoholism and the alcoholic family system. Narcissistic need and entitlement deprivation is the catastrophic common denominator genetic to all alcoholic family systems. Narcissistic injury constitutes the first and foremost family psychodynamic consideration essential to a clinical understanding of the etiology of alcoholism, the alcoholic, and the alcoholic family system.

The alcoholic's family system of origin is (1) decidedly pathological in numerous respects, and (2) often includes a biologic parent or primary parental model who is alcoholic or chemically dependent. This chapter elucidates the global psychopathology of the alcoholic family system involving an alcoholic husband (father) and non-addicted female spouse.

THE ALCOHOLIC FAMILY SYSTEM

The Alcoholic Husband

The alcoholic family system is by no means a singular psychodynamic entity. All alcoholics are relatively unique human beings. Likewise, alcoholic family systems differ and are unique. In spite of the very unique transactional features and psychodynamic characteristics of every family system including a drinking male alcoholic, a number of rather consistent patterns of individual and familial adjustment are associated with these families. The multiplicity of psychodynamic considerations specific to the alcoholic family system spring from both the overt adjustment style and internal psychodynamics of each unique family member within the system. The adjustment style of the alcoholic family system is always a product of the behavioral or transactional characteristics of its individual members. Alcoholic family systems evolve and develop as a function of the overt adjustment styles and internal psychodynamics that each spouse brings to the marital relationship. These factors are associated with mate selection and, thus, the creation of an alcoholic family system.

The male alcoholic has experienced considerable early life narcissistic need and entitlement deprivation. The alcoholic brings to the marriage and family relationship tremendous feelings of inadequacy, inferiority and conflict. Depression, anxiety and diffuse hostility are affects with which the male alcoholic has struggled prior to marriage.

Many male alcoholics harbor a great deal of resentment, anger and rage for women in general (Forrest, 1980c). These conflicts can remain unconscious or pre-conscious in the case of some alcoholics. The hostility and unresolved rage that the male alcoholic harbors for women is associated with the experience of pervasive narcissistic injury involving the mother object. The male alcoholic lives out a pathological repetition compulsion in his relationship with women. He attempts to gain the original mother object's love, concern and narcissistic need and entitlement gratifications through subsequent male-female relationships. However, the male alcoholic unconsciously wishes to destroy women à la lex talionis as a direct result of the mother-object's rejection and narcissistic inadequacy.

These psychodynamic issues are of the utmost relevance to an adequate understanding of the alcoholic marriage. Male alcoholics perpetually act out this repetition compulsion in their encounters with women. Thus, the marital relationship or perhaps numerous marital relationships are destined to involve the same unending struggles and conflicts. It is rational to expect the alcoholic marital relationship to be dysfunctional (Paolino and McCrady, 1977).

Male alcoholics also manifest chronic problems associated with poor impulse control. The alcoholic is an individual of action rather than deliberation and control. Most male alcoholics lack sufficient internal parameters of control. Acting out is basic to the addiction process. Marital discord (Forrest, 1978) is frequently caused by the alcoholic's acting out symptomatology. The acting out rubric involves behaviors pertaining to sexuality, hostility, drinking behavior per se, depression, legal involvement, and vocational difficulties. The alcoholic externalizes and acts out in defense of his precarious self-system. The acting out struggles of the male alcoholic also represent a methodology by which overdetermined dependency conflicts are pathologically resolved.

The male alcoholic neurotically attempts to demonstrate to self and significant others that he is potent, masculine, important, independent, and powerful by acting out. However, the powerful and unresolved dependency conflicts of the male alcoholic predispose him to select a mate who will ultimately meet, tolerate, and reinforce his inordinate dependency needs. The wife of the male alcoholic is a prototypic mother. The addiction process represents an example par excellence of both psychological and physiological dependence. Dependency conflicts (Blane, 1968; Forrest, 1983) incorporate pathological orality, depression and rage.

The male alcoholic is a bipolar person. The identity conflicts of the male alcoholic involve the questions "Who am I?" and "Am I really a male?" The global adjustment style of the alcoholic is in large measure determined by this matter of fragmented identity. Rational and responsible one minute, the alcoholic becomes irresponsible and irrational the next. Classically, this almost Jekyll-Hyde personality change is precipitated and controlled by the ingestion of alcohol. Alcoholics are not individuals of moderation. Alcoholics tend to perceive and behave in an "all or none" fashion. Loving and hating, being depressed or manic, controlling or being controlled, being dependent and independent, and acting out and subsequently experiencing profound guilt are but a few of the bipolar behavioral characteristics of the male alcoholic. Integrated behavior and consistent patterns of living are an impossibility in the absence of a well-developed self-system. In the absence of an adequately consolidated nuclear identity, the alcoholic must constantly vacillate in his world of object relations, fantasy ideation, and perceptions of self and significant others. These processes are markedly neurotic.

The alcoholic has virtually had no chance to be other than a failure. Perceiving oneself as a failure and behaving accordingly is basic to the alcoholic adjustment mode. This process facilitates irresponsible behaviors. The failure oriented experiences of the alcoholic shape and reinforce future failure-oriented transactions, which seem to eventually dictate the creation of a person who can only respond in ways which maintain a failure identity. Most alcoholics have a failure identity. The failure identity can be related to academic matters, material possessions, vocational accomplishments, and marital and family adjustments. Many alcoholics have never learned to be successful, to view themselves as worthwhile and productive. These individuals perceive themselves as failures. Internally and interpersonally, they feel like failures.

The initial living experiences that convey and create a sense of failure in the male alcoholic are potently validated upon entry into the educational system. This situation may not apply to some alcoholics who are bright and have achieved well academically. Unfortunately, the academic experiences of many alcoholics have been disastrous (Ackerman, 1978). Academic failure (Glasser, 1965) synergizes feelings of inferiority, incompetence, and inadequacy. The alcoholic fails academically for a variety of reasons. The emotional climate of the home, parental attitudes regarding the value and worth of a formal education, nutritional factors, alcoholism in the home, and multiple role and work demands placed upon the alcoholic can all contribute to academic failure.

The interpersonal and intrapersonal worlds of the alcoholic involve hurt, rejection, pain and depression. Alcoholics are depressive. Many male alcoholics medicate themselves for endogenous depression (Della-Giustina and Forrest, 1979) vis-à-vis drinking and intoxication. Very often, the alcoholic becomes so adept at self-medication that his depressive trends go unrecognized during courtship and dating. The alcoholic often vehemently denies that he is depressed. The experience of depression may be so well controlled by the drinking process, for such an extended period of time, that it is clinically understandable how the alcoholic can deny and dissociate this particular aspect of his experiential being from conscious awareness. The experience of prolonged narcissistic injury results in the depressive dimensions of the alcoholic character structure.

Anxiety constitutes another salient dimension of the alcoholic character structure. The deprivation experiences of the alcoholic create profound feelings of uncertainty, ambiguity, and a lack of self-structure. The alcoholic lives in a world that is filled with chronic uncertainty, apprehension, a lack of meaningful structure and anxiety. These exigencies facilitate the experience of anxiety. Depression and anxiety are usually coexisting affective states.

Alcoholism is a defense against anxiety. The alcoholic uses alcohol as a defense against depression and anxiety. Eventually, the addiction process becomes a primary source of anxiety and depression. The paradoxical nature of the addiction process (Pursch, 1979) is such that the initial relief and gain facilitated via the ingestion of alcohol eventually breaks down and actually precipitates anxiety, depression and decompensation. This process is extremely difficult for most addicted individuals to comprehend.

The alcoholic male is angry, resentful and often enraged. Such individuals are covertly, if not overtly, angry at the world. In many cases, they are determined to get even with significant others. This process is logical. Alcoholics do not *choose* (Forrest, 1980a) to be unloved, rejected, unwanted, and physically and emotionally abused. Early life narcissistic injury is the direct result of parental or surrogate parental psychopathology. Intense and prolonged narcissistic injury results in an internal frame of reference and behavioral style that is steeped in rage and anger. The interpersonal and attitudinal style of the alcoholic always encompasses a pathologic degree of resentment. Some alcoholics act out their aggressive or hostile feelings. Most alcoholics do not lash out at others in the form of overt attacks or assaults. The alcoholic more typically tends to stew in his or her own rage. Alcoholics are neurotically encapsulated in their own anger, resentment, and hostility. Alcoholics also discharge these powerful negative affects against the self. The net result of this general process is a highly masochistic relationship with self. Headaches, gastrointestinal problems, and other psychosomatic symptoms are associated with the sadomasochistic conflicts of all alcoholics (Evans, 1980).

The sadomasochistic trends of the alcoholic have a tremendous bearing and impact upon the marital relationship. Indeed, the developmental process of alcoholism is singularly one of becoming increasingly sadomasochistic. A basic characterological prerequisite for engagement in the addiction process may be a high pain threshold. The alcoholic has been forced to endure a great deal of physical and emotional pain. Alcoholics also learn to inflict pain upon those closest to them. The alcoholic's sadomasochistic style of behavior involves pain management. The non-alcoholic spouse is very often baffled by the sadomasochistic behaviors of the alcoholic. However, the non-addicted spouse has also been programmed to live and behave within this particular form of interpersonal milieu. Many alcoholic males become so punitive, assaultive, and vindictive that the wife and children can simply no longer tolerate his presence. The guilt and remorse experienced by the alcoholic as a direct result of his sadistic transactions within the family system reinforces his masochistic needs to punish self and precipitates further drinking and intoxication.

This discussion of the male alcoholic has focused upon personality dysfunction and psychopathology. Becoming and being an alcoholic is an extremely unpleasant and painful experience. Presentations of the alcoholic as a happy-go-lucky, carefree, fun-loving individual (Forrest, 1980) are totally unrealistic. The features of the alcoholic discussed thus far are difficult to accept and share with significant others and self. This is why the alcoholic vehemently denies (Clinebell, 1956; Blane, 1968) that he is addicted to alcohol.

The male alcoholic brings to the marital relationship and family system a tremendous ability and need to deny reality factors and interpersonal feedback specific to himself. As the addicted individual becomes increasingly dependent upon alcohol, he congruously becomes less other-person oriented. Many alcoholics utilize alcohol and intoxication in order to meet the demands of interpersonal intimacy that are demanded in courtship and marriage.

This account of the pre-marital psychological makeup of the male alcoholic is truncated and far from complete. Yet, the psychodynamic issues and characterological features that have been discussed are very much a part of what, in reality, the male alcoholic brings to the marriage relationship. A number of the significant psychodynamic issues and experiential realities that pertain to the wife of the male alcoholic will now be discussed.

The Non-alcoholic Wife

The woman who marries an alcoholic does so as a result of other than merely chance or random factors. The woman who chooses an alcoholic spouse seems to be predisposed to this choice. Predisposition is a function of prior experiences in living. Relatively unique experiences in living predispose or somehow make it easier for certain women to select an alcoholic spouse.

The wives of alcoholics are consistently the products of family constellations involving severe narcissistic need and entitlement deprivation. The wife of the alcoholic has experienced consistent early life narcissistic injury. However, she has not usually experienced the same quantity and intensity of emotional and physical deprivation as her husband. Many of these women report that they left home or ran away at an early age in order to escape the physical and emotional abuse of parents. Unfortunately, a primary methodology for escaping from a pathological family system often involves getting married. The wife who had fled from her primary family system to the marriage relationship soon finds that her own emotional difficulties and unresolved conflicts very quickly begin to neurotically determine the transactions and behaviors of her marital relationship. The wives of many alcoholics have experienced a good deal of rejection, hurt and pain at the hands of their parents. Her parents have been quite primitive. They may have "done all they could" in terms of parenting and child care. However, their parenting abilities and skills were limited or parataxic.

The wife of the alcoholic tends to have had a marginal relationship with her father. Frequently, these women indicate that their fathers were extremely punitive and physically abusive toward them during childhood and adolescence. Both parents have covertly conspired to deny the daughter her femininity and freedom to develop as a person during adolescence. These wives have had fathers who were quite concerned about their dating and sexual behaviors. A great deal of emphasis has been placed upon *not* acting out sexually during adolescence. Verbal messages to this effect tend to be communicated by the father in such primitive terms as, "Don't come home to us if you get knocked up." These messages synergize the acting out and rebellious trends of the daughter. The father actually drives the daughter away from him and facilitates her sexual acting out vis-à-vis these transactions.

Some of the wives of alcoholic husbands have had relationships with their fathers that were clearly erotic in nature (Forrest,

1982b). The father who treats his daughter brutally and is physically abusive often does so in order to control or block his own erotic and sexual desires to act out with the daughter. Overt and perhaps extended father-daughter incest occurs in some of these family systems (Wegscheider, 1981; Forrest, 1982b). This psychodynamic issue should always by investigated in the case of early adolescent girls who run away from home. Incestuous father-daughter relationships teach the daughter many pathologic attitudes and beliefs about males in general. The alcoholic male cannot understand or comprehend the opposite sex. The wife of the alcoholic also feels as though she lives in a world that is composed of an inordinate number of strange, incomprehensible, opposite-sexed persons!

The matters of not trusting, feeling inferior, and even fearing males and yet somehow paradoxically remaining markedly dependent upon them is a very significant characterological feature of women who marry alcoholics. These dynamics explain or relate to the marital persistence of the wives of most alcoholics. The wives of alcoholics (Milt, 1969; Forrest, 1980) will tolerate years of verbal and physical abuse at the hands of their alcoholic spouse. Questions of self-worth, feelings of inferiority and inadequacy, and unresolved identity conflicts dictate that these women somehow tolerate the alcoholic behaviors of their husbands. Issues such as these form the basis for dependency. The wife is continually programmed or reinforced into more pathologically dependent marital roles as the marriage progresses. The alcoholic consciously activates and reinforces the dependent behaviors of his wife. This tactic allows him to feel potent, powerful and in control of his wife. As she becomes progressively more dependent, he feels free to drink, remain intoxicated, and act out.

Many of the wives of alcoholics (Forrest, 1978; Wegscheider, 1981) are chronically depressed. The experience of narcissistic need and entitlement deprivation clearly precipitates significant depression in these women. A negative self-concept, low self-esteem, and feelings of inadequacy predispose the wife of the alcoholic to admire and identify with his superficial grandiosity, self-assurance, and an "I can take on the world" attitude. By identifying with him, she can symbiotically transcend her own feelings of inferiority, inadequacy and depression. Living with chronic depression makes living with an alcoholic more tolerable! Marked preoccupation with one's own problems and encapsulation within one's private world of pathology provides a viable form of insulation from the emotional difficulties of significant others. This factor is related to the denial and lack of awareness upon the part of wives that their husbands are alcoholic. Existing in an interpersonal and intrapersonal morass of nearly overwhelming pathology, to include the alcohol addiction of a husband, "numbs" the wife's feelings and awareness. Life for her is an experiential hell. Coping and merely existing are major struggles. Most wives of alcoholics become significantly depressed in the marital relationship (Paolino and McCrady, 1977).

Some of the women who marry an alcoholic have personal difficulties associated with acting out. Problems with authority, with the police, parents, school teachers, administrators, and the church are basic to their *modus operandi*. Running away from home, sexual promiscuity (often with older males), heavy drinking, drug abuse, immaturity, irresponsibility, and poor impulse control relating to many other areas of living characterizes these select wives. Many of these women have been married three or four times. Typically, their previous husbands were floridly alcoholic or problem drinkers. The treatment prognosis in these cases is quite poor. Wives of this type overtly reinforce and synergize the alcoholism of their husbands.

These women are easily identified. Their conflicts are readily apparent. These wives invariably (Pursch, 1979) drink with their husbands. While such women may eventually lose control over their patterns of consumption and also be identified as alcoholic, more typically they remain heavy drinkers who somehow manage to retain some degree of control over their drinking behavior and thus never become labeled alcoholic. Most of these marriages involve a great deal of physical abuse and violence and can be extremely sadomasochistic. These relationships can involve spouse murder. Sexual promiscuity and acting out upon the part of one or both partners often precipitates violent assaults. The wife of the alcoholic also acts out symbiotically vis-à-vis the husband's alcoholism. The wife learns to disdain and abhor much of the behavior of her alcoholic husband. However, pre-consciously and unconsciously she identifies with his defiance of all authority and his ability to say "to hell with it." Thus, the wife symbolically derives a great deal of enjoyment and gain from many of her husband's alcohol-facilitated behaviors. She also derives a great deal of secondary gain from assuming family responsibilities. She is the family martyr. Significant others often perceive her as the good spouse or strong family member who somehow manages to keep the family intact.

The wives of most alcoholics are extremely dependent. The inordinate dependency needs of the wives of alcoholics evolve from their experiences within their families of origin. Many of these women have grown up within a family constellation in which the father was domineering, controlling and aggressive. The wife of the alcoholic appears to have modeled the passive, dependent, withdrawing behaviors of her mother. Their fathers have been tyrannical, domineering, threatening, and overwhelmingly assertive. This extended experience in family living combines dependency with psychological pain, abuse and hurt. Women who emerge from these family milieus usually assert that the last male they would ever marry would be one like their father! Yet, many of them marry an exact or very similar emotional and behavioral replica of their father. These women have spent the majority of their lives learning to live with their father, which predisposes them to seek his prototype in a husband. Their interpersonal skills and adjustments are such that they simply do not know how to relate to males that are essentially better adjusted and more integrated than their father.

The wife of the alcoholic is frequently obese or manifests marked problems in the area of weight control. The majority of these women are overweight. A small percentage of these wives are ectomorphic in body somatotype. Depression, severe anxiety, and other psychophysiological variables can cause significant problems in the area of weight control. The large, big-breasted, overweight female primitively symbolizes dependency and security for the alcoholic. These dynamics in mate selection are related to the pathological dependency needs and oral fixation of the alcoholic and his spouse.

The shy, withdrawn, and introverted ectomorphic wife acts out this same pathological dependency vis-à-vis her body somatotype. She tends to cling to the alcoholic. The more ectomorphic wives of alcoholics can be orally oriented. However, they are more commonly anally fixated or manifest an anal type of characterological structure. The wife brings these overdetermined dependency needs with her to the marital relationship.

Many wives of alcoholics have been parented by an alcoholic father. Research data (Ackerman, 1978; Wegscheider, 1981; Wilsnack, 1982) indicates that 40 to 50 percent of women who marry an alcoholic or heavy drinker have been parented by an alcoholic father. The unique experience of living with an alcoholic father or stepfather for a period of some 15 to 20 years involves consistent teaching, learning and reinforcement with an alcoholic male! This is a simple and yet extremely recondite matter. These women have continually learned and overlearned how to live with a male alcoholic. In spite of the emotional turmoil, pain, hurt, and all of the other negative affective components specific to this experience, the daughter of the alcoholic learns to live with an alcoholic male in one of the most intense and extended of human encounters. These women have not learned how to live and interact with a non-alcoholic male. The experience of learning how to live with a male alcoholic (father or surrogate father) is such a powerful and total experience in living that nearly 50 percent of the women who endure this initial male-female relationship select a marital partner who is alcoholic or chemically dependent.

In the case of the majority of women who have grown up with an alcoholic father and subsequently married an alcoholic, the process of daily living becomes more than a caricature of the past. These women assume the roles and life-style of their mothers. Daughters of alcoholics who marry alcoholics recreate the family system from which they evolved. This familial process is a repetition compulsion.

The programming that takes place within these particular family milieus is contingent upon the behavioral prerequisites and role behaviors that the wife brings with her to the marital relationship. Each additional family member exerts a multifaceted impact upon the emotional style and equilibrium of the alcoholic family system.

Unconsciously and pre-consciously, these women attempt to ritually or magically undo the pathology of their family pasts. Women who have been parented by an alcoholic father and subsequently marry an alcoholic wish to resolve their own father's alcoholism and other psychopathology. Primitively, these women believe this process can be accomplished by being the wife that their mother never was able to be. In choosing an alcoholic husband, the daughter of an alcoholic (Forrest, 1978) attempts to both rescue her own father and simultaneously compensate for her mother's pathology and inability to effect this same successful rescue effort. She demonstrates that she is better integrated and more effective as a woman and wife than her own mother vis-à-vis these processes. These women also primitively believe that their mothers caused their father's alcoholism. The daughter of the alcoholic harbors a great deal of rage relative to her mother's paradoxical impotence or powerlessness within the family system. She attempts to ritually undo these feelings via her marriage to an alcoholic.

These processes involving mate selection are ineffective and maladaptive in a repetition-compulsion fashion. Many women act out this constellation of psychodynamic processes for the duration of their lives. The basic psychodynamics of the alcoholic family system will now be discussed.

PSYCHODYNAMICS OF THE ALCOHOLIC FAMILY SYSTEM

At the point of treatment engagement, the alcoholic family system is stable, if not solidified, with regard to intrafamilial roles, behavior, affect, and transactional style. The alcoholic is usually identified as the family victim and/or scapegoat. The behaviors and role transactions specific to victimizing and scapegoating are essentially the same. The common denominator basic to both of these roles involves being consistently undermined by significant others and continually experiencing threat and anxiety in these relationships. The alcoholic appears to be the chronic "underdog" within the family system. As a result of being a victim or scapegoat, the alcoholic is never right. He is always subject to suspect, his decisions must always be somehow inadequate if not wrong, and his motives must be questioned. The alcoholic family member (scapegoat) affords other family members (Forrest, 1978) various sources of psychological gain. The spouse and children of the alcoholic learn quite early in family life that is very easy to project blame, anger and frustration upon the alcoholic.

Within the contexts of courtship, marriage and parenting, many of the alcoholic's alcohol-related and facilitated decisions, judgments and other problem-solving strategies are inadequate and inappropriate. Thus, the wife and children learn that the alcoholic is an excellent target for many of their personal feelings of frustration, anger, failure and inadequacy. Rather than acknowledging and relating these very negative realities associated with their own behavior and relationships with self and significant others, it is easier for the spouse and children to blame or scapegoat the alcoholic. If the wife has experienced chronic feelings of inadequacy, inferiority, and a personal sense of worthlessness, an alcoholic husband can be an excellent, although neurotic, solution for these negative self-perceptions and feelings. At least she can be "one up" within the context of marriage! The gain afforded the wife via this specific psychodynamic issue eventually facilitates her ability to permit the husband to remain intoxicated. The wife may unconsciously desire that the husband remain intoxicated and covertly reinforce his alcoholism for these very reasons. The wife simultaneously dislikes and rejects her husband's chemical dependence. The marital relationship progressively deteriorates. Some wives will initiate pathological patterns of alcohol consumption (Pursch, 1979) as a means of coping with severe marital and familial conflicts. The majority of women who attempt this solution to marital and family dissonance soon give up or terminate their pathological drinking behavior. They discover that they cannot tolerate the physical and psychological effects of alcohol abuse.

The wives of all alcoholics derive secondary gain from their husband's alcoholism. However, when the wife neurotically derives gain from the husband's alcohol addiction, she also in a concomitant fashion experiences significant guilt and emotional conflict as a result of this process. She experiences considerable anxiety, depression and hostility relative to her husband's alcoholism. However, guilt dictates that she remain within the alcoholic family system. Guilt also actively synergizes her feelings of anxiety, depression and rage. These affects and transactions maintain the homeostatic emotional equilibrium (Haley, 1971) of the alcoholic family system. Pervasive feelings of guilt and the distorted belief that she is somehow responsible for her husband's becoming addicted are basic to the psychopathology of the wife. Consciously, the wife of the alcoholic knows that she has victimized and scapegoated her husband on countless occasions. This conscious realization primitively reinforces her belief that she is responsible for her husband's becoming an alcoholic. In reality, the wife is in no way responsible for her husband's alcoholism.

The children in an alcoholic system (Forrest, 1978; Wegscheider, 1981) are also actively engaged in the familial process of victimizing and scapegoating the alcoholic. Children in alcoholic family systems learn that their addicted father is essentially the "bad guy." In part, this takes place simply as a result of the behavioral style of the alcoholic. Children learn that their alcoholic father is unpredictable. He can also be hostile, angry and possibly violent. He often says mean and hurtful things to them. His promises are never fulfilled. In short, the children of an alcoholic father learn that their father is frequently unreliable and irresponsible. They know that he is a direct source of emotional turmoil, pain and conflict within their lives and the family system.

During early adolescence, the sons and daughters of alcoholics begin to interact and cognitively relate to their alcoholic fathers in a different fashion. Teenagers begin to cognitively and affectively understand familial transactions. The alcoholic can no longer "buy off" his children. He can no longer compensate for his lack of genuine love, care and concern for the children with glib and superficial verbalizations or money. Providing material or monetary symbols for love does not work.

It is not atypical for the mother to begin to overtly encourage her teenagers to side with her in victimizing and scapegoating the father. The wife of the alcoholic encourages the children to scapegoat the alcoholic. The children may have previously supported the mother in her scapegoating transactions. As adolescents, they begin to consciously recognize flaws and parataxic warp in the mother's behavioral style. Many teenagers begin to confront, attack and rebel against their mothers. They also begin to side with their fathers in familial battles. Needless to say, this process is disconcerting for the wife of the alcoholic. She feels as though her own children have turned on her. This process is very confusing for the adolescent entrapped within an alcoholic family system. As children, it was relatively easy to side with the mother in family struggles and conflicts. Teenagers in these family systems vacillate in their parental alliances. At one moment, they may feel strongly that their mother is right. Shortly thereafter, they feel just as strongly about the behavior of their alcoholic father and thus identify with him in his struggles against their mother.

These family systems place a great deal of ambiguity and stress on children. However, many children learn to cope relatively well within these families. In fact, some are better integrated, responsible and more mature than either parent. This appears to be generally true with regard to 20 to 25 percent of children living in an alcoholic familial system (Ackerman, 1978). Unfortunately, the vast majority of children growing up within an alcoholic family system find the experiences of family living to be extremely anxiety producing. These persons feel that they are always in the middle. Many are depressed and guilty. Living in an alcoholic family system for twelve to eighteen years involves consistent learning and conditioning experiences that are maladaptive. Many of these adolescent family members are out of control. Acting out is basic to the symptom structure of many adolescents who have been parented within an alcoholic family system.

The specific issue of becoming consciously aware of personal roles in the processes of scapegoating and victimizing the alcoholic father precipitates much of the guilt and depression that is experienced by children in alcoholic family systems. During adolescence, the children in alcoholic families meaningfully comprehend their unique family living experiences. At this time, the adolescent begins to deal with powerful feelings of guilt and depression associated with having been an integral part of the process of victimizing the addicted father. The many difficulties between the mother and father become more understandable.

Adolescents in alcoholic family systems also realize and comprehend just how disturbed and pathological life is within their particular family constellation. The adolescent consciously resents being trapped within an alcoholic family system. These children begin to act out during adolescence. The acting out pathology of the children in alcoholic families encompasses the fusion of the lust dynamism (sexuality) and aggression or rage. These adolescents act out against their parents and authority figures. The adolescent family member may begin to actively identify with the alcoholic father. Outright rejection of the mother, verbal and perhaps even physical assaults against her, and other more sophisticated psychological games or maneuvers to undermine her controlling or domineering familial roles are frequently a part of the behavioral repertoire of adolescents in alcoholic family systems.

These processes involve sons and daughters engaged in an alcoholic family system. The adolescent daughter questions and eventually rejects her mother for her inability to disengage from the alcoholic father. She also understands her mother's role in victimizing the alcoholic father. Many of these adolescent daughters verbalize, "The last person I would ever marry would be an alcoholic, like my father." She vehemently rejects her mother and the type of relationship her mother has maintained with her father. Adolescent sons are unable to establish any form of close, meaningful relationship with their fathers. Although the son wishes to establish a close relationship with his father, he also ambivalently fears and disdains his father. The father and son can never establish a meaningful interpersonal relationship in the presence of the father's active alcoholism.

The adolescent daughter in an alcoholic family system may run away from home and become pathologically promiscuous. Sons often attempt to physically and verbally challenge both parents. Physical violence, confrontations, and assault against the father may also be acted out by the adolescent son. Some sons leave home prematurely. When the son leaves home, this specific act tends to be premeditated and expected by the family. When the teenage daughter exits from the family system, this event tends to be impulsive and often associated with marriage, pregnancy, or some other form of overt sexual acting out. She dramatically escapes from the family! The direct or connotative sexual issues that are related to the daughter's family exit are repressed and denied within the family system. However, these issues are verbalized and dealt with in a multiplicity of pathological ways within the context of acute familial crisis situations. At these junctures, the adolescent daughter is openly referred to as "a damned whore" or a "no good" by the alcoholic father or other family members.

THE "DOUBLE BIND" AND THE ALCOHOLIC FAMILY SYSTEM

The double bind is one of the major concepts in family pathology and family therapy. There are three essential ingredients in the double-bind situation (Bateson et al., 1956):

> The individual is involved in an intense relationship; that is, a relationship in which he feels it is vitally important that he discriminate accurately what sort of message is being communicated so that he can respond appropriately. . . ; (secondly), the individual is caught in a situation in which the other person in the relationship is expressing two orders of messages and one of these denies the other. . . ; (thirdly), the individual is unable to comment on the messages being expressed to correct his discrimination of what order of message to respond to (i.e. he cannot make a metacommunicative statement) (p. 254).

The double-bind concept was initially proposed as a primary casual factor in the etiology of schizophrenia. A wealth of clinical articles and research publications have been devoted to this issue. The roles of victim and scapegoat involve the double bind. Once the alcoholic or any other member in the alcoholic family system becomes identified as the family scapegoat, he or she is continually the target of double-binding communications and transactions. Many of the double-bind-oriented transactions within an alcoholic family system encompass the alcoholic. Verbally and behaviorally, the non-alcoholic spouse and children appear to want the alcoholic to be sober and recover. However, the spouse and children often suggest or reinforce further intoxication upon the part of the alcoholic. The wife may purchase liquor for her husband. The spouse of the alcoholic may actively suggest that he should be able to drink or control his drinking. Some spouses verbalize that the alcoholic is easier to live with while intoxicated. Messages of this nature represent the example par excellence of a double bind.

The alcoholic family system can be characterized as homeostatically double-binding. The double-binding process differs significantly between alcoholic family systems and schizophrenic family systems (Haley, 1971). Consistent role reversals and "role slippage" characterizes the double-binding process within alcoholic family systems. Communication (Haley, 1963) and overt behavioral transactions within the alcoholic family system are homeostatic with regard to the *chronic* presence of the double bind. Although double binding is one of the fundamentals of behaving and communicating within the alcoholic family system, the matter of *who* is being placed in the actual double-bind situation is inconsistent. This is in contrast to family systems that include a schizophrenic child or adolescent (Zuk, 1967). In schizophrenic family systems, it is the "unique" family member who is consistently and chronically placed in the double-bind situation. Double binding in schizophrenic familial systems seems to focus upon one primary family member. This matter is of the utmost clinical significance.

It appears that the alcoholic is the primary recipient of the double bind within the alcoholic family system. In actuality, this is not the case. Every member of the alcoholic family system is involved in role reversals or "role slippage" into and out of the double-bind situation.

Parents in alcoholic family systems conjointly double bind and scapegoat their children (Satir, 1964). The wife of the alcoholic may consistently attempt to ally the children with her in her attempts to victimize the husband. The alcoholic may pathognomically attempt this same process. It is even more pathological when the alcoholic and his spouse both scapegoat or double bind the children. These issues have received little attention in the clinical and research alcoholism literature (Emrick, 1980). Fortunately, children in the alcoholic family system are only subjected to tolerable "doses" of double binding. The role slippage in these families prevents each family member from becoming floridly psychotic or schizophrenic. The scapegoating, victimizing, and double-binding transactions that homeostatically take place in the alcoholic family system are extremely psychonoxious. However, the processes of role reversal and role slippage that occur in these family systems are paradoxically adaptive and neurotic. This transactional process serves to deter the development of primary thought-disorder pathology among family members trapped within alcoholic family constellations. The role-reversal process also reinforces persistence within the alcoholic family system. The social learning, conditioning and reinforcement specific to living and behaving within these family systems dictate familial persistence.

Another major psychodynamic component of the alcoholic family system involves the inability of the *wife* to maintain a sufficient degree of identity differentiation (Bowen, 1978). The wife of the alcoholic tends to create and maintain her identity within these family systems vis-à-vis her symbiotic relationship with (1) her husband and (2) the children. This process is normal within the context of marriage and family living. However, wives of alcoholics symbiotically and pathologically fuse their identities with their husbands and children. The wife's "good" identity tends to evolve from her relationship with the children during the later stages of the addiction process. Early in the addiction process, she secures and maintains a sense of goodness and adequacy via the marital relationship. The non-addicted spouse solidifies a functional identity within the context of the alcoholic marriage and family system. Yet, the wife's consolidated identity becomes increasingly pathologic and fused with the alcoholic as the addiction process unfolds. The non-addicted spouse's identity is precarious.

As the husband begins to alcoholically decompensate, she also symbiotically becomes progressively more dysfunctional. Covering up, lying, paying bills, assuming generalized responsibility, social withdrawal and familial isolation, pathological drinking, sexual acting out, and emotional and physical abuse of the children are indications of the wife's symbiotic fusion with the alcoholic. The wife gives up her more healthy or "good" identity introjects and assumes a familial and personal identity that becomes increasingly pathological and dysfunctional. The processes of symbiosis and decompensation also include the children. Children involved in alcoholic family systems become pathologically fused with the alcoholic father and the addiction process. These processes neurotically shape and determine the marital and family adjustments of children of alcoholics.

EGO FUSION AND THE ALCOHOLIC FAMILY SYSTEM

Regression and ego-fusion dynamics enmesh every member of the alcoholic family system. Alcoholic family members often appear to be inadequate, powerless, impotent, and overwhelmed within the family system. In reality, the alcoholic is an inconsistent family dictator! In many respects, the non-addicted spouse and children allow themselves to be controlled. Yet, the alcoholic does shape and determine patterns of familial communication, emoting, behaving and interacting.

The addiction process also shapes and determines the global adjustment style of individual family members as well as the family system (Forrest, 1980). The alcoholic facilitates familial isolation. As these pathological transactions evolve within the alcoholic family system, the non-addicted family members give up their individuality, emotional well-being, and separate identities. An ego fusion (Forrest, 1978) takes place within the alcoholic family system. Non-addicted family members fuse their identities with the alcoholic and the addiction process. Non-addicted family members become emotionally and behaviorally fused with the alcoholic. On some occasions, family members angrily attack and confront the alcoholic. Yet, they also support him, feel sorry for him, and may even drive to the liquor store in order to protect him from the dangers of drinking and driving. Eventually, the family is "stuck" or encapsulated in the bottle. This familial process is regressive.

Many spouses of alcoholics are pathologically dependent, depressive, and orally fixated prior to marriage. Nonetheless, the spouse of the alcoholic experiences gross behavioral regression within the confines of the alcoholic marriage and family system. It is also difficult for the children in these family systems to developmentally, emotionally, and cognitively transcend the alcoholic's global level of adjustment. The processes of ego fusion and regression within these family systems are often so total and all encompassing that at least 40 percent of the children in these families eventually become addicted. The ego fusion and symbiotic ties within the alcoholic family system do not singularly precipitate the chemical dependencies of the children that evolve within these family constellations. However, these are basic psychodynamic components in alcoholism and the alcoholic family system.

The alcoholic family system establishes a family ego (Forrest, 1978) or nuclear family identity. This pathologic and symbiotic family ego precludes the development and establishment of healthy, individual identities upon the part of the individuals that live in an alcoholic family system. Alcoholic family systems have a homeostatic emotional climate that is pathologic. The blurring of individual ego boundaries within these family systems creates a symbiotic familial ego fusion that is a defense against more primitive, regressive patterns of individual adjustment. When family members leave these family systems, they consistently experience intense anxiety and personality disorganization. They also consciously and pre-consciously attempt to recreate replicas of their original family system. The recreation of a similar family system establishes stability, binds anxiety, and precipitates personality integration for members of alcoholic family systems. A few individuals who escape from alcoholic family systems consciously work at not creating a family system that is akin to their original family. Regression or movement in the direction of effecting an alcoholic family system are ever-present realities for all individuals who have grown up within an alcoholic family system.

VIOLENCE AND THE ALCOHOLIC FAMILY SYSTEM

Alcoholism is a disorder of anger and violence. The life-style of the alcoholic is steeped in violence. Violence is also an ever-present ingredient in the alcoholic family system. Everyone involved with the alcoholic (Forrest, 1980) becomes entrapped in the violence of the addiction process. The violence of alcoholism is reflected via numerous demographic variables. Automobile deaths and accidents, arrests and legal involvements, divorce and marital discord, child abuse and neglect, job losses and poor job performance, rape, suicide, self-inflicted physical and medical problems, and emotional disorders represent but a few of the violent products of alcoholism and problem drinking.

The violence of alcoholism is often focused within the context of the alcoholic family system. As a result of the initial pathology of the mother-son relationship, the male alcoholic is destined to experience chronic and marked difficulties within the realm of male-female relationships. This reality becomes floridly manifest within the confines of the marital relationship. Male alcoholics experience multiple marriages, numerous affairs, or perhaps gross discord within the context of an apparently successful marriage encompassing thirty or forty years. The chronic male-female-oriented struggles and battles of the male alcoholic represent his talion-oriented attempts to retaliate and "get even" with his mother. The mother object has narcissistically injured the alcoholic, and his adjustment style with women is congruous with the talion principle. These struggles also reflect the alcoholic's attempt to resolve or work through these very powerful conflicts and struggles having to do with women and male-female relationships. Some alcoholics verbalize that they "can't get along with women." These verbal messages are usually quite glib and fail to take into account his very real unconscious and pre-conscious concerns about his inadequacies and conflicts in this specific realm.

The male alcoholic eventually actualizes one of three possible alternatives within the context of relationships with women and marriage: (1) he remains single and avoids the initimacy of a marital relationship; (2) he marries, perhaps to remarry any number of times (but within the context of these alternatives he maintains a series of extramarital affairs), and (3) he persists in one marital relationship without being involved in extramarital affairs or promiscuous sexual acting out. This third possibility rarely occurs. Alcoholics that fall in the final category are usually better adjusted than those addicted individuals who fall within the first two categories. All of these solutions for the alcoholic's male-female dilemmas are destined to fail.

Unconsciously or pre-consciously, the male alcoholic is determined to destroy or annihilate the female object. In choice number one, the alcoholic symbolically destroys all women by denying their very existence. He denies women entry into his intimate interpersonal world. Thus, they cannot hurt or destroy him, as he will not even admit their being! Choice two involves a more concrete attack against women. Sexual exploitation, destruction, retaliation, and attempted resolution of this pathology are central ingredients in the processes of divorce and extramarital sexual acting out. Choice three is indicative of a better-integrated character structure. However, this form of marital adjustment is frequently sadomasochistic (Schad-Somers, 1982). Unconsciously, the alcoholic persists in marriage in an attempt to win over the spouse in a life-death-oriented fashion. In these marriages, the alcoholic male quite frequently punishes his wife (mother substitute) for the entirety of the marriage in retaliation for his mother's primary role in early life narcissistic injury. At the same time, the alcoholic masochistically punishes himself (Forrest, 1983) for somehow being so unlovable, inadequate, and worthless initially within the context of mother-self, father-self, and familial-self relationships. These processes include the unconscious or preconscious attempt and wish to work through and resolve these dimensions of characterological warp. These processes are also associated with much of the alcoholic's violence and violent acting out within the family system. Many alcoholics are consistently angry and violent toward their wives. Ultimately, it is very difficult for the alcoholic male to live effectively with a wife whom he wishes to murder. The unconscious and pre-conscious talion needs of the alcoholic are also fused with the needs to love and be loved. These processes dictate rather radical affective, behavioral, and cognitive vacillation within the marital relationship.

The wife of the alcoholic also experiences considerable difficulty with the management of anger, resentment, and oral rage within the marital relationship. Quite typically, the wife of the alcoholic chooses an addicted husband as a result of unconscious and preconscious, rescue-oriented needs. Many of these women were parented by an alcoholic father. As mentioned earlier, these women also wish to magically undo their mother's inadequacy and ineffectual parenting. In short, the wife of the alcoholic attempts to take her mother's place within the alcoholic family system so that she might somehow effect dramatic family change.

Daughters of alcoholics also harbor a great deal of rage and anger for their fathers. Daughters of alcoholics learn to fear and distrust men in general. Moreover, they unconsciously and preconsciously wish to attack, retaliate, and get even with their alcoholic fathers. These dimensions of the wife's character structure and adjustment style account for her potential for violent acting out within the alcoholic marriage and family system. The experience of living with a drinking alcoholic for a prolonged interval of time precipitates an exacerbation of these sources of anger and rage. Women who persist within an alcoholic marriage eventually become violent. Some of these women masochistically internalize their feelings of anger and rage. However, many of these women violently retaliate against their alcoholic husbands for their alcoholism per se and the crazy behaviors that accompany the addiction process. Quite simply, the marital and familial *modus operandi* of the wife of the alcoholic tends to include a good deal of poorly controlled, violent acting out.

Violence is an ever-present reality within the alcoholic family system. Most alcoholic marital relationships are overtly violent. Alcoholic marriages are also covertly violent. Both spouses may physically and verbally attack each other on a daily or perhaps even hourly basis! Covert violence in the alcoholic family system can be manifested via psychosomatic symptoms. Migraine headaches, gastrointestinal problems, low-back pain, chronic depression, tissue destruction, and heart attacks are but a few of these symptoms (Evans, 1980). Alcoholism is always a form of violence acted out against the self. All of the members of the alcoholic family system are usually poorly controlled. Physical assaults take place in these families. Anger, rage and resentment are continually acted out in the form of verbal confrontations and verbal assaults in these family constellations. Persistence within the alcoholic family system is often pre-consciously and unconsciously equated with winning upon the part of all or various family members. In a sadomasochistic sense, the ultimate form of winning in this context means living while destroying significant others. The alcoholic may secretly wish that his wife would die. Likewise, the wife and children often wish that the alcoholic would be killed in a car wreck or in some other manner. It is common for an act of violence, such as murder, to take place within alcoholic families. The alcoholic family system is an emotional and physical battleground.

Acting out is also basic to the alcoholic family system. Violence, rage, aggression, and hostility are very destructive negative affects when acted out in socially inappropriate ways. Every member in the alcoholic family system is prone to pathological acting out. Control is an interpersonal and intrapersonal ingredient that is missing within the members of an alcoholic family system. The alcoholic family system is consistently out of control. The various checks and balances that are operational within reasonably well-adjusted family systems are not functional within alcoholic family systems. These checks and balances are contructed vis-à-vis individual ego strength, personal identities, defined roles and role-appropriate behaviors, and effective experiences in the realm of socialization. These ingredients have not been a part of the life experience of the alcoholic and members of the alcoholic family system.

Alcoholic family systems are chaotic (Forrest, 1978). Feelings, behaviors, communications, and familial transactions are chaotic in a paradoxically systematic, predictable fashion within the alcoholic family system. The violence, acting out, double binding and scapegoating, familial role reversals and role slippage, and family ego fusion within these families are all realities that contribute to the chaotic dimensions of these families.

In spite of these sources of pathology, the alcoholic family system can be surprisingly malleable once engaged in an effective program of family treatment. This is another characteristic of most alcoholic family systems. Following the termination of drinking upon the part of the alcoholic, the family must make a long-term commitment to the treatment process.

PSYCHOTHERAPEUTIC CONSIDERATIONS

Family and marital therapies are especially germane to the treatment of alcoholism. Family and conjoint therapies are aimed at modifying family and marital relationships. Alcoholism is a family disorder. Every member of the alcoholic family system is emotionally conflicted. These family and marital relationships are diffusely pathological.

Family therapy with alcoholic family systems begins with a focus upon the alcoholic's drinking behavior. Indeed, it is imperative that the alcoholic family member terminate his or her addiction in order for the family therapy process to facilitate global treatment gains. The family therapist meets with the entire alcoholic family system on a weekly basis for four to ten months. Sessions are one hour to one-and-one-half hours in length. The therapist needs to consistently point out transactional, behavioral, communicative, and affective distortions that take place within the therapy sessions and home environment.

A primary goal of family therapy with alcoholic family systems is that of facilitating a more stable and adaptive familial homeostatic equilibrium. Scapegoating and victimizing transactions need to be extinguished. Familial patterns of violence, sabotaging, and controlling need to be modified. Role consistency and rational patterns of emoting need to be established.

The family therapist will need to set concrete limits early in the treatment process. Verbal and physical abuse of any family member will not be tolerated. It is important to avoid family blowups early in the process of family therapy. Family therapy is the treatment of choice in incestuous alcoholic family systems (Forrest, 1982b). Successful family therapy requires continued work and commitment upon the part of each family member. An important goal for the family therapist is that of helping the alcoholic family system to reengage itself with the larger community. Family involvement in the Alcoholics Anonymous community (Alcoholics Anonymous, Al-Anon, and Alateen) is a very effective adjunct to family treatment.

The family therapist actively teaches and reinforces new and more adaptive patterns of family living. The work of family therapy with alcoholic family systems is accomplished vis-à-vis the therapist's relationship *within* the family. Alcoholism is a cancerous familial disorder. Family therapy represents a viable treatment methodology for modifying the cancerous familial dynamics of alcoholism. Family treatment strategies may also be longitudinally preventative.

SUMMARY

The primary psychodynamics of the alcoholic family system were discussed in this chapter. The pathology and adjustment dynamics of both the alcoholic and non-alcoholic spouse prior to marriage and the establishment of an alcoholic family system were elucidated. The unresolved conflicts and struggles of the alcoholic and his spouse floridly color and determine the emotional climate and adjustment style of the alcoholic family system.

The alcoholic family system continues to be poorly understood by clinicians and psychotherapists. Indeed, there is very little research literature available that considers the adjustment style, psychodynamics, and patterns of behavioral interaction and communication that are operational within alcoholic families. This chapter is limited. Only those alcoholic family systems in which the husband was alcoholic are discussed. Therefore, this chapter is devoted to the exploration of a particular type of form of alcoholic family system. Hopefully, other clinicians and authors will consider these issues in forthcoming articles, research and textbooks.

The alcoholic family system is a difficult emotional milieu in which to live and experience family life. These families are turbulent and chaotic with regard to feelings, behavioral transactions, patterns of interaction, and communication. Roles within these families vacillate. Persistent role slippage characterizes the role behaviors of all family members. Scapegoating, victimizing, and double binding are ever-present transactional realities within the alcoholic family system. Family members within alcoholic family systems manifest an ego fusion with the alcoholic. As the ego boundaries of the non-alcoholic family members regressively fuse with those of the alcoholic, a pathological family ego evolves. These families are symbiotic, and individual identity boundaries are blurred (Bowen, 1978). These processes reinforce interdependence within the family system and dictate persistence within the family milieu. The alcoholic family system is a rather pathologically static system. Pathognomic persistence within the alcoholic marriage and family system is often a function of the primitive sadomasochistic trends of both spouses. The alcoholic family system is also violent. Alcohol addiction per se is invariably a violent process. Hostility, poorly controlled aggression, oral rage, and violent acting out are ever-present realities within alcoholic family systems.

Many alcoholic family systems are capable of rather radical positive change once they are engaged in family therapy and a rehabilitation program. The initiation and maintenance of radical adaptive family change is contingent upon the ability of the alcoholic to terminate drinking and enter treatment. If the alcoholic continues to drink while in family therapy, it is very difficult, if not impossible, to initiate behavioral change and long-term therapeutic gains in any of the primary areas discussed in this chapter. Periodic drinking episodes can be expected during the process of therapy with the alcoholic family. However, these regressions are helpful grist for the therapeutic process. Alcoholic family systems are often surprisingly malleable.

Chapter Fourteen

ALCOHOLISM AND ADAPTATION

INTRODUCTION

THIS text deals with the basic psychodynamic and behavioral characteristics of the alcoholic. Psychotherapeutic and rehabilitation strategies for working with alcoholic persons have been a secondary focus throughout the book. The study of the alcoholic is always a study of the individual.

The adaptive dimensions of the alcoholic will be considered in this chapter. The adaptive dimensions of the alcoholic relate to the secondary gain that these individuals obtain from the addiction process. Alcoholics manifest a character structure that provides a surprising number of adaptive strengths. However, some alcoholics do not manifest the various strengths that will be discussed in the following pages. The addiction process always operates in a quid pro quo manner. However, the alcoholic consistently comes out on the short end of the quid pro quo arrangement!

ALCOHOLISM AND THE PARAMETERS OF ADAPTATION

Many of my alcoholic patients have been chronically intoxicated for twenty to thirty years. It is difficult to understand how these persons can remain chronically intoxicated for such an extended period of time and remain reasonably sane. Many behavioral scientists who are unfamiliar with the actual drinking behavior of alcoholics find it hard to believe that these individuals can physically remain chronically intoxicated for twenty to thirty years. In spite of these factors, the vast majority of alcoholics are simply capable of recovery. Recovery means a radically changed life-style (Forrest, 1978 & 1979b). Alcoholics who commit themselves to a psychotherapy relationship, Alcoholics Anonymous, spiritual involvement, or possibly even Antabuse® maintenance are capable of actualizing radically adaptive life-style changes.

The character structure and adjustment style of the alcoholic are relatively malleable. Healthy vocational changes, marital changes, modified patterns of familial interaction and communication, and self-concept changes do occur after the alcoholic is committed to sobriety and psychotherapy. Alcoholics can learn to live honestly, responsibly, and within the dictates of reality.

In order for the alcoholic to begin the process of responsible and rational living, he or she must terminate drinking. The fundamental task of terminating alcohol dependency can be viewed as indicative of characterological malleability.

The alcoholic adjustment style includes psychotic elements. Alcoholics live essentially non-reality-oriented life-styles. The alcoholic loses his or her identity as a result of being trapped in the addiction process. Paradoxically, the addiction process both gives and takes away identity. The alcoholic identity is always a sick identity. More precisely, this identity is continually at loggerheads with reality (Glasser, 1965). Alcoholics avoid the reality of their personal being. The behaviors of the alcoholic are clearly irrational or bizarre. The fantasies, dreams, and intrapersonal adjustments of alcoholics are also pathological. Alcoholics are often perceived as emotionally sick and labeled by the community as deviants. The addicted person is out of control. These clinical features are also basic to the diagnosis of thought disorder or psychosis.

Recovery from chronic alcoholism may well parallel recovery from a long-term psychosis. While this analogy is limited, it is important to realize that the recovery rate from a psychosis or a schizophrenic episode of 5 to 20 years duration is less than the rate of recovery from alcoholism. The primary symptomatology of chronic schizophrenics does not go into significant remission in 50 to 80 percent of treated cases. It is realistic to expect primary symptom remission in at least 70 percent of alcoholics who enter an extended (6 months to 1 year) psychotherapy relationship.

The capacity of the alcoholic to reestablish meaningful and functional interpersonal attachments is the key to the rather radical recoveries that many of these individuals actualize. Alcoholics are capable of making a healthy movement toward and with people. Following the establishment of sobriety, a major thrust of the treatment relationship involves getting the patient back to the world of people. Many alcoholics are capable of stepping out of their addiction and the inappropriate behavioral repertoire that supports the addiction process. Chronically schizophrenic individuals are rarely capable of initiating and maintaining these changes. The interpersonal styles of many neurotics and sociopaths are also recalcitrant to change. Neurotic adjustments are often rather static in nature.

The secondary gain afforded the alcoholic via this particular symptom choice is often cut short. At some point in the addiction process, the alcoholic can no longer live with himself or herself. Significant others reach a point at which they will no longer tolerate the alcoholic's alcoholic behaviors. The alcoholic adjustment style is one in which a number of built-in factors operate to create many crisis situations. These crisis situations can facilitate movement toward physical and psychological health.

The alcoholic is frequently pushed, forced, or coerced into sobriety (Bratter, 1982) and treatment. However, the ability of the alcoholic to respond positively to a crisis situation is demonstrative of malleability. It can be easy to overlook this factor. Frequently, alcoholism therapists become so entrenched with paperwork and tremendous caseloads that they selectively attend to the recidivistic behaviors of their patients. Some counselors are simply not successful in their treatment relationships with alcoholic patients (Forrest, 1979c & 1982a). These counselors may work with a large number of patients over a period of months or even years and never see any of them modify their drinking behavior or get better. In any event, many alcoholics initiate positive behavioral change as a result of external pressures.

Adjusting to a crisis can result in the modification of socially deviant roles and behaviors. The ability to recover from alcoholism can also result in a process of rebirth (Forrest, 1978). The rebirth process can be a physical rebirth in the actual sense of living rather than dying. Rebirth encompasses interpersonal change. Once the alcoholic begins to physically recover, a psychological process of rebirth begins. Spiritual rebirth may be central to this process.

A crucial ingredient in the alcoholism recovery process is that of role change. Many alcoholics are perceived as madmen or social deviants within their communities. Every alcoholic who recovers has been able to *behave* his or her way out of socially deviant roles. This may sound simple. To the contrary, one of the most difficult tasks confronting the newly sober and recovering alcoholic is that of transcending his or her deviant role within the community. By behaving non-alcoholically, responsibly and rationally, the recovering alcoholic is able to gradually modify the perceptions and transactional behaviors of the system that has identified and labeled him an alcoholic and a lunatic. As the alcoholic begins to recover, those closest to him or her also begin to behave more rationally. However, the alcoholic family system and the community in a more generic sense continue to *expect* the recovering alcoholic to behave in a bizarre and deviant manner. In this realm, the alcoholic again proves surprisingly adaptive. Many alcoholics recover in spite of messages to the effect, "I liked you better when you were drinking." It is important for the police, employer, neighbors, and extended family members to learn that the recovering alcoholic is no longer a drinking madman!

The recovery process is synergistic. It requires significant psychological strength to effect the recovery process. In effect, the alcoholic must be responsible for initiating and maintaining personal growth and health. However, the process of personal change and growth often facilitates healthy changes upon the part of significant others! Most, if not all, alcoholics must be the recipient of some form of interpersonal intervention in order to begin the journey into psychological growth and health. In large measure, alcoholics become symptomatic as a result of chronically disturbed interpersonal relationships. Eventually, the alcoholic makes himself or herself psychologically upset, disturbed, and addicted. People contribute very significantly to the adjustment style of the alcoholic in a "sick" sense. People also play a very crucial role in the emotional recovery of the alcoholic. Psychotherapy, involvement with a minister, priest or religious group, self-help groups such as Alcoholics Anonymous, positive addictions, and a healthy love relationship are the primary people-oriented modalities that help the alcoholic recover (Forrest, 1980).

As indicated earlier, it is the ability to move toward and with others that helps many alcoholics change or recover. It is imperative that the recovering alcoholic reestablish meaningful and healthy interpersonal relationships in order to transcend his or her deviant history. A few recovering alcoholics mendaciously reject this point. Healthy relationships do help the recovering alcoholic modify or alter deviant role behaviors. Chronic alcoholics who merely stop drinking very often persist in various inappropriate role behaviors and continue to be psychologically disturbed. These individuals remain unhappy and neurotic. Alcoholics Anonymous (1939) members indicate that these alcoholics have not found serenity. Some of these persons do maintain "white-knuckled" sobriety.

There are many paradoxical aspects to the recovery process. In order to change, the alcoholic must accept his or her alcoholism. This process involves accepting self as a deviant! In other words, the alcoholic recovers and terminates deviant, alcohol-facilitated behaviors by accepting and coming to grips with the reality of his or her alcoholic deviancy. Many alcoholics are able to recover via the medium of involvements with such "deviant" groups as therapy groups, Alcoholics Anonymous, or a religious group! It is pain that very often pushes or forces the alcoholic into recovery. Within the confines of a psychotherapy relationship or Alcoholics Anonymous, the alcoholic learns new and more appropriate social behaviors. The recovering alcoholic needs to learn how to interact and behave with others in an adult and rational manner. These are not easy tasks. Learning how to behave rationally (Ellis, 1979) and appropriately demands work, commitment, persistence and *sobriety*. The pathological network of interpersonal relations that maintains and reinforces the behavioral symptomatology of the alcoholic must be changed. The alcoholic must be responsible for these changes!

Most therapists (Freud, 1953; Reich, 1961) stress the importance of being able to love and work as prerequisites to mental health. General mental health is associated with the abilities to love and work. Psychotherapists agree that the abilities to work and love are extremely important to the adjustment and mental health of most, if not all, people (Ellis, 1979). The majority of drinking alcoholics are capable of neurotically loving and working. The drinking alcoholic loves and works ineffectively. Many alcoholics reach a point in their addiction careers where they must drink alcoholically in order to function on the job and with people. However, the addiction process very often destroys the alcoholic's ability to work and love. The addiction process cripples the alcoholic to the extent of making him or her grossly ineffective in the realms of loving and working. In order to recover, the alcoholic (Forrest, 1980) must reestablish the abilities to love and work. Alcoholics who are unable to return to the world of work and establish healthy, loving relationships after achieving sobriety often give up and initiate careers as chronic mental patients.

Terminating alcoholism and addictive behaviors is difficult. It is even more difficult to learn how to love and work effectively. The majority of people who become addicted to alcohol have never learned how to love effectively. Rather than exploring a number of elaborate and esoteric definitions of love, suffice it to say that love is basically an intimate, meaningful and very *special* form of human relationship. In order to be capable of loving, the alcoholic must significantly resolve or work through his or her parataxic interpersonal *modus vivendi*. The change process requires considerable work, pain and commitment. Many alcoholic persons neurotically attempt to love via sexual promiscuity. Alcoholic males often attempt to love by *over*-idealizing a woman or any number of women. This process results in a pathological love relationship in which the alcoholic is both overdependent and sadomasochistic. Some alcoholics are simply not capable of establishing the most rudimentary of love relationships. Many of these individuals avoid intimate relationships, courtship and marriage.

The drinking alcoholic male is intensely angry at women. Many drinking male alcoholics radiate a deep hatred for women. These men devaluate women. Rejecting women or men, the flight into ephemeral heterosexual promiscuity, and even the inability to maintain a meaningful, in-depth love relationship are issues that the alcoholic and the psychotherapist must effectively resolve within the confines of the psychotherapeutic alliance. These patients are often engaged in an endless repetition compulsion that is none other than a desperate search for human love. In an adaptive sense, many alcoholics are able to learn how to love vis-à-vis a successful psychotherapy relationship.

In order to learn how to love more effectively, the alcoholic must first of all establish sobriety. Beyond this prerequisite, the psychotherapist and alcoholic must spend considerable time in the therapeutic relationship dealing with the psychogenic roots of the alcoholic's inability to love. The psychotherapeutic process (Forrest, 1979a & 1983) always encompasses more than the here and now. Genetic reconstruction of the patient's past must be integrated with a here-and-now focus. Brief psychotherapy is ineffective in the treatment of alcoholism. It can be relatively easy for many recovering alcoholics to never accomplish the tasks of learning how to love and tolerate interpersonal intimacy. Unfortunately, a significant number of alcoholics change very little beyond achieving sobriety. Many alcoholics return to the bottle for this very reason. Many alcoholics also benefit most from psychotherapeutic treatment *after* they have established sobriety. The alcoholic may not be *ready* to commit himself or herself to a psychotherapy relationship prior to having established several months or years of abstinence. The capacity to learn how to love is indicative of characterological strength and adaptation.

Recovery from alcoholism also involves learning more healthy and active patterns of family loving and relating. Drinking alcoholics are incapable of healthy loving within the contexts of marriage and the family. Alcoholics are psychologically and emotionally divorced from their families. Chronic intoxication results in a progressive detachment and withdrawal from the world of interpersonal relations. The alcoholic becomes encapsulated in a bottle (Forrest, 1978). In essence, the alcoholic is married to the bottle. Drinking alcoholics feel isolated, alone and alienated in spite of living with a spouse and family. The alcoholic is an outsider within the alcoholic family system. Following the establishment of sobriety, the alcoholic must learn how to reestablish himself or herself within the family system. This is a critical and difficult task. In order to successfully accomplish this task, the alcoholic must learn how to love his or her spouse and children. The alcoholic needs to learn how to love more effectively within the family context. In the event that the recovering alcoholic fails to develop more adaptive patterns of relating, communicating and loving within the family system, marital separation and divorce may well follow. The spouse and children of the alcoholic must also accomplish the task of more fully and adaptively loving, relating and communicating within the family sytem!

The following brief case study demonstrates how the recovering alcoholic and the alcoholic family system are capable of actualizing adaptive change and growth.

> NP was a fifty-year-old retired army first sergeant. During his military career, NP drank alcoholically for some ten years. He had been "dried out" no less than six times in various military hospitals. In spite of a successful military career, this patient had been unsuccessful in his attempts to secure employment following completion of his military service. At the time of treatment engagement, NP was discouraged and depressed because of his vocational difficulties, marital relationship, and general family life. He had been married for twenty-six years to the same woman and had a family which included a sixteen-year-old son and a thirteen-year-old son.
>
> In the course of extended individual and group therapy with the author, the patient's addiction behavioral style was explored in-depth. Following military retirement, NP had been treated within the confines of numerous alcoholic rehabilitation centers. He had been to one state hospital and three Veterans Administration hospitals for alcoholism treatment. It was difficult for NP to accept the fact that he was an alcoholic. He would remain totally abstinent for as long as six to ten months, only to once again initiate drinking and remain alcoholically dysfunctional for as long as three or four months. Needless to say, NP's world of "alcoholic significant others" reinforced his alcoholic behaviors.

Early in the psychotherapeutic process, NP noted that during the past three or four years, he had resumed drinking only when his wife had been in the hospital (Mrs. P had been hospitalized some six times in three years as a result of a broken leg and other bona fide medical problems). At this juncture in the treatment process, I recommended to the patient that both he and his wife involve themselves in a marital couples' therapy group. This group was composed of four other couples with marital difficulties associated with the alcoholism of one spouse. The P's committed themselves to the treatment group and, thereafter, NP was rarely seen in individual therapy. Within the marital couples' group, NP and his wife almost immediately began to deal with their marital and relationship conflicts. Although the alcoholism and alcoholic behaviors of NP constituted an ever-present red thread in the treatment process, a very major focus for this couple (as well as the other couples comprising this group) was that of *their* relationship and the family relationship. Early in the group process, NP revealed that his recent episodic alcoholism bouts were accompanied with the fantasy and intrapersonal ideation that his wife would "die while on the operating table." As soon as Mrs. P entered the hospital, Mr. P would ruminate about her death and then begin an alcoholic drinking spree that would last for a month or longer. At this time, the patient would drink a fifth of vodka or more per day. His drinking was terminated after admission to a hospital or "detox" facility.

This disclosure upon the part of NP initiated an intense group process of dealing with the couple's mutual love and hate for each other. The couple began to actively explore their dislikes for each other, mutual resentments, communication difficulties, and an entire gamut of other relationship difficulties that at core pertained to the matter of love and hate. An issue that NP began to deal with in therapy was his own familial background and more specifically his relationship with his mother. Within a matter of three months, the therapeutic dialogue of this couple shifted to the here and now. In a rather typical fashion, Mrs. NP had been responsible for parenting, paying bills, and other family management matters throughout much of the marriage. At this time, NP described himself as "a stranger in my own house." As NP began to deal with this issue in therapy, he experienced considerable guilt and depression. The process of family reentry was a difficult one for NP, his wife and both sons. Depression was experienced by Mrs. NP as she began to experience feelings in therapy associated with having been abandoned in marriage by her husband. She began to realize that she had missed much of what marriage is all about for many years. Anger, hostility and resentment were affects that Mrs. NP began to deal with more effectively in the marital relationship.

The oldest son was best able to accept his father's active and sober role within the family constellation. A number of factors were responsible for this. This son was developmentally separated from the family. Additionally, he did well in school, had established a number of relationships outside of the family, and was described by both parents as a rather independent sort of chap. However, the younger son began to evidence a number of symptoms. He began to fail in school, broke into a neighbor's home and took, among other things, a shotgun, began a pattern of chronic lying to the parents and others, and evidenced other acting out symptoms.

Clearly, NP's behavioral change within the family system disrupted the family emotional equilibrium. In many respects, NP's adjustment change created a trauma within the family system that was evidenced most vividly via the symptomatic acting out of the youngest son. It was clinically significant that NP verbalized his feelings toward his youngest son's symptomatic behavior by telling him over and over again, "I'm here to stay." This message meant that his son's crazy behaviors were not going to result in NP's resumption of drinking and the pathological behaviors that had accompanied his alcoholism. The family relationship became the focus of therapy for several months. Every member in the family began to learn that "change" meant change upon the part of all family members.

During the course of some eighteen months of treatment, NP radically changed his behavior and role within the family system. This change demonstrates the malleability of the alcoholic. NP assumed more and more responsibility within the family. He became a real father. He was able to emotionally tolerate the behavior problems of his youngest son, his interpersonal skills improved, he was better able to verbally communicate with all of the family members, and he was better able to tolerate interpersonal intimacy. Additionally, NP no longer needed to drink in order to cope with family living. As NP began to "grow up," in his words, he became increasingly less angry and physically abusive toward his acting out son.

For the first time since his military retirement, nearly ten years earlier, NP was able to secure meaningful employment. NP decided to go to college after having been in group therapy for approximately eighteen months. He enrolled in an alcoholism counselor training program, completed this program, looked for a position for nearly ten months, and finally became employed in an alcohol services division of a community mental health center. Following military retirement, NP had worked as a "carry-out boy" for a large supermarket. He has also worked as a cement finisher and did construction work. In reality, he had failed to establish a rewarding and meaningful vocational identity.

A number of very significant changes were effected by NP during the period in which he was in psychotherapy. Once NP became capable of loving himself in a more adaptive sense, he was more and more capable of loving his wife and children. The family relationship soon encompassed such activities as going on outings and picnics *together*, sharing in the activities of the children, and developing *mutual* friendships outside the immediate family constellation. Communication, behavior, and emotive relating within the family system changed rather radically in a more healthy and adaptive direction. This case history depicts rather well the basic ability of the chronic alcoholic to change in a multifaceted manner.

This case study demonstrates the pervasive change potential that the alcoholic manifests. The patient was able to become a more effective husband and parent. The change process within these families can often be radical in scope and certainly not an ambiguous process. Adaptive change begins when the alcoholic makes a commitment to sobriety and the psychotherapy process. However, the alcoholic is always responsible for the lion's share of the work of changing!

Vocation and career development have very important impacts upon adjustment and self-concept. Recently in the United States, several multiple homicides have been committed by men who were fired or who had just lost their jobs. Suicide, heavy drinking, marital problems and psychiatric disorders have long been associated with job loss. Alcoholics often experience chronic vocational problems juxtaposed to their drinking problem. Frequent job changes, career instability, missed raises and promotions, interpersonal difficulties with supervisors and peers, job absenteeism, and poor work performance are but a few of the facets of the behavioral style of the drinking alcoholic within the world of work (Forrest, 1979b). Many alcoholics have never learned how to work productively. Unfortunately, many of these persons have received very little career guidance.

Some alcoholics are successful within the professions. Alcoholic professionals often seek help when their alcoholism begins to seriously affect their career and job performance. At this juncture, the alcoholic professional may be in the midst of an alcohol-facilitated career crisis. It is imperative that the matters of work and career be managed within the context of the psychotherapy relationship with the alcoholic. A career crisis can result in heavy drinking or the outcropping of florid alcohol addiction. The termination of a career can also be accompanied by the development of alcoholism. The structural breakdown in life-style that results from retirement compounds the loss of control over drinking.

The ability to productively reengage oneself in a career or the world of work is an important indicator of adaptive internal resources. Alcoholics often actualize the ability to become productive within a career. Some alcoholics must regain the capacity to work effectively and productively. Others need to establish their first stabilized career pattern. Vocational productivity begins with sobriety. A major rehabilitation and therapeutic task in the treatment of alcoholics (Forrest, 1979c), therefore, involves helping the patient learn how to work effectively and productively.

Paradoxically, recovering alcoholics can become too productive within the world of work! Work can become a compulsion in the case of the recovering alcoholic. Working compulsively is characterologically congruous with the alcoholic's overdetermined need to bind anxiety. Thus, the psychotherapist must closely assess the qualitative dimensions of the alcoholic's work adjustment. The work compulsion can also be a defensive strategy that serves the purpose of avoiding marital problems, family problems and other sources of conflict. The work process can become a ritualized and obsessive-compulsive behavioral pattern. Effective psychotherapeutic work with alcoholics will resolve this trend toward switching addictions. This process also indicates the presence of change potential.

The alcoholic is able to change, modify and give up various psychological symptoms and behaviors not touched upon in this chapter. Many alcoholics are capable of modifying their depressive symptomatology. The symptoms of anxiety, guilt, rage and overdetermined orality can be changed vis-à-vis a productive psychotherapy experience. The symptom structure of the alcoholic is never completely ameliorated. However, most alcoholics are capable of adaptively changing their symptom structure and behavioral repertoire. Even the alloplastic symptomatology of the alcoholic goes into marked remission following the establishment of sobriety and psychotherapeutic treatment. As the recovering alcoholic begins to grow and change within the context of a psychotherapy relationship, the therapist will find that one of the most observable areas of change is very often in the realm of narcissistic disturbance.

When the alcoholic no longer relies solely upon such primitive defenses as denial, distortion and projection, he or she begins to be capable of looking at self in a reality-oriented manner. At this point, the patient may initiate a more transparent and self-disclosing adjustment style (Forrest, 1978 & 1980; Hountras and Forrest, 1970). Self-disclosure is an essential ingredient in healthy emotional adjustment. Openness and self-disclosure facilitate similar behaviors upon the part of others, thus creating interpersonal movements toward and with significant others. Alcoholics who reach the stage of being able to move toward and with significant others in the absence of drinking and being intoxicated become progressively more capable of giving up maladaptive narcissistic behaviors.

Most alcoholics are compassionate, empathic, understanding, and giving. The need structure of the alcoholic (Huba, Segal and Singer, 1977) is complex. Alcoholics Anonymous provides a number of very viable and concrete methods for the recovering alcoholic to resolve or modify the overdetermined narcissistic dimensions of his or her character structure. Having a sponsor, being a sponsor, "twelve stepping" or making twelve-step calls, and focusing upon "taking someone else's inventory" and "rigorous honesty" are but a few of the strategies employed by AA to deal with the alcoholic's problem of narcissism (Emrick, 1979). Coming to grips with the issue of a "higher power" can certainly create a rupture in the alcoholic's narcissistic defense system! At any rate, many alcoholics are capable of changing the pathologically narcissistic aspects of their behavior.

It is important for the counselor or psychotherapist to focus upon the alcoholic's grandiose power strivings (Forrest, 1978 & 1983). The alcoholic needs to learn how to give in a healthy manner. As the alcoholic travels the road to recovery, he or she progressively becomes more able to give up self-centered patterns of behavior. Giving up a life-style characterized by manipulation, hedonism, and immediate instinctual gratification is difficult. Yet, the narcissistic characterological makeup of the alcoholic is amenable to change. Sober alcoholics who do not resolve their overdetermined narcissistic need structure tend to remain unhappy, isolated, and without friends. In sum, the *drinking* alcoholic is incapable of emotional concern, warmth, compassion and loving in his or her interpersonal relationships. One barometer of the alcoholic's characterological malleability involves the ability to resolve or modify narcissistic conflicts. Many alcoholic persons are able to significantly modify their narcissistic conflicts.

One of my first alcoholic patients stressed the point time and again in therapy that he had survived in life. This point has been emphasized rather felicitously by many of my alcoholic patients. Infancy, childhood, adolescence and the various other developmental stages of life have been difficult in a multiplicity of ways for the alcoholic. Many alcoholics are simply lucky to be alive. Juxtaposed to this point is the fact that many alcoholic persons do not survive. Thousands of alcoholics die annually as a result of suicide, automobile accidents, cirrhosis of the liver and other medical complications. Experiencing life as a drinking alcoholic is less than surviving! In spite of these realities, the ability of many alcoholics to survive, endure and subsequently change is rather astounding. The capacity to change is the critical point of emphasis. Aside from merely surviving in a static sense, the alcoholic can begin the change and recovery processes at virtually any point in the addiction process. Life in the bottle is a static process. Survival is the most basic prerequisite to the change process.

SUMMARY

In this chapter, a number of the more adaptive dimensions of the alcoholic were explored. These adaptive dimensions reveal a very different aspect of the alcoholic character structure. Very few, if any, textbooks dealing with the subject of alcoholism touch upon the characterological and adaptive strengths of the alcoholic. Research and clinical studies do not generally indicate that the alcoholic is the possessor of positive personality features or characterological strengths. There are no research data dealing with the adaptive dimensions of the alcoholic. Researchers and clinicians study drinking alcoholics and psychopathology! Most psychotherapists do not have the opportunity to investigate in-depth and *know* alcoholics who have attained prolonged sobriety and recovered.

The ability of the alcoholic to modify various behaviors following the establishment of sobriety was also considered in this chapter. Sobriety is the basic precursor to recovery and global behavior change upon the part of alcoholics. The alcoholic is capable of changing! Many clinicians continue to believe that "once an alcoholic, always an alcoholic" in a drinking sense. Alcoholic persons consistently demonstrate an ability to change in the following ways: (1) terminating drinking and the morass of crazy behaviors genetic to the addiction process, (2) giving up socially deviant role behaviors, thus becoming capable of healthy and adaptive interpersonal engagement, (3) establishing functional roles within the family system, which include the development of an ability to love and more effectively manage the affective dimensions of interpersonal living, (4) becoming productive within the world of work, and (5) giving up a rather wide range of basically internal psychological problems associated with the alcoholic symptom choice. The depressive, obsessive-compulsive, acting out, and narcissistic symptoms of the alcoholic go into significant remission following successful psychotherapeutic treatment (Forrest, 1983). The case study included in this chapter demonstrates rather well a number of the adaptive dimensions and characterological strengths of the alcoholic. Most alcoholics manifest an uncanny ability to simply survive!

The alcoholic character structure is malleable. Many chronic alcoholics can return to a life of responsibility and rational living (Ellis, 1979). Hopefully, this chapter will stimulate new research and prove heuristic. The recent increases in teenage alcohol abuse (Forrest, 1983) and collective patterns of alcoholism are associated with economic instability, unemployment, possible war and nuclear holocaust, and various social realities. Alcohol abuse and alcoholism are neurotically adaptive solutions to these social realities for hundreds of thousands of Americans.

BIBLIOGRAPHY

Ackerman, R.J.: *Children of Alcoholics: A Guidebook for Educators.* Holmes Beach, Florida, Learning Publications, 1978.

Ackerman, R.J.: Alcoholism and Child Abuse. Lecture, Psychotherapy Associates, P.C. Sixth Annual Advanced Winter Workshop, "Treatment and Rehabilitation of the Alcoholic, " Colorado Springs, Colorado, Feb. 7, 1980.

Armor, D.J., Polich, J.M., and Stambul, H.B.: *Alcoholism and Treatment.* New York: John Wiley & Sons, 1978.

Bandura, A.: *Principles of Behavioral Modification.* New York: Holt, Reinhart, and Winston, 1969.

Banks, R.: Alcoholism and Violent Behavior. Lecture, Psychotherapy Associates, P.C. Eighth Annual Advanced Winter Workshop, "Treatment and Rehabilitation of the Alcoholic," Colorado Springs, Colorado, Feb. 2, 1982.

Bateson, G., Jackson, D.D., Haley, J. and Weakland, J.: Toward a theory of schizophrenia. *Behavioral Science, 1*:251-265, 1956.

Beckman, L.J.: Women alcoholics. *Journal of Study on Alcoholism, 36*: 797-824, 1975.

Bellwood, L.R.: *Alcoholism: The Common Neurosis of Our Time.* Denver: Bell-Hart Publishing Co., 1973.

Bergler, E.: *Homosexuality: Disease or Way of Life?* New York: Collier Books, 1956.

Blane, H.T.: *The Personality of the Alcoholic: Guises of Dependency.* New York: Harper and Row, 1968.

Blum, E.M., and Blum, R.H.: *Alcoholism: Modern Psychological Approaches to Treatment.* San Francisco: Jossey-Bass, Inc., 1969.

Bowen, M.: *Family Therapy in Clinical Practice.* New York: Jason Aronson, 1978.

Bratter, T.E.: The psychotherapist as a twelfth-step worker in the treatment of alcoholism. *Family and Community Health, 2*(2):31-58, 1979.

Bratter, T.E.: Advanced Reality Therapy Techniques in the Treatment of Alcoholism and Substance Abuse. Lecture, Psychotherapy Associates, P.C. Sixth Annual Advanced Winter Workshop, "Treatment and Rehabilitation of the Alcoholic," Colorado Springs, Colorado, Feb. 5, 1980.

Bratter, T.E.: Confrontation groups: the therapeutic community's gift to psychotherapy. In Vanos, P., and Devlin, J. (Eds.): *Proceedings of the First World Conference on Therapeutic Communities.* Montreal: Potage Press, 1976, pp. 164–174.

Bratter, T.E.: Confrontation: a group psychotherapeutic orientation with heroin addicts. In Uchtenhagen, A., Battegay, R., and Friedemann, A. (Eds.): *Group Therapy and Social Environment.* Switzerland: Hans Huber, 1975, pp. 360–367.

Bratter, T.E.: Responsible therapeutic eros: the psychotherapist who cares enough to define and enforce behavioral limits with potentially suicidal adolescents. *The Counseling Psychologist, 5*:97-104, 1975d.

Bratter, T.E.: Some pre-treatment group psychotherapy considerations with alcoholic and drug-addicted individuals. *Psychotherapy: Theory, Research and Practice, 18*(4):508-515, 1982.

Burnett, M.M.: Toward a model for counseling alcoholics. *The Psychotherapy Bulletin,* pp. 9, 4, 31-33, 1976.

Byers, A.P.: Clinical Hypnosis Training. Lecture, Psychotherapy Associates, P.C. Eighth Annual Advanced Winter Workshop, "Treatment and Rehabilitation of the Alcoholic," Colorado Springs, Colorado, Feb. 5, 1982.

Cameron, N.: *Personality Development and Psychopathology: A Dynamic Approach.* Boston: Houghton Mifflin Co., 1963.

Castor, D.U.: Treatment of the Adolescent Alcoholic. Lecture, Psychotherapy Associates, P.C. Eighth Annual Advanced Winter Workshop, "Treatment and Rehabilitation of the Alcoholic," Colorado Springs, Colorado, Feb. 4, 1982.

Catanzaro, R.J.: *Alcoholism: The Total Treatment Approach.* Springfield: Thomas, 1968.

Chafetz, M.: The Drug scene: I. Is there a safe way to drink? *Reader's Digest,* July 1977, pp. 100-103.

Chapman, A.H., and Chapman H.S.: *Sullivan: The Man and His Work.* New York: G.P. Putnam's Sons, 1976.

Cleckly, H.M.: *The Mask of Sanity,* 4th ed. St. Louis: C.V. Mosby, 1964.

Clinebell, H.J., Jr.: *Understanding and Counseling the Alcoholic.* Nashville: Abingdon, 1956.

DeLint, J.E.: Alcoholism, birth bank and parental deprivation. *American Journal of Psychiatry, 120*:1062-1065, 1964.

Della-Giustina, V.E., and Forrest, G.G.: Depression and the dentist. *GA Journal of Dentistry,* August 1979, pp. 15-17.

Della-Giustina, V.E., Brooks, J.D., and Forrest, G.G.: Stress management techniques for the practicing dentist. *GA Journal of Dentistry,* August 1978, pp. 18-20.

Ellis, A.: Rational-Emotive Therapy Training. Lecture, Psychotherapy Associates, P.C. Fifth Annual Advanced Winter Workshop, "Treatment and Rehabilitation of the Alcoholic," Colorado Springs, Colorado, Feb. 1, 1979.

Ellis, A.: Rational-Emotive Therapy and the Treatment of the Alcoholic. Lecture, Psychotherapy Associates, P.C. Third Annual Advanced Winter Workshop, "Treatment and Rehabilitation of the Alcoholic, Colorado Springs, Colorado, Feb. 5, 1976.

Ellis, A.: Rational-emotive therapy: research data that supports the clinical and personality hypotheses of RET and other modes of cognitive-behavior therapy. *The Counseling Psychologist, 7*:2-42, 1977.

Ellis, A.: Constitutional factors in homosexuality: A reexamination of the evidence. In Biegel, Hugo (Ed.): *Advances in Sex Research.* New York: Hoeber Medical Division, Harper and Row, 1963.

Emrick, C.D.: A review of psychologically oriented treatments of alcoholism, I: The use and interrelationships of outcome criteria and drinking behavior following treatment. *Quart Journal Study on Alcoholism, 35*: 523-549, 1974.

Emrick, C.D.: A review of psychologically oriented treatment of alcoholism. II: The relative effectiveness of different treatment approaches and the effectiveness of treatment versus no treatment. *Quart Journal Study on Alcoholism, 36*:88-108, 1975.

Emrick, C.D.: Perspectives in clinical research: relative effectiveness of alcohol abuse treatment. *Family and Community Health, 2*(2):71-88, 1979.

Erickson, E.: Identity and the life cycle. *Psycho Issues, I*:1-164, 1959.

Evans, J.H.: Alcoholism and Psychosomatic Illness. Lecture, Psychotherapy Associates, P.C. Sixth Annual Advanced Winter Workshop, "Treatment and Rehabilitation of the Alcoholic," Colorado Springs, Colorado, Feb. 1, 1980.

Fann, W.E., Karacan, I., Pokorny, A.D., and Williams, R.L.: *Phenomenology and Treatment of Alcoholism.* New York: SP Medical and Scientific Books, 1980.

Fenichel, O.: *The Psychoanalytic Theory of Neurosis.* New York: W.W. Norton, 1945.

Fenichel, O.: *The Collected Papers of Otto Fenichel: Second Series.* New York: W.W. Norton, 1954.

Forrest, G.G.: *The Diagnosis and Treatment of Alcoholism.* Springfield: Thomas, 1975.

Forrest, G.G.: *The Diagnosis and Treatment of Alcoholism.* Rev. 2nd ed. Springfield, Thomas, 1978.

Forrest, G.G.: "Motivating Alcoholic Patients for Treatment." Lecture, Fourth Annual Colorado Summer School on Alcoholism, Glenwood Springs, Colorado, June 11, 1978a.

Forrest, G.G.: Alcoholism, Object Relations and Narcissistic Theory. Lecture, Psychotherapy Associates, P.C. Fifth Annual Advanced Winter Workshop, "Treatment and Rehabilitation of the Alcoholic," Colorado Springs, Colorado, Jan. 29, 1979d.

Forrest, G.G.: Setting alcoholics up for therapeutic failure. *Family and Community Health, 2*(2):59-64, 1979b.

Forrest, G.G.: *Confrontation in Psychotherapy with the Alcoholic.* Holmes Beach, Florida: Learning Publications, 1982a.

Forrest, G.G.: Negative and positive addictions. *Family and Community Health, 2*(1): 103-112, 1979d.

Forrest, G.G.: *How to Live with a Problem Drinker and Survive.* New York: Atheneum, 1980.

Forrest, G.G.: Alcoholism, Identity and Sexuality. Lecture, Psychotherapy Associates, P.C. Sixth Annual Advanced Winter Workshop, "Treatment and Rehabilitation of the Alcoholic," Colorado Springs, Colorado, Feb. 4, 1980a.

Forrest, G.G.: "Transparency as a Prognostic Variable in Psychotherapy." Unpublished doctoral dissertation, University of North Dakota, Grand Forks, North Dakota, 1970.

Forrest, G.G.: "A Model for Training Addiction Counselors." Paper presented at the Rocky Mountain Counselor Education and Supervision Convention, Denver, Colorado, Oct. 3, 1976.

Forrest, G.G.: Group Psychotherapy Techniques in the Treatment of Alcoholism. Lecture, Psychotherapy Associates, P.C. First Annual Southeastern Fall Workshop, "Treatment and Rehabilitation of the Alcoholic," Savannah, Georgia, Oct. 4, 1977.

Forrest, G.G.: *Alcoholism and Human Sexuality.* Springfield: Thomas, 1982b.

Forrest, G.G.: *How to Cope With a Teenage Drinker.* New York: Atheneum, 1983.

Forrest, G.G.: "Psychotherapy with the Alcoholic." American Personnel and Guidance Association Pre-Convention Workshop, Atlanta, Georgia, Mar. 28, 1980b.

Forrest, G.G.: "Alcoholism Treatment Techniques and Principles." Lecture, 24th Annual International School of Alcohol Studies. University of North Dakota. Grand Forks, North Dakota, July 23, 1982c.

Forrest, G.G.: Alcoholism, Schizophrenia and Defense. Lecture, Psychotherapy Associates, P.C. Eighth Annual Advanced Winter Workshop, "Treatment and Rehabilitation of the Alcoholic," Colorado Springs, Colorado, Feb. 1, 1982d.

Forrest, G.G.: Psychodynamically oriented treatment of alcoholism and substance abuse. In Bratter, T.E., and Forrest, G.G. (Eds.): *Current Management of Alcoholism and Substance Abuse.* New York: The Free Press, 1983.

Freud, S.: The future prospects of psychoanalytic therapy. In *Collected Papers.* London: Hogarth, 1953, vol. II.

Gade, E.M., and Goodman, R.E.: Vocational preference of daughters of alcoholics. *The Vocational Guidance Quarterly*, Sept., 1975, pp. 41-47.

Gaylin, W.: *The Meaning of Despair*. New York: Science House, Inc., 1968.

Gilberstadt, H., and Duker, J.: *A Handbook for Clinical and Acturial MMPI Interpretation*. Philadelphia: Saunders, 1965.

Glasser, W.: *Reality Therapy: A New Approach to Psychiatry*. New York: Harper and Row, 1965.

Glasser, W.: *Positive Addiction*. New York: Harper and Row, 1976.

Goldman, L.: Toward more meaningful research. *The Personnel and Guidance Journal, 55*(6):363-368, 1977.

Haley, J.: Marriage therapy. *Arch Gen Psychiatry, 8*:213-224, 1964.

Haley, J.: *Changing Families: A Family Therapy Reader*. New York: Grune and Stratton, 1971.

Harper, R.A.: Stress Management Training. Lecture, Psychotherapy Associates, P.C. Eighth Annual Advanced Winter Workshop, "Treatment and Rehabilitation of the Alcoholic," Colorado Springs, Colorado, Feb. 4, 1982.

Harris, T.: I'm Ok – You're Ok: A Practical Guide to Transactional Analysis. New York: Harper and Row, 1969.

Hartocollis, P. (Ed.): *Borderline Personality Disorders*. New York: International Universities Press, Inc., 1977.

Hill, H.E., Haertzen, C.A., and Davis, H.: An MMPI factor analytic study of alcoholics, narcotic addicts and criminals. *Quart Journal of Study on Alcoholism, 23*:411-431. 1963.

Hoffman, H., Jackson, D.N., and Skinner, H.A.: Dimensions of psychopathology among alcoholic patients. *Quart Journal Study on Alcoholism*, 1975, pp. 36, 825-837.

Hountras, P.T., and Forrest, G.G.: Personality characteristics and self-disclosure in a psychiatric outpatient population. College of Education Record, University of North Dakota, *55*:206-213, 1970.

Huba, G.J., Singer, J.L., and Segal, B.: Organization of needs in male and female drug and alcohol users. *J Consulting and Clinical Psych, 45*(1): 33-44, 1977.

Jacobson, E.: *Depression*. New York: International Universities Press, Inc., 1971.

Jellinek, M.E.: Heredity and alcohol: science and society. *Quart Journal Study on Alcoholism*, pp. 104–114, 1945.

Jourard, S.M.: *The Transparent Self*. Princeton, New Jersey: D. Van Nostrand Co., Inc., 1964.

Kaestner, E., Rosen, L., and Appel, P.: Patterns of drug abuse: relationships with ethnicity, sensation seeking and anxiety. *J Consult and Clin Psych, 45*(3):462-468, 1977.

Kernburg, O.: *Borderline Conditions and Pathological Narcissism*. New York: Jason Aronson, Inc., 1975.

Kernburg, O.: *Object Relations Theory and Clinical Psychoanalysis.* New York: Jason Aronson, Inc., 1976.

Kernburg, O.: *Internal World and External Reality.* New York: Jason Aronson, Inc., 1980.

Kister, G.W.: *The Disorganized Personality.* New York: McGraw-Hill Book Company, 1964.

Klein, M.: A contribution to the psychogenesis of manic-depressive states. In Gaylin, W. (Ed.): *The Meaning of Despair.* New York: Scientific House, Inc., 1968.

Knauert, A.P.: The treatment of alcoholism in a community setting. *Family and Community Health, 2*(1):91-102, 1979.

Knauert, A.P.: Differential Diagnosis in the Treatment of Alcoholism. Lecture, Psychotherapy Associates, P.C. Sixth Annual Advanced Winter Workshop, "Treatment and Rehabilitation of the Alcoholic," Colorado Springs, Colorado, Feb. 8, 1980.

Knauert, A.P.: The Alcoholic Personality: Myth or Reality? Lecture, Fourth Annual Advanced Winter Workshop, "Treatment and Rehabilitation of the Alcoholic," Colorado Springs, Colorado, Jan. 30, 1978.

Knauert, A.P.: Methods for Maintaining the Sanity of Addiction Counselors and Therapists. Lecture, Fifth Annual Advanced Winter Workshop, "Treatment and Rehabilitation of the Alcoholic," Colorado Springs, Colorado, Jan. 31, 1979.

Knauert, A.P.: The Differential Diagnosis of Alcoholism. Lecture, Psychotherapy Associates, P.C. Eighth Annual Advanced Winter Workshop, "Treatment and Rehabilitation of the Alcoholic," Colorado Springs, Colorado, Feb. 2, 1982.

Knauert, A.P.: Alcoholism and Brain Damage. Lecture, Psychotherapy Associates, P.C. Third Annual Advanced Winter Workshop, "Treatment and Rehabilitation of the Alcoholic," Colorado Springs, Colorado, Jan. 31, 1977.

Kohut, H.: *The Analysis of the Self: A Systematic Approach to the Psychoanalytic Treatment of Narcissistic Personality Disorders.* New York: International Universities Press, 1971.

Kohut, H.: *The Restoration of the Self.* New York: International Universities Press, 1977.

McGahee, B.: Treatment of the Inhibited Neurotic Alcoholic. Lecture, Psychotherapy Associates, P.C. Second Annual Southeastern Fall Workshop, "Treatment and Rehabilitation of the Alcoholic," Savannah, Georgia, Oct. 1, 1978.

Martin, J.C.: Alcoholism and the Family. Lecture, Psychotherapy Associates P.C. Second Annual Southeastern Fall Workshop, "Treatment and Rehabilitation of the Alcoholic," Savannah, Georgia, Oct. 1, 1978.

Martin, J.C.: Alcoholism. Lecture, Psychotherapy Associates, P.C. First Annual Advanced Winter Workshop, "Treatment and Rehabilitation of the Alcoholic," Colorado Springs, Colorado, Feb. 1, 1974.

Martin, J.C.: Guidelines for Alcoholism Counselors. Lecture, Psychotherapy Associates, P.C. Fifth Annual Advanced Winter Workshop, "Treatment and Rehabilitation of the Alcoholic," Colorado Springs, Colorado, Jan. 29, 1979.

Masterson, J.F.: *The Narcissistic and Borderline Disorders: An Integrated Developmental Approach.* New York: Brummer/Mazel, 1981.

Matuschka, E.: Alcoholism and Sociopathy. Lecture, Psychotherapy Associates, P.C. Second Annual Southeastern Fall Workshop, "Treatment and Rehabilitation of the Alcoholic," Savannah, Georgia, Oct. 1, 1978.

Matuschka, E.: Bioenergetic Training. Lecture, Psychotherapy Associates, P.C. Fifth Annual Advanced Winter Workshop, "Treatment and Rehabilitation of the Alcoholic," Colorado Springs, Colorado, Feb. 1, 1979.

Matuschka, E.: Advanced Transactional Analysis Techniques in the Treatment of Alcoholism. Lecture, Psychotherapy Associates, P.C. Fifth Annual Advanced Winter Workshop, "Treatment and Rehabilitation of the Alcoholic," Colorado Springs, Colorado, Feb. 4, 1980.

Meissner, W.W.: *The Paranoid Process.* New York, Jason Aronson, 1978.

Menninger, K.: *Man Against Himself.* New York: Harcourt, Brace and World, Inc., 1938.

Milt, H.: *Basic Handbook on Alcoholism.* New Jersey: Scientific Aids Publications, 1969.

Mowrer, O.H.: *The Crisis in Psychiatry and Religion.* Princeton, New Jersey: D. Van Nostrand Co., Inc., 1961.

Mowrer, O.H.: *The New Group Therapy.* Princeton, New Jersey: D. Van Nostrand Co., Inc., 1964.

Paolino, T.J., and McCrady, B.S.: *The Alcoholic Marriage: Alternative Perspectives.* New York: Grune and Stratton, 1977.

Pattison, E.M.: Differential treatment of alcoholism. In Fann, W.E. et al.: *Phenomenology and Treatment of Alcoholism.* New York: SP Medical and Scientific Books, 1980.

Pursch, J.: Alcohol, Pills and Recover. Lecture, Psychotherapy Associates, P.C. Fifth Annual Advanced Winter Workshop, "Treatment and Rehabilitation of the Alcoholic," Colorado Springs, Colorado, Jan. 29, 1979.

Rachman, S.J., and Hodgson, R.J.: *Obsessions and Compulsions.* Princeton, New Jersey: Prentice-Hall, Inc., 1980.

Rathod, N.H., and Thompson, I.G.: Women alcoholics: a clinical study. *Quart Journal Study on Alcoholism, 32*:45-52, 1971.

Reich, W.: *Character Analysis.* New York: The Noonday Press, 1961.

Reich, W.: *The Discovery of the Orgone: The Function of the Orgasm.* New York: The Noonday Press, 1942.

Reik, T.: *Listening with the Third Ear.* New York: Pyramid Books, 1948.

Reik, T.: *The Compulsion to Confess.* New York: Grove Press, Inc., 1961.

Roe, A.: Children of alcoholic parents raised in foster homes: alcohol, science and society. *Quart Journal Study in Alcoholism,* pp. 115-128, 1945.

Rogers, C.R.: *Client-Centered Therapy.* Boston: Houghton Mifflin, 1952.

Ruggles, W.L., et. al.: A Follow-up Study of Clients at Selected Alcoholism Treatment Centers Funded by NIAAA. Stanford Research Institute, May, 1975.

Saltzman, L.: *The Obsessive Personality*. New York: Science House, 1968.

Satir, V.: *Conjoint Family Therapy: A Guide to Theory and Technique*. Palo Alto: Science and Behavior Books, 1964.

Schad-Somers, S.P.: *Sadomasochism: Etiology and Treatment*. New York: Human Sciences Press, Inc., 1982.

Schafi, M., Lavely, R., and Jaffe, R.: Medication and the prevention of alcohol abuse. *Am Journal Psychiatry, 132*(9):942-945, 1975.

Scott, E.M.: Death and Dying in the Alcoholic. Lecture, Psychotherapy Associates, P.C., Fifth Annual Advanced Winter Workshop, "Treatment and Rehabilitation of the Alcoholic," Colorado Springs, Colorado, Jan. 30, 1979.

Sena, D.: Basic Counselor Skills Training. Lecture, Psychotherapy Associates, P.C. Sixth Annual Advanced Winter Workshop, "Treatment and Rehabilitation of the Alcoholic," Colorado Springs, Colorado, Feb. 4, 1980.

Shostrom, E.L.: *Man the Manipulator*. New York: Bantam Books, 1967.

Silverstein, L.M.: Motivating Alcoholics for Treatment. Lecture, Psychotherapy Associates, P.C. Sixth Annual Advanced Winter Workshop, "Treatment and Rehabilitation of the Alcoholic," Colorado Springs, Colorado, Feb. 7, 1980.

Sobell, L.C., and Sobell, M.B.: The Use of Behavioral Analysis in the Treatment of Alcohol Problems. Lecture, Psychotherapy Associates, P.C. Third Annual Advanced Winter Workshop, "Treatment and Rehabilitation of the Alcoholic," Colorado Springs, Colorado, Feb. 2-6, 1976.

Spitz, R.A.: Anaclitic depression: an inquiry into the genesis of psychiatric conditions in early childhood. In Gaylin, W. (Ed.): *The Meaning of Despair*. New York: Science House, Inc., 1968.

Steiner, C.: *Games Alcoholics Play*. New York: Grove Press, 1971.

Stekel, W.: *Patterns of Psychosexual Infantilism*. New York: Washington Square Press, Inc., 1952.

Sternburg, D.P.: Treatment of alcoholics in private practice: Inclusion of the family or other support system. *The Psychotherapy Bulletin, 9*:13-17, 1976.

Strupp, H.H.: Clinical psychology: irrationalism and the erosion of excellence. *American Psychologist, 31*(8):561-571, 1976.

Sullivan, H.S.: *Schizophrenia as a Human Process*. New York: W.W. Norton and Co., Inc., 1953.

Sullivan, H.S.: *Clinical Studies in Psychiatry*. New York: W.W. Norton and Co., Inc., 1956.

Sutker, P.B.: Personality differences and sociopathy in heroin addicts and non-addicted prisoners. *Journal of Abnormal Psychology, 78*:247-251, 1971.

Szasz, T.S.: *The Myth of Mental Illness*. New York: Dell Publishing Co., 1961.

Szasz, T.S.: *Schizophrenia: The Sacred Symbol of Psychiatry.* New York: Basic Books, Inc., 1976.

Vogler, R.E., Weissback, T.A., Comptom, J.V., and Martin, G.T.: Integrated behavior change techniques for problem drinkers in the community. *Journal Consult and Clin Psych, 45*(2)267-279, 1967.

Vraa, C.W.: Treatment of the Human Sexual Dysfunctions. Lecture, Psychotherapy Associates, P.C. Sixth Annual Advanced Winter Workshop, "Treatment and Rehabilitation of the Alcoholic," Colorado Springs, Colorado, Feb. 5, 1980.

Wanberg, K.: Alcoholism Types and Dimensions: Differential Diagnosis and Treatment Implications. Lecture, Psychotherapy Associates, P.C. Fifth Annual Advanced Winter Workshop, "Treatment and Rehabilitation of the Alcoholic," Colorado Springs, Colorado, Feb. 1, 1979.

Wegscheider, S.: Family Dynamics and Family Therapy with the Alcoholic. Lecture, Psychotherapy Associates, P.C. Sixth Annual Advanced Winter Workshop, "Treatment and Rehabilitation of the Alcoholic," Colorado Springs, Colorado, Feb. 7, 1980.

Wegscheider, S.: *Another Chance: Hope and Health for the Alcoholic Family.* Palo Alto, California: Science and Behavior Books, Inc., 1981.

Wellman, L.E.: Applied Social Learning Theory in the Treatment of the Alcoholic. Lecture, Psychotherapy Associates, P.C. Fifth Annual Advanced Winter Workshop, "Treatment and Rehabilitation of the Alcoholic," Colorado Springs, Colorado, Feb. 1, 1979.

Wellman, L.E.: Positive Self-Image Training. Lecture, Psychotherapy Associates, P.C. Sixth Annual Advanced Winter Workshop, "Treatment and Rehabilitation of the Alcoholic," Colorado Springs, Colorado, Feb. 5, 1980.

Wilsnack, S.C.: Femininity by the bottle. *Psychology Today,* pp. 39-43, April 1973.

Wilsnack, S.C.: Issues in the Treatment of Alcoholic Women. Lecture, Psycotherapy Associates P.C. Sixth Annual Advanced Winter Workshop, "Treatment and Rehabilitation of the Alcoholic," Colorado Springs, Colorado, Feb. 4, 1980.

Wilsnack, S.C.: Alcohol and Women. Lecture, Psychotherapy Associates, P.C. Eighth Annual Advanced Winter Workshop, Treatment and Rehabilitation of the Alcoholic," Colorado Springs, Colorado, Feb. 2, 1982.

Wolpe, J.: *Psychotherapy by Reciprocal Inhibition.* Stanford: Stanford University Press, 1958.

Wooddell, W.J.: Medical Detoxification of the Alcoholic. Lecture, Psychotherapy Associates, P.C. Sixth Annual Advanced Winter Workshop, "Treatment and Rehabilitation of the Alcoholic" Colorado Springs, Colorado, Feb. 6, 1980.

Wooddell, W.J.: Why Boozers Burp Blood. Lecture, Psychotherapy Associates, P.C. Eighth Annual Advanced Winter Workshop, "Treatment and Rehabilitation of the Alcoholic," Colorado Springs, Colorado, Feb. 4, 1982.

Yochelson, S., and Samenow, S.E.: *The Criminal Personality: A Profile for Change.* New York: Jason Aronson, Inc., 1976, vol. I.
Yochelson, S., and Samenow, S.E.: *The Criminal Personality: The Change Process.* New York: Jason Aronson, Inc., 1977, vol. II.
Zuk, G.H.: Family therapy. *Arch Gen. Psychiatry, 16*:71-79, 1967.

INDEX